COLLEGE DICTATION
FOR TRANSCRIPTION

LOUIS A. LESLIE
Editor in Chief, Gregg Shorthand Publications

CHARLES E. ZOUBEK
Coauthor, Gregg Shorthand, Series 90

A. JAMES LEMASTER
Coauthor, Gregg Shorthand, Series 90

KAY MENDENHALL
Instructor, Department of Business Education,
Mountain View High School, Orem, Utah

LORRINE B. SKAFF
Professor of Business, Southern Oregon State
College, Ashland

Shorthand written by Jerome P. Edelman

COLLEGE DICTATION
FOR TRANSCRIPTION

Gregg Division/
McGraw-Hill Book Company

New York   Madrid
Atlanta   Mexico
Dallas   Montreal
St. Louis   New Delhi
San Francisco   Panama
Auckland   Paris
Bogotá   San Juan
Guatemala   São Paulo
Hamburg   Singapore
Johannesburg   Sydney
Lisbon   Tokyo
London   Toronto

College Dictation for Transcription, Series 90
Copyright © 1981, 1975 by McGraw-Hill, Inc. All
Rights Reserved. Printed in the United States of
America. No part of this publication may be reproduced,
stored in a retrieval system, or transmitted, in any
form or by any means, electronic, mechanical,
photocopying, recording, or otherwise, without
the prior written permission of the publisher.

1 2 3 4 5 6 7 8 9 0 DODO 8 9 8 7 6 5 4 3 2 1

Library of Congress Cataloging in Publication Data
Main entry under title:
College dictation for transcription, series 90.

    Edition of 1975 published under title: College
dictation for transcription.
    Correlated with Gregg shorthand for colleges,
series 90, by L. A. Leslie, and others.
    1. Shorthand—Gregg—Exercises for dictation.
I. Leslie, Louis A., date   II. Leslie,
Louis A., date   Gregg shorthand for colleges,
series 90. III. College dictation for transcription.
Z56.2.G7A43   653'.427042'4   79-27124
ISBN 0-07-037765-0

83, 660

CONTENTS

1 Employment 1

2 Personnel and Training 22

3 Energy and Ecology 44

4 Motor Vehicles 65

5 Printed Media 89

6 Communications 111

7 Homes 133

8 Agriculture and Food 156

9 Finance 180

10 Credit 202

11 Sales 224

12 Travel and Transportation 243

13 Recreation and Leisure 263

14 Business Equipment 282

15 Goodwill and Public Relations 301

16 General 321

College Dictation for Transcription, Series 90, is a teacher's source book of carefully written business letters and memorandums that are ideal for developing and testing transcription skill. It may be used in any advanced shorthand class, regardless of the textbook the students use.

However, *College Dictation for Transcription, Series 90,* will be of greater value to the teacher whose students are using *Gregg Shorthand for Colleges, Transcription, Series 90,* as their advanced textbook because the material and the transcription instruction are closely correlated with the lessons of that book.

FEATURES OF COLLEGE DICTATION FOR TRANSCRIPTION, SERIES 90

Organization   This book contains 480 new, previously unpublished business letters and memorandums. The material is divided into 4 parts, 16 chapters, and 80 lessons, which corresponds to the organization of *Gregg Shorthand for Colleges, Transcription, Series 90.* The letters and memorandums in each chapter relate to the same topic, business, industry, or department of a business as do the corresponding chapters in the text.

Related Letters   The first three letters in each lesson in this book reply to or relate to the first three letters of the corresponding lesson in the textbook. Consequently, when the students have read and copied the letter in Lesson 6 of *Gregg Shorthand for Colleges, Transcription,* for example, they are actually getting a preview of the vocabulary and subject matter of the letters from this book that the teacher will dictate the following day. This simulates the conditions under which the students will work in a business office, where secretaries usually have an opportunity to read incoming correspondence before taking dictation for replies. In addition, the dictation and transcription of related letters helps to maintain student interest.

The last three letters in each lesson pertain to the same subject matter.

Punctuation Control To make the students' early transcription efforts easy and successful, the introduction of punctuation problems in the material has been carefully controlled. The letters in Lesson 1 of *College Dictation for Transcription, Series 90*, contain no internal punctuation marks. In Lesson 2, only parenthetical commas are used within the sentences. In Lesson 3, the appositive comma is introduced. Latter lessons follow the same pattern.

No punctuation mark is included in the letters in this book until it has either been covered or in the text.

Typing Style Control The first problems of typing style are reviewed before Lesson 16 in *Gregg Shorthand for Colleges, Transcription, Series 90*. Beginning with Lesson 16, the letters in this book include problems of typing style. No new applications of typing style are included in these letters until they have been either reviewed or introduced in the student textbook.

Shorthand Preview Each letter or memorandum is accompanied by a shorthand preview, followed by the type key, of more difficult words and phrases that occur in that letter or memorandum. This preview enables the teacher to eliminate the shorthand stumbling blocks in the material before dictating it.

Transcription Preview A helpful feature of this book, is the inclusion of a transcription preview with each letter or memorandum (with the exception of office-style letters) in the first 50 lessons and in selected material in Lessons 51 through 80. These transcription previews help to eliminate the *nonshorthand* stumbling blocks from the dictated material, just as the shorthand previews help to eliminate the *shorthand* stumbling blocks. The transcription previews contain spelling words, punctuation reminders, and typing style tips. They call the students' attention to the types of errors that secretaries frequently make so that the students will not make them in their own transcription.

Each new element is called to the students' attention in the punctuation and typing style preview. In most cases, where no new element is introduced in the text, a more difficult element from a previous lesson is reviewed.

Office-Style Dictation In the student text, the principles of office-style dictation are introduced, one in each chapter beginning with Chapter 6. Beginning with Lesson 29, this dictation book supplies an office-style letter in each lesson. Each type of problem is reviewed a number of times after it has been presented.

The office-style letters have been written so that teachers can include or eliminate the office-style problems when they dictate.

Alertness Exercises The importance of alertness on the part of the secretary is stressed in the student text. In Part 4 of this book the fifth letter in each lesson contains an alertness exercise in which there is an error that students should detect and correct.

It is suggested that students be warned that the first alertness exercise contains an error and that they should be alert to catch it and correct it. Later, however, these exercises should be dictated without any warning that the material contains an error, and the students should be held responsible for correcting the error.

Addresses for Transcription Addresses for the letters and memorandums in this dictation book are given in the back of *Gregg Shorthand for Colleges, Transcription, Series 90.* Thus, after teachers have dictated, say, Letter 15 in *College Dictation for Transcription, Series 90,* they can simply tell the students to use address No. 15 in the text. In this way the students follow fairly closely the practice that prevails in the business office, where addresses are seldom dictated and the secretary obtains them from the correspondence being answered.

Suggested Procedure

1. Place on the chalkboard or overhead projector the shorthand preview for the material, having the students read in concert each outline as you write it. This preview should not require more than 1 minute.

2. Dictate the letter at a rate about 20 words a minute below the average dictation progress speed test of the class. For example, if most of the students can take a 3-minute speed test dictated at 80 words a minute and transcribe it with 95 percent accuracy, letters for transcription might be dictated at 60 words a minute.

3. Discuss the problems brought up in the transcription preview. Be careful to keep these discussions brief.

4. Ask the students to tell you whether the letter is short, average, or long; what margins they should use; and how many lines from the letterhead they should start the inside address. This will be easy if they have read carefully the "Letter Placement by Judgment" suggestions in the textbook.

5. Tell the students the letter style you want them to use.

6. Tell them the number of the address they should use.

As the transcription course progresses and the students' transcription skill develops, these steps should gradually be eliminated until the students are able to transcribe without any assistance from the teacher.

The authors are confident that *College Dictation for Transcription, Series 90,* will be of great help in teaching students to become rapid and accurate transcribers.   *The Authors*

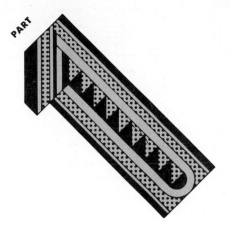

PART

It is suggested that students transcribe the letters in Part 1 in blocked style with standard punctuation. This gives students an opportunity to develop skill in typing a letter form that is frequently used in business. Have the students study the letter-placement suggestions on pages 30 and 31 of *Gregg Shorthand for Colleges, Transcription, Series 90*.

To keep the students' problems to a minimum, punctuation and typing style are introduced on a step-by-step basis, shown in the following outlines:

Chapter 1
EMPLOYMENT
Lesson 1   No internal punctuation
Lesson 2   Comma parenthetical
Lesson 3   Comma apposition
Lesson 4   Comma series
Lesson 5   Comma *and* omitted; Comma
  conjunction

Chapter 2
PERSONNEL AND TRAINING
Lesson 6   Commas *as, if,* and *when*
  clauses
Lesson 7   Comma introductory
Lesson 8   Comma nonrestrictive
Lesson 9   Comma geographical

Chapter 3
ENERGY AND ECOLOGY
Lesson 11   Semicolon no conjunction
Lesson 12   Period courteous request
Lesson 13   Hyphen
Lesson 14   Apostrophe

Chapter 4
MOTOR VEHICLES
Lesson 16   Dates and numbers
Lesson 17   Time
Lesson 18   Capitalization of company
  names and divisions and compass
  points
Lesson 19   Money
Lesson 20   Addresses

LESSON 1

❮ LETTER 1 ❮ (Related to Lesson 1, Letter 3)

NOTE: All letters and memorandums indicated as "related to" are answers to or are related to letters in *Gregg Shorthand for Colleges, Transcription, Series 90.*

Interview, necessary, arrangements, arrive, to begin, requested.

Dear Mr. Franklin: It will be convenient for me to come to your office for an interview on the date you[1] suggested. My travel agent has made all the necessary arrangements for me. I will keep an accurate[2] record of my expenses and mail it to you at a later date.

My plane will land in Houston early in the[3] morning. I should arrive at your office about the middle of the morning to begin the interview you have[4] requested.

I look forward to meeting with you and learning about your operations. Cordially yours, [98]

TRANSCRIPTION PREVIEW

Spelling. Interview, arrangements, accurate, requested.
Punctuation. There is no internal punctuation in any of the sentences.

◖ LETTER 2 ◗ (Related to Lesson 1, Letter 4)

Impressed, data, practical, qualifies, recruiting, definite.

Dear Mr. Freeman: Thank you for your letter requesting an interview for a position with our firm. I was[1] very much impressed by the information you presented in your personal data sheet. It appears that you[2] have the kind of practical experience that qualifies you for a position of responsibility[3] with a major company.

We are planning a recruiting trip to your section of the country next month. We expect[4] to spend several days in your area. We will contact you when we have made definite plans so that you[5] can arrange to meet with us at that time.

We are eager to meet you to discuss the possibility of your[6] joining our firm. Yours very truly,   [127]

TRANSCRIPTION PREVIEW

Spelling.   Impressed, practical, definite, eager.
Punctuation.   There is no internal punctuation in any of the sentences.

◖ LETTER 3 ◗ (Related to Lesson 1, Letter 5)

Always, worthy, responsibility, individuals, prompts, recommendation.

Dear Mr. James: It is always difficult to select a person from several worthy candidates to fill[1] a position of responsibility and trust with our company. We met a large number of capable[2] individuals who appear to be well qualified for the positions we have available.

There is[3] generally some little thing that prompts us to select a person over several others. The letters of[4] recommendation you solicited and sent to us a few days ago turned the tide in your favor. This action[5] represents the kind of initiative and creativity that we are seeking in those we interview.

Please[6] call me collect at my office within the next day or so. I would like to discuss the details of our offer[7] with you personally. Cordially yours,   [147]

TRANSCRIPTION PREVIEW

Spelling.   Candidates, recommendation, solicited, initiative.
Punctuation.   There is no internal punctuation in any of the sentences.

◖ LETTER 4

Indicated, currently, aggressive, vacancies, commercial, channels.

Dear George: Last week I was visiting a friend of mine who works for a major company. He indicated that[1] his firm currently is looking for a person to fill a vacancy.

I have done business with this company[2] for several years. The company impresses me as one of the fastest growing and most aggressive firms in[3] the industry. They do not find it necessary to advertise their vacancies through any of the commercial[4] channels because their employee termination rates are so low.

I recall that you have been interested in[5] a new position for several months. Perhaps this opening is just the thing you are looking for. It would[6] certainly be worth checking out. Cordially yours,   [128]

TRANSCRIPTION PREVIEW

Spelling.   Aggressive, channels, termination, certainly.
Punctuation.   There is no internal punctuation in any of the sentences.

ℂ LETTER 5

Memorandum, requirements, resignation, numerous, minimum.

Mr. Calvin: I trust that this memorandum will satisfy your requirements for a written notice of my[1] resignation.

There are numerous good reasons why I should stay on here at your company. There is only one[2] good reason why I should leave. The opportunity for me to take a job that requires a minimum of travel[3] is one that I cannot reject. That is the reason for my leaving.

I have certainly enjoyed the years I[4] have worked here. The experience has been positive and worthwhile. Thanks for providing me the opportunity[5] of working for your company. John Pratt

[107]

TRANSCRIPTION PREVIEW

Spelling. Numerous, minimum, experience, worthwhile.
Punctuation. There is no internal punctuation in any of the sentences.

ℂ LETTER 6

Assistant, informed, temporary, limit, exception, competent, details.

Dear Mrs. Clyde: This morning my executive assistant informed me of your request for a temporary[1] secretary for a period of several months beginning next month.

Our policy here is to limit[2] the services of our temporary secretaries to no more than a month at a time with any employer.[3] We are willing to make an exception in your case because you have used our services several times in[4] the past.

We are sending you one of our most competent secretaries. We will contact you in several days[5] to get some details on the assignment. Sincerely yours, [110]

TRANSCRIPTION PREVIEW

Spelling. Temporary, exception, competent, assignment.
Punctuation. There is no internal punctuation in any of the sentences.

LESSON 2

❊ LETTER 7 ❊ (Related to Lesson 2, Letter 3)

Disappointed, candidate, impressed, excellent, application, session.

Dear Mrs. Oliver: I am, of course, quite disappointed that you selected another candidate to fill[1] the opening for which I interviewed. I was certainly impressed by your employees. I am sure that your[2] company would be an excellent organization with which to associate.

Please keep my application in[3] your files. I would be willing to discuss any further opportunities in my field that may develop[4] within your firm.

Thank you again for the time you generously spent with me during our interview session.[5] Sincerely yours, [103]

TRANSCRIPTION PREVIEW

Spelling. Disappointed, impressed, excellent, discuss.
Punctuation. Commas before and after *of course* (, parenthetical).

⊄ LETTER 8 ⊄ (Related to Lesson 2, Letter 4)

[shorthand symbols]

Flattering, comments, aware, extensive, additional, pertaining.

Dear Mrs. Smith: Thank you for your flattering comments regarding my recent interview for a position with[1] your firm.

You are aware, of course, that I have had extensive training in the field of credit management. My[2] experience in this line of work has given me a strong desire to pursue my original career objectives.[3] I would be willing to consider the position you have in mind if it is within the credit field. Would[4] you, therefore, provide me some additional information pertaining to the job opening you have in mind.[5]

Please let me know as soon as possible so that I can plan to come to your office for further testing. Cordially[6] yours,   [121]

TRANSCRIPTION PREVIEW

> **Spelling.** Flattering, extensive, pursue, career.
> **Punctuation.** Commas before and after *of course* and *therefore* (, parenthetical).

⊄ LETTER 9 ⊄ (Related to Lesson 2, Letter 5)

[shorthand symbols]

Detailed, adequate, opportunity, subsequently, challenging, rewarding.

Dear Ms. Young: I have prepared a detailed data sheet that provides the information you need. I hope that the data[1] related to my work experience is adequate for your purposes, Ms. Young.

My employment record[2] shows that I have held only one position during the past few years. My present employer, however, has given[3] me the opportunity to work in all departments of our firm. I began as a typist and subsequently[4] advanced to my present position as an executive secretary. My current job is a[5] challenging and rewarding one.

The position you have open would provide an opportunity for me to[6] develop further my skills and talents in the secretarial field.

I hope to hear from you soon in regard to[7] this matter. Sincerely yours, [145]

TRANSCRIPTION PREVIEW

Spelling. Experience, subsequently, challenging, develop.
Punctuation. Commas before *Ms. Young;* before and after *however* (, parenthetical).

❿ LETTER 10

Completed, schedules, agencies, believe, proposed, to provide.

Mr. Brown: We have completed our research on the fee schedules used by private employment agencies in the[1] state. It appears that our schedule is well below the state average. I suggest that we adjust our schedule[2] immediately.

I believe that our basic fee should be increased significantly. We probably should charge the[3] equivalent of the gross salary for one week. Most of the companies we surveyed charge this amount.

I would like[4] you to express your point of view on this proposed adjustment at our next staff meeting. Please consider the matter[5] carefully and be prepared to provide some constructive input, Mr. Brown. Jane Williams [116]

TRANSCRIPTION PREVIEW

Spelling. Appears, adjust, surveyed, carefully.
Punctuation. Comma before *Mr. Brown* (, parenthetical).

Request, resources, reminded, circumstances, assist, available.
center, through, recruit, directly, existence.

Dear Kathy: It seems only yesterday that I was looking for my first job just as you are today. Your request[1] for information on job resources reminded me of my circumstances many years ago when I was[2] a new graduate of a local business school.

There are several resources available to assist you[3] in finding suitable employment. The newspapers generally contain current listings of local positions[4] that are available. Many of the larger companies advertise in their related trade journals. These[5] journals may be available either in your school library or in the public library.

There are also[6] private and public employment agencies operating within most larger communities. Your school probably[7] has a placement center through which you may be able to find a job. Many firms recruit directly through these[8] centers. The larger companies may also have their own personnel offices where you can directly apply[9] for a position. Contacts with friends and relatives can often reveal the existence of available jobs.[10]

You may be sure, Kathy, that I will keep my eyes open for the kind of job you are seeking. Good luck in this[11] important endeavor. Sincerely yours, [227]

TRANSCRIPTION PREVIEW

Spelling.   Resources, suitable, library, reveal.
Punctuation.   Commas before and after *Kathy* (, parenthetical).

◖ **LETTER 12**

Interviewing, several months, positions, negative, instituted, requiring, counselors.

Dear Mrs. Tate: I have been interviewing for a position in advertising during the past several[1] months. I have not received any good offers in spite of a rather large number of available positions.[2] I believe there must be something in my personal file that is having a negative influence on prospective[3] employers.

I understand that regulations have been instituted requiring schools to make the information[4] in personal files available to students on request. I would like to inspect my records if this[5] is the case.

Please indicate, therefore, when I could meet with one of your counselors to go over the material[6] in my file. I would prefer to come in the afternoon because of my heavy morning class schedule. Cordially[7] yours,   [141]

TRANSCRIPTION PREVIEW

Spelling.   Negative, counselors, prefer, schedule.
Punctuation.   Commas before and after *therefore* (, parenthetical).

LESSON 3

ℂ LETTER 13 ℂ (Related to Lesson 3, Letter 3)

Pleasant, acquainted, personality, knowledge, territory, association.

Dear Mr. Phillips: Yesterday I had the pleasant experience of getting acquainted with your representative,[1] Miss Ann Baker. Miss Baker appears to be everything you said she would be. Her personality and[2] her knowledge of your products make her a very effective sales representative. I am certain that she will[3] do a very good job for your firm in this territory.

Miss Baker left our offices with one of the largest[4] orders we have given one of your people. We are looking forward to our association with her.

Please[5] convey our best wishes for a speedy recovery to Mr. Robert Jones, your former representative[6] in our territory. Sincerely yours, [127]

TRANSCRIPTION PREVIEW

Spelling. Acquainted, personality, knowledge, convey.
Punctuation. Commas after *with your representative* and *Mr. Robert Jones* (, apposition).

❡ LETTER 14 ❡ (Related to Lesson 3, Letter 4)

Candidates, narrowed, qualifications, require, conclusion, coordinate.

John Foster: We have interviewed many candidates for the position you have open in your department. We[1] have narrowed the field down to several individuals who appear to have the credentials and qualifications[2] you require. We are impressed by the training and background of these people. It will be a difficult job[3] selecting one of them.

We have invited each candidate to spend one day next week with members of your department.[4] We would like you to give us your recommendations at the conclusion of that day.

We have asked Mary Billings,[5] my assistant, to act as host for the day. She will coordinate her activities with you. Fred Roberts[6]
[120]

TRANSCRIPTION PREVIEW

Spelling. Narrowed, credentials, recommendations, coordinate.
Punctuation. Commas before and after *my assistant* (, apposition).

ℭ LETTER 15 ℭ (Related to Lesson 3, Letter 5)

Discussed, assignment, among, considerable, significantly, prospects.

A. L. Franks: My wife and I have discussed your offer to open a new sales territory in the Providence[1] area.

I requested my present assignment in Los Angeles because both our families live here. The[2] past few years have been among the most pleasant of our lives. We are, therefore, quite firmly opposed to changing our[3] residence.

The company has enjoyed considerable success in Los Angeles during these past few years. The[4] annual sales reports show that our business has increased significantly each year. Prospects for the future have[5] never been brighter. I must, therefore, decline your fine offer, Mr. Franks.

You may be sure that I will continue[6] to do the best job possible in representing our company here in California. You might wish to ask[7] Ms. May White, the former representative here, if she would like to open the sales territory in Providence.[8] George Farmer

[163]

TRANSCRIPTION PREVIEW

Spelling. Discussed, assignment, residence, considerable.
Punctuation. Commas before and after *the former representative here* (, apposition).

ℭ LETTER 16

Involved, orientation, interviewed, individually, input, evaluation.

To the Staff: The hiring procedures in our organization have often involved several staff members.[1] Interested applicants are generally given a casual orientation to our basic procedures[2] at the time they are interviewed. Then they meet individually with each department head and other key[3] personnel for further discussion.

In the past we have contacted many of you personally to provide[4] important input when we make our employment decisions. In the future, however, we would like each of you to[5] prepare a written evaluation of each prospective employee immediately after the interview.[6] The review should be submitted to our personnel secretary, Miss Byers.

Your cooperation in[7] this matter will be genuinely appreciated.
James Sherman   [153]

❡ LETTER 17

Photocopied, dismissal, supervisor, memorandum, occasions, consistently, quotas.

Lois Layton: I have photocopied the records you requested concerning the dismissal of our former[1] shipping room supervisor, Mr. Bill Young. They are attached to this memorandum.

Mr. Young was informed in[2] writing on several occasions that his performance was consistently below par. He achieved the minimum[3] standards that have been set for his department only one month during the past year. We suggested that he take[4] another position within the company. He refused to do so, however. Our other employees relied[5] upon Mr. Young to meet the quotas of the department. It was unfair to them to keep him on the payroll.[6]

I felt it necessary, therefore, to terminate his services.

Please let me know if you need any other[7] information. Bill Rogers [146]

TRANSCRIPTION PREVIEW

    Spelling. Dismissal, memorandum, consistently, necessary.
    Punctuation. Comma before *Mr. Bill Young* (, apposition).

⟨ LETTER 18

Entire, text, employment, positions, guidelines, functions.

    To the Staff: I have just finished reading the entire text of a law recently enacted by the federal[1] government. The section covering equal opportunity in employment has left me with some concern. It[2] appears that our company is not following the employment practices required by law. We have too few women[3] in management positions. There are also too few women working in the production area.

    Mr.[4] James, an expert in government regulation of business, and I are working on some procedures that we believe[5] will help us meet the requirements of the law before the end of the year.

    We will make these guidelines available[6] to everyone involved in the employment functions of our company in a few weeks. May Green [138]

TRANSCRIPTION PREVIEW

    Spelling. Equal, management, women, procedures.
    Punctuation. Commas before and after *an expert in government regulation of business* (, apposition).

LESSON 4

ℂ **LETTER 19** ℂ **(Related to Lesson 4, Letter 3)**

[shorthand]

Informative, agency, procedures, enabled, sponsoring.

Dear Mr. Taylor: Thank you for your informative letter on the services your agency renders.

We have[1] used the services of your agency in our classes on many occasions in the past. Your testing procedures,[2] guidance programs, and placement services have enabled many of our students to find positions in the[3] business world.

Next month we are sponsoring a business education workshop for the students in our department.[4] We will be sponsoring activities designed to help our students become personally acquainted with[5] valuable community resources. We would be happy to have someone from your organization make a[6] presentation to our students. Cordially yours, [128]

TRANSCRIPTION PREVIEW

Spelling. Renders, occasions, placement, sponsoring.
Punctuation. Commas after *procedures* and *programs* (, series).

ℂ **LETTER 20** ℂ **(Related to Lesson 4, Letter 4)**

[shorthand]

Recommendation, extraordinary, design, creativity, already.

Dear Mr. Samuels: Thank you for your letter of recommendation for Miss Alice Hawkins, a former employee[1] of your company. We thought you might like to know how Alice is doing with our company since we hired her[2] several months ago.

Her record has been extraordinary. Her knowledge of modern design, her creativity,[3] and her ability to work with our other employees have already made her one of our most[4] valuable staff members. We have great plans for Alice. We think our company will provide her an opportunity[5] to become one of the leading people in the design business.

Please feel free to call on us anytime we[6] can be of help to your organization. Cordially yours,   [131]

TRANSCRIPTION PREVIEW

> **Spelling.** Extraordinary, knowledge, design, creativity.
> **Punctuation.** Commas after *design* and *creativity* (, series).

❲ LETTER 21 ❲ (Related to Lesson 4, Letter 5)

Interviewing, impressed, cordial, helpful, graduates, degree.

Dear Mr. Taylor: Thank you for the opportunity of interviewing for a secretarial position[1] in your organization. I was impressed by your cordial, helpful, and friendly personnel.

Would you please,[2] however, remove my name from consideration. I have decided to continue my education rather[3] than take a position at this time. The opportunities for college graduates are excellent. I have been[4] given a grant which will enable me to obtain my degree in only one more year.

Please let me know if you[5] would be interested in considering me for employment for next year. Cordially yours,   [116]

TRANSCRIPTION PREVIEW

> **Spelling.** Cordial, decided, graduates, excellent.
> **Punctuation.** Commas after *cordial* and *helpful* (, series).

◁ LETTER 22

[shorthand symbols]

Directive, position, senior, enjoyed, transfer, discuss, details.

Edward Farley: We received a directive from our Gary office indicating that a position as senior[1] designer is open at the plant
there. The head of the department requested that you be given the[2]
opportunity of filling that job.

We have enjoyed working with you here in the Chicago plant.
We recognize,[3] however, that a position such as this could mean
a great deal to you, your wife, and your children. We will be glad[4]
to arrange a transfer for you if you decide to move to Gary.

Please come to my office on either Monday[5] or Tuesday to discuss some of the details of this offer. Allen Ames   [113]

TRANSCRIPTION PREVIEW

Spelling. Designer, recognize, discuss.
Punctuation. Commas after *you* and *wife* (, series).

◁ LETTER 23

[shorthand symbols]

**Thank you for your, incentive, encouraged, developed, seminars,
workshops.**

Dear Ray: Thank you for your letter requesting information on
how to set up your own business.

Your concern that[1] too little information and incentive are currently available to those who wish to work for themselves[2] is certainly a valid one. We believe that more people should be encouraged to take the option of self-employment.[3]

There is considerable help available to people like you. Our company, in fact, has developed[4] several timely publications deal-ing with the subject of starting a business. We also hold regular[5] evening seminars, training sessions, and workshops in which you might be interested. I have included a[6] circular that provides de-tailed information on our various programs.

Please let us know if we can be of further[7] service to you. We will be pleased to hear from you. Sincerely yours,   [153]

TRANSCRIPTION PREVIEW

Spelling.   Encouraged, developed, seminars.
Punctuation.   Commas after *seminars* and *sessions* (, series).

❰ LETTER 24

To serve, assistant, efficiency, dependability, integrity.

Dear Mr. Smith: I am very glad to serve as a reference for Mr. Bill Brown. Mr. Brown served as an[1] assistant in my office for several years. He is a person of efficiency, dependability, and[2] in-tegrity.

I am very happy to give him my unqualified recommendation. Sincerely yours,   [59]

TRANSCRIPTION PREVIEW

Spelling.   Reference, assistant, efficiency, integrity.
Punctuation.   Commas after *efficiency* and *dependability* (, series).

LESSON 5

❮ LETTER 25 ❯ (Related to Lesson 5, Letter 3)

**Apologize, omission, graduate, suitable, position,
as soon as possible.**

   Dear Mr. Elton: I must apologize for the omission you noted on my personal data sheet.

   I[1] have had a long, rather steady career in the airline industry. I was not employed, however, during the[2] years in question. I spent that time in graduate school at a local college.

   I hope this information will allow[3] you to proceed with my application for employment. I am eager to find a suitable position[4] as soon as possible. Very truly yours,   [88]

TRANSCRIPTION PREVIEW

   Spelling.   Omission, graduate, proceed.
   Punctuation.   Comma after *long* (, *and* omitted).

❮ LETTER 26 ❯ (Related to Lesson 5, Letter 4)

Interviewed, throughout, area, impressive, techniques, research.

   Dear Mr. Strong: It was certainly a pleasure to interview your graduating business education students[1] for teaching positions in our school district. We have interviewed students on many campuses throughout the[2] area. None have been more impressive than the students at your college.

   Your students were skilled in interviewing[3] techniques. They had accurate, complete files. They had done their research on our school district. Their verbal: skills were excellent.[4] We made job offers to several of the students.

Thank you for your help, Mr. Strong. Cordially yours, [98]

TRANSCRIPTION PREVIEW

Spelling. Campuses, impressive, techniques, verbal.
Punctuation. Comma after *accurate* (, *and* omitted).

❲ LETTER 27 ❲ (Related to Lesson 5, Letter 5)

Development, terminations, purchasing, rather, challenging, vacancy.

Mr. Frost: We have just had a development in one of our departments that might be of interest to you.

We[1] have been busy changing work assignments because of our recent employee terminations. One of our purchasing[2] agents decided to quit rather than accept a different, more challenging work load. This action created[3] a vacancy in that department. We feel you would be qualified to fill the vacancy.

This action would,[4] of course, enable you to stay with the company and retain the benefits you have accumulated. Please[5] call my secretary for an appointment to discuss the matter with me in detail if you are interested.[6] Betty Parsons [123]

TRANSCRIPTION PREVIEW

Spelling. Development, challenging, accumulated.
Punctuation. Comma after *different* (, *and* omitted).

❡ LETTER 28

Considerable, profitable, experience, helpful, capacity, effectively.

Dear Ms. Mason: I have had considerable time to reflect on my extensive, profitable work experience[1] with your company since I terminated my services.

You were particularly helpful to me[2] at all times, Ms. Mason. You encouraged me to increase my capacity to function effectively as an[3] executive secretary, and you helped me to develop an ability to work with others. I feel[4] I am a better worker because of my association with you, and I thank you sincerely.

I hope to[5] be able to drop in occasionally to see you and the other employees of the company. Cordially[6] yours, [121]

TRANSCRIPTION PREVIEW

Spelling. Extensive, profitable, particularly, occasionally.
Punctuation. Commas after *extensive* (*, and* omitted); after *secretary* and *with you* (*,* conjunction).

❡ LETTER 29

Division, Madison, frankly, supervisor, substantially, transfer.

Mr. Walker: Next week Mr. Gary Smith will begin working for your division in Madison. He has[1] completed several years of service with our branch in Chicago, and, frankly, we will miss him.

Gary has worked closely[2] with our production supervisor in developing better, more efficient methods for the operation[3] of our assembly line. On several occasions his ideas have increased our output substantially. His[4] friendly, concerned manner has enabled him to work effectively with others in implementing changes. Our[5] loss is certainly your gain, but we know the best interests of the company are served by this transfer.

We are sure[6] you will enjoy working with Gary as much as we have. Ann Brown [132]

TRANSCRIPTION PREVIEW

Spelling. Developing, efficient, implementing.
Punctuation. Commas after *Chicago* and *gain* (, conjunction); after *better* and *friendly* (, *and* omitted).

ℂ LETTER 30

Congratulations, cooperation, solicited, accelerate, unnecessary.

To the Staff: Congratulations to all of you for your helpful, willing cooperation during the past few[1] weeks. The large number of orders our sales representatives solicited during May, June, and July forced us[2] to accelerate our production substantially. It was, fortunately, unnecessary for us to hire[3] any additional employees during this short period of time because of your willingness to work[4] overtime.

We hope that the necessity for overtime will not occur again in the near future. You may be[5] sure we will never purposely impose such a demanding work schedule on any of you. Sharon Jones [118]

TRANSCRIPTION PREVIEW

Spelling. Solicited, accelerate, unnecessary.
Punctuation. Comma after *helpful* (, *and* omitted).

PERSONNEL AND TRAINING

LESSON 6

◖ LETTER 31 ◖ (Related to Lesson 6, Letter 3)

Program, discount, instituted, elated, accounting.

To the Staff: Our program for making discount purchases at local retail stores has now been in effect for[1] several months. When we instituted the plan, we were concerned that it could take more than a year to begin functioning[2] smoothly.

We are elated, however, at the reaction of our employees. It appears that most of you[3] are already taking advantage of the program. The complex accounting system for crediting your bank accounts[4] with a percentage of your purchases has worked even better than we anticipated.

We encourage[5] each of you to shop at participating stores whenever possible. In this way you will be assuring the[6] survival of this exciting, worthwhile program. Dorothy Marks [132]

TRANSCRIPTION PREVIEW

Spelling. Instituted, elated, assuring, worthwhile.
Punctuation. Comma after *plan* (*, when* clause).

◖ LETTER 32 ◖ (Related to Lesson 6, Letter 4)

Grievances, differences, intention, satisfaction, recommendations.

Mr. Miller: We held a meeting last week with several of our dissatisfied employees and their union[1] representative, Mr. Charles Allen. When Mr. Allen presented me with a list of major grievances,[2] I thought we would have a difficult time resolving our differences. His intention, however, was merely to[3] work out the problems as quickly as possible to the satisfaction of both parties. If we are to settle[4] the matter quickly, I believe we will have to make some changes in our management policies. My recommendations[5] are attached. I have set up a meeting for next month with Mr. Allen to review our progress in this[6] matter. I will keep you informed as important developments occur. Sue Phillips   [135]

TRANSCRIPTION PREVIEW

Spelling. Dissatisfied, grievances, management, recommendations.

Punctuation. Commas after *grievances* (*, when* clause); after *quickly* (*, if* clause).

◖ LETTER 33 ◖ (Related to Lesson 6, Letter 5)

Scheduled, speaker, serious, disappointed, associates.

To the Staff: We regret to inform you that Betty Miller, our scheduled speaker at our management conference,[1] will not be able to be with us on that occasion. She has been having serious health problems, and her doctor[2] advises her to avoid all travel for a few months.

When we received her letter, we were disappointed.[3] She suggested, however, that we contact one of her associates, James Washington. Mr. Washington serves[4] as regular consultant with several large manufacturing firms, lectures to management groups on a[5] regular basis, and is the author of several important publications. He is available and has[6] consented to replace Mrs. Miller.

We are certain he will be an excellent substitute speaker for our[7] conference. We are looking forward to hearing the stimulating ideas he has to offer. T. J. Peterson[8]   [160]

TRANSCRIPTION PREVIEW

Spelling.   Occasion, disappointed, associates, consented.
Punctuation.   Comma after *letter* (, *when* clause).

⟪ LETTER 34

Effective, competent, participate, excellent, anxious, coordinators.

Dear Miss Madison: One of the most effective ways to assure your company of an adequate supply of[1] competent employees in the future is to participate in cooperative education programs.

As[2] you may know, there are several local high schools that have developed excellent cooperative programs. Their[3] programs provide young people with vocational training in a wide variety of technical areas.[4] These students are anxious to work, and they have the skills necessary to perform successfully elementary[5] tasks in their selected vocational fields.

The coordinators in each of these schools are seeking business[6] executives to work with them in providing job placement opportunities for the students involved. If your[7] plant or office could accommodate several of these students, we would be delighted.

When you are contacted[8] sometime next month by a local program coordinator, we hope you will take the opportunity to[9] discover the many advantages of cooperative education. Sincerely yours,   [197]

Spelling. Effective, adequate, developed, technical, successfully, coordinators.

Punctuation. Commas after *As you may know* (, *as* clause); after *these students* (, *if* clause); after *program coordinator* (, *when* clause).

❴ LETTER 35

Allotment, executives, discovered, somewhat, benefited.

Mr. Baker: I received a request for a travel allotment from Frank Baker, a senior executive[1] in our firm. Frank would like to attend a meeting of advertising executives in Denver next month.

When I[2] checked our records, I discovered that Frank has not attended a professional convention in several years.[3] As you know, we try to budget enough money for each of our management personnel to attend a major[4] convention at least every other year.

We would prefer that our people attend meetings somewhat closer to home.[5] This convention is an important one, however, and I feel that the company would be benefited in[6] several ways by sending Frank.

I recommend, therefore, that you approve this request. Edith Davis   [138]

TRANSCRIPTION PREVIEW

Spelling. Received, allotment, discovered, benefited.

Punctuation. Commas after *our records* (, *when* clause); after *As you know* (, *as* clause).

❡ LETTER 36

Purchased, applicable, postage, indicated, commitments.

Dear Mr. Roberts: When I received your request recently for sales training films, I instructed my secretary[1] to look through our files and compile a list of suitable materials. We have purchased several films during[2] the past several years that might be applicable to your program. The complete list is enclosed for your[3] convenience.

The rental price of our films is shown on the attached sheet. We pay the shipping costs to your office, but you[4] must provide the return postage. If you wish, you may use the films several times during the rental period.[5] It is important, however, that you return them on the dates indicated to allow us to honor our[6] commitments to our other customers.

We hope you find these films helpful in your training program. Cordially yours,[7]   [140]

TRANSCRIPTION PREVIEW

Spelling.   Through, suitable, applicable, commitments.
Punctuation.   Commas after *sales training films* (, *when* clause); after *If you wish* (, *if* clause).

LESSON 7

❡ LETTER 37 ❡ (Related to Lesson 7, Letter 3)

Employee, justified, adapted, himself, potential, recommendation.

Dear Mr. Drake: Your faith in Larry Franklin, the new employee in our department, was certainly justified.[1] Larry has adapted himself to our work routine in record time. In fact, he shows real potential for leadership[2] in our department. He has made several suggestions thus far which we have adopted.

As you will notice[3] on his monthly evaluation report, Larry appears to be very happy with his new assignment.[4] Everyone in the department seems to like him, and we are confident that he will have no problems with our other[5] employees.

Thanks for your recommendation. Sincerely yours,   [111]

TRANSCRIPTION PREVIEW

Spelling.   Faith, justified, routine, evaluation.
Punctuation.   Comma after *In fact* (, introductory).

❡ LETTER 38 ❡ (Related to Lesson 7, Letter 4)

Regarding, afforded, terms, significant, replacement.

Mr. Williams: I have the report of the retirement committee regarding your request for early retirement.[1] They recommended that you be placed on early retirement with all the benefits afforded under the[2] terms of your contract.

We will miss you here at the company. You have made a significant contribution to[3] our operations over the years. Your leadership and enthusiasm have been important factors in the[4] success of our company.

As soon as you can make proper arrangements with your department supervisor, please[5] give us your termination date. Of course, we will need to begin looking for your replacement as soon as your[6] retirement plans have been finalized. T. L. Stockton   [129]

TRANSCRIPTION PREVIEW

Spelling.   Recommended, significant, enthusiasm, termination.
Punctuation.   Comma after *Of course* (, introductory).

◀ LETTER 39 ◀ (Related to Lesson 7, Letter 5)

Attended, workshop, enthusiasm, obviously, adjustments, participate.

Dear Mr. Church: Last week several of our employees attended your workshop on new methods of data[1] processing.

The success of any training program can usually be measured by the enthusiasm of the[2] participants. Your workshop was obviously an unqualified success judging from the reaction of our[3] staff members. After they returned last Monday, they requested a general staff meeting to discuss the new methods[4] they had learned. We have already benefited from their experience by making some adjustments in our[5] existing procedures.

Thank you for inviting us to attend your workshop. We would be glad to participate[6] in one of your outstanding programs anytime in the future. Sincerely yours,   [134]

TRANSCRIPTION PREVIEW

Spelling.   Obviously, unqualified, judging, procedures.
Punctuation.   Comma after *Monday* (, introductory).

◀ LETTER 40

Union, management, committee, employees, detail.

Mr. Blair: As you know, many of the employees here at the company would like to join a credit union.[1] Because there is no credit union at our company, we hope that the management will help us to start one.

We[2] are asking that a committee of employees meet with representatives from management next week to discuss[3] the matter in detail. Please let me know when it will be convenient for someone from the general management[4] office to meet with us. Ann Moore

[86]

TRANSCRIPTION PREVIEW

Spelling. Employees, union, committee, discuss.
Punctuation. Comma after *our company* (, introductory).

◖ LETTER 41

Recommendations, suggestions, surprised, evaluate, willingness.

Mr. Morton: Enclosed are the recommendations and suggestions you requested for our new office building.[1] We were surprised at the interest our employees had in the new construction project.

As you will observe, some of[2] the suggestions appear to be impractical. We have made no attempt to edit them or evaluate their[3] merit. However, you will derive some general ideas from these comments to help you in your planning.

We[4] appreciate your willingness to accept input from those of us who will be using the new office building. We[5] will look forward to the opportunity of examining and discussing the preliminary building[6] design. Larry Miller

[124]

TRANSCRIPTION PREVIEW

Spelling. Recommendations, impractical, evaluate, willingness.
Punctuation. Comma after *However* (, introductory).

Discussed, facilities, disruptions, disadvantages, trend.

Mr. Fields: I have discussed with my staff the contents of your recent memorandum concerning educational[1] field trips and tours through our facilities. Of course, these groups do cause some disruptions to our employees as they[2] move through our plant. We try to minimize these disruptions as much as possible, but we know they cannot be[3] completely eliminated.

The question is whether or not the benefits of these tours outweigh the disadvantages.[4] We believe they do.

Our company is expected to play a positive role in community and[5] educational affairs. In fact, more and more of our employees are coming from the local community.[6] We feel that our attempt to acquaint our citizens with our facilities is responsible for this trend.

Our[7] recommendation, therefore, is that we continue to offer this important public service. Rosa Lopez[8]   [160]

TRANSCRIPTION PREVIEW

Spelling.   Minimize, disruptions, eliminated, outweigh, acquaint.
Punctuation.   Commas after *Of course* and *In fact* (, introductory).

LESSON 8

C LETTER 43 C (Related to Lesson 8, Letter 3)

Initiated, report, how much, carefully, program, adjusting.

Dear Member: We initiated a plan for making discount purchases several months ago. At that time[1] we promised that we would provide a quarterly report to all participants. Your statement, which is enclosed, shows[2] where your purchases were made, how much you spent, and how much you saved.

If you will study it carefully, you will be[3] able to determine the value of this program to you and your family. Notice that some stores give a higher[4] discount than others. You can save more by adjusting your shopping patterns.

We hope you are enjoying this service[5] provided by your association. We are anxious to serve our members in any way possible. Yours[6] very truly,   [123]

⊄ LETTER 44 ⊄ (Related to Lesson 8, Letter 4)

Facilities, gratified, institute, procedures, sustained, consequently.

To All Employees: Many of you have been using the exercise facilities we constructed in our office[1] building. We are gratified that you are benefiting from this service.

We have encountered a problem,[2] however, that has required us to institute some changes in procedures. Several of you have sustained minor[3] injuries while using our equipment. This has resulted in an unusually high absenteeism[4] rate.

Consequently, we have hired John Roberts, who is a local physical education instructor, to be[5] on hand for an hour each day to give instructions to those who desire to use our facilities. He will set up[6] an individualized program for each employee that will be appropriate to his or her present physical[7] condition.

If each of you adhere to this simple guideline, we can increase your enjoyment of these facilities[8] and reduce the risk of injury.
Don Anderson   [171]

Spelling.   Exercise, gratified, absenteeism, individualized.
Punctuation.   Commas before and after *who is a local physical education instructor* (, nonrestrictive).

❡ LETTER 45 ❡ (Related to Lesson 8, Letter 5)

Understand, maintained, interest, business, speakers, advisory, let us know.

Dear Mr. Sanchez: I understand that you are in charge of business education for your school district. My firm,[1] which is located here in Atlanta, has always maintained an interest in local education programs. We[2] are specifically concerned that the schools provide the necessary training for young people to become qualified[3] for the secretarial, stenographic, and clerical positions available in business.

If we[4] can be of service to the schools in your district, we would be happy to do so by providing guest speakers,[5] sponsoring field trips to our offices, and serving on advisory committees.

We have a number of staff members[6] who are eager to serve you. Please let us know how we may assist you. Yours truly,   [135]

Spelling.   Always, maintained, stenographic, sponsoring, advisory.
Punctuation.   Commas before and after *which is located here in Atlanta* (, nonrestrictive).

❡ LETTER 46

Employees, proposal, twice, discussed, objection, encounter.

Ms. Miller: Last month several employees from the accounting department approached me with a proposal to[1] change our current payroll procedures. They had circulated a petition requesting that we change our pay[2] period from once a month to twice a month. They had the signatures of a majority of our salaried[3] employees.

I have discussed the matter with Mr. Harvey Baker, who is our data processing coordinator,[4] and he feels there is no serious objection to making the requested change. If you will get together[5] and work out the details with Mr. Baker sometime next week, perhaps we can make the necessary changes before[6] our next payroll.

Let me know if you encounter any difficulties with this plan. Roger Best   [138]

TRANSCRIPTION PREVIEW

Spelling.   Approached, payroll, petition, coordinator.
Punctuation.   Commas before and after *who is our data processing coordinator* (, nonrestrictive).

◖ LETTER 47

Obtain, encourages, self-development, specifically, accompany, printed.

Dear Mrs. Casey: A close friend of mine, Mrs. Helen Smith, recommended that I contact you for suggestions[1] as to where I might obtain materials on management training. My present employer encourages[2] everyone in trainee positions to seek outside help for self-development. Unfortunately, our company[3] library, which was opened only a few months ago, has little material that might be useful in helping[4] me further my goals with the company.

I specifically need materials geared to an individualized[5] approach. If there are tapes, filmstrips, or records that accompany any printed materials, I would[6] be willing to rent or purchase them.

Please send your catalog as soon as possible to my address printed at[7] the top of this letter. Cordially yours,   [147]

TRANSCRIPTION PREVIEW

Spelling.   Recommended, encourages, trainee, catalog.
Punctuation.   Commas before and after *which was opened only a few months ago* (, nonrestrictive).

❬ LETTER 48

Reviewed, available, steadily, leadership, trend, efficiency, prominence.

To the Staff: The board of directors recently reviewed our production records for the past year. Their report, which[1] is available in our executive office, shows the reasons why we are steadily losing our position[2] of leadership in the textile manufacturing industry.

Our sales increased only a small percentage[3] during the past year, but our costs went up significantly. If this trend continues, our company will be in[4] very serious financial straits.

We are, therefore, asking all our employees to do whatever they can to[5] increase their personal efficiency and to decrease expenses. A united effort will be required by[6] everyone to rebuild our company to its former position of prominence. Harry Gordon   [138]

TRANSCRIPTION PREVIEW

Spelling.   Losing, percentage, significantly, efficiency.
Punctuation.   Commas before and after *which is available in our executive office* (, nonrestrictive).

⊄ LETTER 49 ⊄ (Related to Lesson 9, Letter 3)

Sabbatical, justify, elsewhere, provision, reassignments, financial.

Dear Mr. Blair: We have reviewed your request for a sabbatical leave to work in Providence, Rhode Island. We[1] feel that your circumstances would justify our granting you a regular leave of absence rather than a[2] sabbatical leave because you are accepting employment elsewhere.

This type of leave does not include a provision[3] for financial remuneration or a requirement that employees return to their former positions.

Even[4] though your absence will result in some rather difficult reassignments in your department, we are pleased to[5] give you a leave of absence. We hope that this period of time will enable you to meet some important[6] financial goals you have set for yourself and your family. Cordially yours,   [133]

TRANSCRIPTION PREVIEW

Spelling.   Sabbatical, absence, remuneration, reassignments.
Punctuation.   Comma after *Providence* (, geographical).

⊄ LETTER 50 ⊄ (Related to Lesson 9, Letter 4)

Memorandum, supervisors, clarifications, projection, guideline, distribution.

To All Employees: A few months ago we released a memorandum

outlining the provisions of our current[1] benefits package. Since that time many of you have directed questions to your department supervisors[2] concerning the relationships of fringe benefits to salary. The following clarifications may help[3] you understand how decisions affecting your benefits are made.

When our board reviews our financial picture[4] each year, a projection is made concerning the amount of money that will be available for salary[5] increases and benefits. This basic figure serves as a guideline when new contracts are written. The money[6] available can be spent only one time, of course. It may be spent for either salary increase or fringe benefits.[7] It cannot be spent for both.

If you are concerned about the distribution of these funds, please contact Mr.[8] James in our Birmingham, Alabama, office. I am sure he will be happy to help you. Mary King   [178]

TRANSCRIPTION PREVIEW

Spelling.   Memorandum, benefits, financial, distribution.
Punctuation.   Commas before and after *Alabama* (, geographical).

◖ LETTER 51 ◖ (Related to Lesson 9, Letter 5)

Gratified, absenteeism, significant, previous, cooperation, maintaining.

Mr. Mann: We have been gratified by the progress you have made during the past month in reducing your[1] absenteeism at our Provo, Utah, plant. Although you have missed one day of work during the past month, this is a significant[2] improvement over your previous record.

Your continued cooperation in maintaining a good[3] attendance record will be sincerely appreciated. J. R. Kent   [73]

TRANSCRIPTION PREVIEW

Spelling. Gratified, absenteeism, although, significant.
Punctuation. Commas before and after *Utah* (, geographical).

❮ LETTER 52

Announce, foremost, impressive, representatives, advocates, enable.

To the Staff: We are pleased to announce that Randy Gray, one of the foremost lecturers in America on time[1] management, will be our speaker at the November sales training workshop in Houston, Texas.

Mr. Gray has an[2] impressive list of credentials. He has been the recipient of many awards in the field of management.[3] Because of his efforts, thousands of sales representatives have increased their sales records by applying the[4] principles he advocates.

We are certain that his message will enable all of us to achieve greater[5] productivity. Jane Patton   [104]

TRANSCRIPTION PREVIEW

Spelling. Foremost, lecturers, credentials, recipient.
Punctuation. Comma after *Houston* (, geographical).

❮ LETTER 53

Intricate, frustration, proficient, orientation, solution, modified, results.

Dear Mr. Davis: Do your new employees have a difficult time mastering the intricate details of your[1] business operations? Do they express frustration at the complexity of your many office rules, procedures,[2] and regulations? Does it often take them months to become proficient in performing their jobs?

If you are[3] spending too much time in the orientation and training of your new employees, perhaps we have a solution[4] to your problem. We have developed a training program which can easily be modified to any[5] particular business. The packet includes an illustrated booklet, a timely filmstrip, and accompanying[6] cassette tapes.

We are sending you this training program free of charge. Try it with your next new employee. If you like[7] the results, send us your check for the proper amount. If you are not satisfied, simply return the packet of[8] materials to our Tulsa, Oklahoma, office. You will be under no obligation. Cordially yours,[9]   [180]

Spelling.   Intricate, frustration, complexity, orientation, cassette.
Punctuation.   Commas before and after *Oklahoma* (, geographical).

ℂ LETTER 54

Personally, cafeteria, morale, decision, delicious, realized.

Mr. James: I want to tell you personally what a fine job our cafeteria staff has been doing during[1] the past year. Since we began opening the cafeteria in our Jackson, Mississippi, plant for breakfast[2] as well as lunch everyday, I have noticed a great improvement in employee morale. I firmly believe[3] that it was a very wise decision for us to open this facility.

I am pleased to report that the[4] cafeteria has been operating quite efficiently during the first year. We have managed to prepare[5] delicious, nourishing meals for all employees at a cost that is well below what we had expected. Although[6] we never intended to make a profit on the operation, we have actually realized a small surplus.[7]

We have several reasons to believe that we will be able to run the cafeteria in the years ahead[8] with the same efficiency that we have during the past year. Lee Davis   [174]

TRANSCRIPTION PREVIEW

Spelling. Cafeteria, breakfast, morale, quite.
Punctuation. Commas before and after *Mississippi* (, geographical).

LESSON 10

◖ LETTER 55 ◖ (Related to Lesson 10, Letter 3)

Invitation, attend, substantially, conference, supervises, programs, arrangements.

Dear Mr. Marks: Thank you for your invitation to attend your training seminar on the latest developments[1] in electronic equipment. I am sure that our employees could benefit substantially from your[2] presentation.

Unfortunately, we will be involved in a government audit during that time and will be[3] unable to release any of our staff for that training session.

Would it be possible for you to set up a[4] conference here at our Dearborn, Michigan, plant sometime next month? If it is possible, please contact Mr. Ralph[5] Jackson, who supervises all training programs, to make the necessary arrangements. Sincerely yours,   [118]

Spelling. Seminar, developments, substantially, audit.
Punctuation. Commas after *Unfortunately* (, introductory); before and after *Michigan* (, geographical).

❐ LETTER 56 ❐ (Related to Lesson 10, Letter 4)

Schedule, implement, adopt, impressed, previous, appreciated.

To the Staff: Last month we introduced the new work schedule in our department. Our intention was to implement[1] gradually this shorter work week, but the response from the members of the other departments has been so[2] enthusiastic that we are preparing to adopt the program throughout the company next month.

The home office staff[3] in Chicago, Illinois, has been impressed thus far with the results of our schedule change. The morale of our[4] personnel has shown a decided improvement, their rate of production has increased, and the quality of their work[5] has remained at their previous high level.

Your support of this program is appreciated. Doris Johnson[6]
[120]

Spelling. Introduced, enthusiastic, adopt, appreciated.
Punctuation. Commas after *week* (, conjunction); before and after *Illinois* (, geographical); after *improvement* and *increased* (, series).

❐ LETTER 57 ❐ (Related to Lesson 10, Letter 5)

Appreciated, conducting, somewhat, summarized, advisor, indicate.

Dear Mr. Bradley: We appreciated the efforts of your staff in setting up and conducting a workshop[1] on new tax laws. You may be interested in the comments of several of our employees who attended this[2] training program.

They felt that the program was somewhat too long. The information you gave could have been summarized[3] in a brief publication and sent to businesses for their individual use. Mr. Hastings, the former[4] government tax advisor, provided a great deal of information on specific tax laws. However, he[5] failed to indicate what impact each specific change would have on current business procedures.

We hope these suggestions[6] might be helpful in your planning of future seminars. Sincerely yours,   [134]

TRANSCRIPTION PREVIEW

Spelling.   Workshop, somewhat, brief, advisor.
Punctuation.   Commas before and after *the former government tax advisor* (, apposition); after *However* (, introductory).

⟨ LETTER 58

Decided, position, headquarters, extensive, personnel, forward.

Dear Mr. Bradford: We are pleased that you have decided to take a position with us in our Salem, Oregon,[1] office. You are scheduled to begin your employment next month.

We would like you to report to our company[2] headquarters in Los Angeles for extensive training. Our personnel director, Mr. James Cunningham, will[3] make all travel arrangements for both your trip to Los Angeles and your final move to Salem.

We are looking[4] forward to our association together. Sincerely yours,   [92]

Spelling.   Headquarters, extensive, personnel, forward.
Punctuation.   Commas before and after *Oregon* (, geographical);
before and after *Mr. James Cunningham* (, apposition).

ℂ LETTER 59

Congratulations, remarkable, establish, production, offered.

Mr. Church: Congratulations on your recent achievement with our company. The number of products you sold[1] in November is truly a remarkable accomplishment. We are always delighted when someone is able[2] to establish new sales records. It gives our other employees greater incentive to produce.

Since you have[3] won our top production prize, you may begin making plans for your vacation trip to Paris, France. This trip, which was[4] set up by our travel department, is one of the finest prizes we have ever offered.

We hope you will enjoy[5] yourself in France and that you will be ready to set new records when you return. Joan Harrington   [118]

Spelling.   Congratulations, remarkable, incentive, offered.
Punctuation.   Commas after *prize* (, introductory); after *Paris* (, geographical).

ℂ LETTER 60

Recently, considered, perspective, satisfied, in addition, warmer.

Dear Mr. Blair: A friend of mine, Ms. Jane Davis, told me recently that you are seeking someone to direct the[1] operations of your training department. I would very much like to be considered for employment with your[2] fine company. My data sheet is enclosed for your examination.

I have worked for several executives[3] during the past few years. Each of them has given me a valuable perspective for training employees. Although[4] I am very satisfied with my current position, I would welcome the opportunity to work for[5] a larger company. In addition, my family and I would like to move to a warmer climate.

I would[6] be happy to make arrangements for an interview at your convenience. I hope to hear from you soon. Cordially[7] yours, [141]

TRANSCRIPTION PREVIEW

Spelling.   Considered, examination, perspective, welcome.
Punctuation.   Commas before and after *Ms. Jane Davis* (, apposition); after *current position* and *In addition* (, introductory).

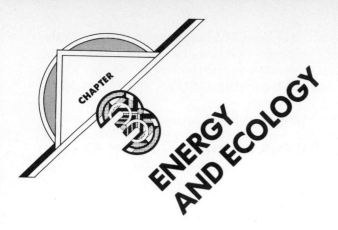

CHAPTER

ENERGY AND ECOLOGY

LESSON 11

❨ **LETTER 61** ❨ (Related to Lesson 11, Letter 3)

President, local, attempt, excessive, pollution, satisfactory.

Dear Ms. Garcia: Last month I was elected president of our local farm bureau. One of my pledges to[1] our members was to work with all levels of government in an attempt to reduce the burdening effect of[2] excessive controls.

Our governing board objects to your attempts to regulate the burning of weeds from our fields.[3] This is an example of the controls that make it difficult for us to continue farming.

I personally[4] believe that the matter of air pollution is an important one and must be dealt with effectively.[5] However, we must maintain the right to regulate this practice among our own members.

We believe we can do a[6] satisfactory job; we hope you agree. Because the planting season is rapidly approaching, we need to[7] come to an agreement on this issue soon. Cordially yours,   [151]

Spelling. Pledges, burdening, excessive, pollution.

Punctuation. Semicolon after *a satisfactory job* (; no conjunction).

❆ LETTER 62 ❆ (Related to Lesson 11, Letter 4)

Indicating, gasoline, exclusively, cutback, quotas.

Dear Mr. Maxwell: Yesterday I received your letter indicating that all gasoline supplies would be cut[1] beginning next month. As you know, the cold months are critical to the success of my operation. I rely[2] almost exclusively on the sale of gasoline products during these months.

I have decided, therefore, to seek[3] another supplier rather than accept the cutback you propose. I have reviewed our contract, and it specifies[4] that I can seek other suppliers if you fail to meet your quotas.

Please terminate your distribution to[5] my station at the end of this month. Please let me know if your situation changes; I would be glad to reconsider[6] my decision. Cordially yours, [127]

TRANSCRIPTION PREVIEW

Spelling. Success, exclusively, supplier, propose.

Punctuation. Semicolon after *if your situation changes* (; no conjunction).

❆ LETTER 63 ❆ (Related to Lesson 11, Letter 5)

Cooperation, discontinue, reaction, adjustment, terminating, attrition.

To All Store Managers: Thank you for your cooperation in our recent decision to discontinue keeping[1] our grocery stores open all night.

The reaction from the public appears to be favorable. The only[2] real problem within our operations has been the adjustment of work schedules. Please do whatever is[3] necessary to avoid terminating any employee because of this change. Within a few months, the normal[4] attrition rate should allow you to bring your staff down to desirable levels.

Thank you again for your[5] cooperation; it is sincerely appreciated. Jill Smith   [111]

TRANSCRIPTION PREVIEW

Spelling.   Adjustment, terminating, attrition, desirable.
Punctuation.   Semicolon after *your cooperation* in the last paragraph (; no conjunction).

❰ LETTER 64

Recent, concrete, evaporation, indicates, supported, project.

Dear Member: In a recent government bulletin a proposal was made to place a concrete dam at the end[1] of Farmington Lake. The contention is that this operation will save the thousands of gallons of water that[2] are lost through evaporation each year.

Our own research indicates that this contention is not supported by[3] fact. The actual net water savings from this operation will be minimal.

If you wish to express your[4] concern over this project, please write to your local and state government officials; their addresses are attached.[5] Only through a united effort can we bring the actual facts to light. Cordially yours,   [117]

Spelling. Concrete, contention, through, evaporation, minimal.
Punctuation. Semicolon after *government officials* (; no conjunction).

⓵ LETTER 65

Lexington, recreation, development, reconsider, residential, commissioners.

Dear Miss Roberts: For many years the city of Lexington has been purchasing land outside the city for park[1] and recreation development. I suggest that we reconsider this plan and try to bring recreation[2] sites closer to the people.

Much of our existing vacant land inside the city is very valuable because[3] it can be developed for residential purposes. However, there are a number of sites within the[4] city limits that are priced quite reasonably.

Locating more of our parks within the city boundaries would[5] be a real convenience to our citizens. In addition, the residents would save time and energy in[6] traveling to recreation sites.

I hope you and the other commissioners will consider this idea and be[7] prepared to discuss your recommendations at the next meeting. Thank you for your consideration; I genuinely[8] appreciate it. Yours truly,   [167]

Spelling. Recreation, residential, boundaries, traveling.
Punctuation. Semicolon after *your consideration* (; no conjunction).

◖ LETTER 66

Controlling, successful, effective, allowable, effectiveness, unused, cheerfully.

Dear Home Gardener: The chances are good that your experience in controlling insects during the past few years has[1] not been too successful.

The basic problem is that most effective sprays have been banned by the government. The[2] allowable sprays are effective only for a short time and rapidly break down within a few days.

We have[3] developed a new spray that might be the solution to your problem. This spray has the immediate killing effect[4] of other commercial products, but it retains its effectiveness for more than a month.

Your local dealer now[5] has this spray. We hope you will try it this year. If you are not satisfied, return the unused portion to your dealer;[6] your money will be cheerfully refunded. Cordially yours, [132]

TRANSCRIPTION PREVIEW

Spelling. Controlling, allowable, effectiveness, unused.
Punctuation. Semicolon after *to your dealer* (; no conjunction).

LESSON 12

◖ LETTER 67 ◖ (Related to Lesson 12, Letter 3)

Delicate, environment, vigorous, regulations, variance.

College Dictation for Transcription

Dear Mr. Willis: Achieving the delicate balance between a healthful environment and a vigorous[1] economy is not an easy matter. While we want everyone to cooperate in achieving the[2] objectives of recent government regulations, it is not our intent that the law threaten the survival of[3] any business.

There is a provision in the law that does not allow us to provide a variance due to[4] special circumstances. We would be willing to meet with you and discuss your situation at a time that will[5] be convenient for you.

Will you please let us know when you would like to meet with us. Sincerely yours,   [117]

TRANSCRIPTION PREVIEW

Spelling.   Achieving, vigorous, variance, circumstances.
Punctuation.   Period after the last sentence (. courteous request).

⊄ LETTER 68 ⊄ (Related to Lesson 12, Letter 4)

Research, ecology, hydrogen, flammable, unclassified.

Dear Mr. Lopez: The information you sent regarding your research was just what I needed for my report.[1] The members of my ecology class were quite interested in the information I presented.

One of the[2] class members raised a question concerning the safety of hydrogen. Because it is an extremely flammable[3] substance, how can problems of storing it in an airplane be overcome?

Will you please tell me about any research[4] that is currently being done in that area. Any leads you can provide on the location of[5] unclassified information will be sincerely appreciated. Cordially yours,   [115]

TRANSCRIPTION PREVIEW

Spelling.   Ecology, hydrogen, flammable.
Punctuation.   Period after *in that area* (. courteous request).

❰ LETTER 69 ❰ (Related to Lesson 12, Letter 5)

Appointment, terminate, will you please, conversation, ecological.

Dear Mr. Samuels: I am very much pleased with my appointment in your organization. I have made arrangements[1] with my present employer to terminate my services at the end of January. Will you please let[2] me know if I may begin work in your company in February.

As I indicated in our previous[3] conversation, I have always been interested in helping to restore the ecological balance of[4] the area lakes. The recent improvements in the lakes are evidence of what can be done through cooperation[5] of government, business, and private individuals.

You may be sure that I am enthusiastic over[6] the opportunities afforded me through an association with your organization. Cordially[7] yours,   [141]

TRANSCRIPTION PREVIEW

Spelling.   Previous, ecological, balance, cooperation.
Punctuation.   Period after *February* (. courteous request).

❰ LETTER 70

Range, announce, system, carburetor, foreign, self-addressed.

Dear Customer: Over the years our wholesale company has been providing our dealers a wide range of products[1] for automobiles. We have sold devices to make them safer, quieter, and more comfortable.

We are now[2] happy to announce that we have available for immediate delivery a new fuel system that mounts[3] easily to the carburetor of almost any foreign or domestic automobile. This device could[4] save your customers a great deal on their fuel costs. The system comes with an unconditional guarantee.

We know[5] you will want to carry the new system along with our other products. We will be happy to send you a free[6] demonstration model. To order one, just fill out and return the enclosed self-addressed card. May we hear from you[7] soon. Sincerely yours,

[144]

TRANSCRIPTION PREVIEW

Spelling. Carburetor, foreign, domestic, guarantee.
Punctuation. Period after the last sentence (. courteous request).

◖ LETTER 71

Followed, atmosphere, presentation, environmental, contribution.

Dear Mr. Ellsburg: I have followed with interest the work you and your research team have done on the effects of burning[1] certain fuels on our atmosphere.

Our college is conducting a workshop next month on energy research, and[2] we would be delighted if you would make a presentation at one of our meetings. We are not a political[3] group; our only purpose is to keep business, government, and civic leaders informed on important[4] environmental issues.

I have included a tentative schedule of our meetings with this letter. If you can be[5] with us, please indicate the time and date you prefer.

We would be honored by your contribution to our workshop[6] series. May we have your answer by return mail. Cordially yours,

[132]

Spelling.   Fuels, delighted, environmental, honored.
Punctuation.   Period after the last sentence (. courteous request).

⊄ LETTER 72

[shorthand]

Homeowner, stockholders, unique, insulation, commercial, seriously.

Dear Homeowner: Our stockholders approved a unique arrangement at our last general meeting. They authorized[1] us to offer our customers financing for the addition of insulation to their homes at very low[2] interest rates. This plan is our way of encouraging our customers to use less energy while increasing the[3] comfort of their homes.

Our customers can make arrangements with any commercial installer on our approved list[4] to bring their insulation up to the proper levels in their ceilings and walls. The interest charge will be[5] considerably less than that offered by most commercial banks.

We hope you will consider seriously taking[6] advantage of this fine opportunity to save energy. In order to take advantage of this unusual[7] opportunity, all you need do is fill out, sign, and return the enclosed form. May we hear from you soon.[8] Sincerely yours,

[162]

TRANSCRIPTION PREVIEW

Spelling.   Stockholders, unique, insulation, considerably.
Punctuation.   Period after the last sentence (. courteous request).

LESSON 13

⊄ LETTER 73 ⊄ (Related to Lesson 13, Letter 3)

[shorthand]

Review, modifications, adapted, influence, unauthorized, decision.

Dear Ms. Allen: Enclosed is a sample of the newly developed environmental education materials[1] you requested for review. I hope you find them suitable for your needs.

With just a few modifications,[2] the materials we are sending you can be adapted to almost any ecology course. We believe[3] that these materials have done a great deal to influence our students.

I want to caution you about[4] duplicating materials for classroom use. The material is copyrighted by a major publisher[5] and can be reproduced only with permission of that company. Any unauthorized reproduction of[6] the material will, of course, violate the copyright law.

We hope to hear from you soon in regard to your[7] decision on using our materials. Cordially yours,   [151]

TRANSCRIPTION PREVIEW

Spelling.   Developed, suitable, permission, unauthorized.
Punctuation.   No hyphen after *newly* (no hyphen after *-ly*).

❦ LETTER 74 ❦ (Related to Lesson 13, Letter 4)

Up-to-date, radiation, attorney, expect, liability, lawsuits.

Dear Mr. Lane: We have studied your up-to-date report on the radiation levels in your area. In[1] addition, I have gone over the legal aspects of the case with the state attorney, George Morris; I expect[2] an opinion from his office before the end of the month.

The circumstances surrounding this situation[3] are unfortunate. We are, of course, concerned over the health of our residents, but we must also be concerned[4] over the question of legal liability. We fully expect that there will be a number of lawsuits[5] initiated.

Please keep me well informed of future developments in this situation. Yours truly,   [119]

Spelling.   Radiation, levels, aspects, unfortunate.
Punctuation.   Hyphenate *up-to-date* (hyphenated before noun); no hyphen in *well informed* (no noun, no hyphen).

ℂ LETTER 75 ℂ (Related to Lesson 13, Letter 5)

Announcing, committee, flattered, offshore, committed.

Dear Mr. Martin: Your letter announcing my appointment as head of the energy research committee arrived[1] at the office yesterday. I am flattered by this appointment. Since my last contact with you, however, I[2] have had second thoughts about accepting such a great responsibility.

I was hired by my employer here[3] in Houston, Texas, to help develop our offshore oil operations. We set some very important objectives[4] to which I committed myself. Since these objectives have only been partially realized, I feel that I should[5] devote all my time to this project.

I must, therefore, decline your fine offer. I know you will be able to find[6] a well-qualified person to carry out your important research project. Sincerely yours,   [137]

Spelling.   Appointment, flattered, accepting, offshore.
Punctuation.   Hyphenate *well-qualified* (hyphenated before noun).

ℂ LETTER 76

Recently, associate, tentative, exploration, project, as soon as possible.

Ms. Brown: Recently I received an interesting letter from James Lexington, a former associate of mine.[1]

Mr. Lexington purchased several thousand acres of land in Arizona, New Mexico, and Utah[2] a few years ago. He hopes to be able to drill oil or gas wells on the property, but he needs a great deal[3] of technical advice before he begins work. At the present time he has a tentative agreement with a[4] well-known bank to provide financing for the exploration.

I think it would be a good idea for our company[5] to work with Mr. Lexington on this project. Would you like to go with me to see him sometime in the next[6] few weeks? If you would, please let me know as soon as possible. I will make arrangements for the trip. Marie Yates   [139]

TRANSCRIPTION PREVIEW

Spelling.   Associate, acres, advice, tentative, arrangements.
Punctuation.   Hyphenate *well-known* (hyphenated before noun).

ℂ LETTER 77

Monthly, yourself, insulated, furnace, sole, comfortable.

Dear Mrs. Sparks: Do you shudder when you receive your monthly heating bills during the cold months? If you do, ask yourself[1] these questions.

Do you have proper insulation in your attic? Are your walls also well insulated? Do[2] you feel drafts in your house when the winds blow? Do your windows steam up when you are cooking? Does your furnace turn on[3] repeatedly during the night?

Our firm has been in business for many years in this city. Our sole purpose is to[4] make your home more comfortable and cost less to heat and cool.

If you will return the enclosed self-addressed envelope,[5] one of our representatives will call on you and give you a free estimate on how you can save substantially[6] on your present heating bills. Sincerely yours,   [130]

Spelling. Insulation, attic, steam, substantially.
Punctuation. No hyphen in *well insulated* (no noun, no hyphen).

ℂ LETTER 78

Newly, evaluate, determine, modifications, themselves, obligation.

Dear Homeowner: Enclosed is a newly written checklist that will enable you to evaluate the energy[1] efficiency of your home. Go over this checklist with your family. You will appreciate the many[2] factors that determine how much your fuel costs are in a given year.

Begin making improvements now by adding[3] extra insulation, weather stripping, or storm doors and windows to your home. By making these modifications,[4] your home will be a more comfortable place in which to live, and the improvements will pay for themselves in fuel savings[5] in just a few years.

The checklist is yours with no obligation. It is our way of encouraging you to[6] join the fight to save our dwindling fuel resources. Cordially yours, [132]

TRANSCRIPTION PREVIEW

Spelling. Checklist, enable, evaluate, insulation.
Punctuation. No hyphen after *newly* (no hyphen after *-ly*).

LESSON 14

ℂ LETTER 79 ℂ (Related to Lesson 14, Letter 3)

Chemical, analyze, impurities, inhibit, pollution, rather.

Ms. Washington: I have been working on the problem of the chemical and radiation levels in our plant[1] as you directed.

Last week I hired Mr. Lee Davis, a local chemist, to take and analyze several[2] air samples in those areas where our employees work. His report was quite interesting; it revealed that harmful[3] conditions exist in only one area.

Mr. Davis suggested that we could take one of two specific[4] steps. We could replace the equipment in the area, or we could equip each person with a special mask[5] to filter out impurities. This mask, however, may inhibit each employee's effectiveness.

If we decide[6] to replace the equipment to reduce pollution levels, the project could be rather long and costly. Please[7] let me have your ideas on the matter. George Fox   [149]

TRANSCRIPTION PREVIEW

Spelling. Chemical, radiation, harmful, exist.
Punctuation. Employee's (singular possessive).

ℂ LETTER 80 ℂ (Related to Lesson 14, Letter 4)

Challenge, prescribed, community, stockholders, appointment.

Dear Mr. Ward: The challenge of reducing industrial pollution to the levels prescribed by law is a[1] concern to each of us. The responsibility is ours as well as yours. The people in your community[2] want clean air to breathe. The workers in your plant want to continue to make a living. Your stockholders want your[3] operations to return a dividend to them. And government officials would like to satisfy everyone.[4]

Meeting all these goals within a year's time may be an impossible task. It is a well-known fact, however, that[5] without goals it is hard to make any progress.

If you would like to call my office to set up an appointment[6] to discuss the current regulations, I will be glad to meet with your representative. Sincerely yours,   [139]

Spelling. Challenge, prescribed, stockholders, representative.

Punctuation. Ours, yours (no apostrophe in possessive pronoun); year's (singular possessive).

◁ LETTER 81 ◁ (Related to Lesson 14, Letter 5)

Article, agree, enjoy, perspective, / meditate, contribution.

Dear Mrs. Yates: In a recent article I stated that walking is perhaps the most effective, safe exercise[1] for most people. As you will remember, I based the article on a letter of yours. I have received many[2] responses from people who agree with us.

Hundreds of people wrote to me about how much they enjoy walking[3] as a form of daily exercise. Many people commented that walking gives them a fresh perspective on[4] things. It provides them an opportunity to meditate as they have not done for years. Several even mentioned[5] the fuel they save because they use their automobiles less frequently.

The letter you submitted was most[6] intriguing. I am writing another article on the same subject; it will be published in next week's newspaper.[7] Thank you for your contribution, Mrs. Yates. Sincerely yours, [151]

TRANSCRIPTION PREVIEW

Spelling. Article, effective, enjoy, perspective.

Punctuation. Yours (no apostrophe in possessive pronoun); week's (singular possessive).

◁ LETTER 82

Resulting, encouraging, requires, unfortunately, token, modify.

Dear Mr. Strong: I have been reviewing your report dealing with the cleanup operations resulting from oil[1] spills along our state's highways; the success of these operations is not encouraging.

The current law requires[2] companies responsible for the spills to do the cleanup operations themselves. Unfortunately, it is[3] difficult to enforce this law, and often only a token effort is made to do the job right.

I recommend[4] that we petition the legislature to grant us administrative power to modify the current[5] regulations. I would like to see us hire private contractors to do the work and then bill the responsible[6] companies for the cost.

Do you think we could persuade the executive committee to grant us this much-needed[7] change? Sincerely yours, [144]

TRANSCRIPTION PREVIEW

Spelling. Encouraging, token, petition, persuade.
Punctuation. State's (singular possessive).

◖ LETTER 83

Undoubtedly, fortunately, appears, information, enough.

Dear Mrs. Cunningham: Undoubtedly, you have read about the flooding that occurred in our state a few years ago.[1] This disaster was the result of inadequate flood-control planning. The property damage was very[2] great; fortunately, there were no lives lost.

It appears from recent publications that many areas throughout[3] our region have inadequate flood-control plans. Do you have any current information on our state's current[4] plans? If you do, I hope you will be good enough to share the information with me. Sincerely yours, [98]

TRANSCRIPTION PREVIEW

Spelling. Occurred, inadequate, fortunately, enough.
Punctuation. State's (singular possessive).

❰ LETTER 84

Inventive, conserving, consequently, appliances, electricity, dishwashers.

Dear Homemaker: The inventive capacity of America's researchers is almost incredible. A[1] few years ago everyone became concerned with conserving our energy resources. Consequently, our[2] engineers and designers began working on plans for more efficient home appliances. We think you will be impressed[3] by their achievements.

Our newest line of refrigerators consumes even less electricity than last[4] year's models; our ranges are even more efficient. Our dishwashers will do a more thorough cleaning job on your[5] dishes and pans at less cost than previous models.

We are proud of our record and would like the opportunity[6] to help you save money on your energy bills.

Drop in to one of our appliance centers soon and ask for[7] a demonstration of our new line. We think you will be glad you did. Cordially yours,   [155]

TRANSCRIPTION PREVIEW

   Spelling.   Inventive, designers, efficient, impressed.
   Punctuation.   America's (singular possessive).

LESSON 15

❰ LETTER 85 ❰ (Related to Lesson 15, Letter 3)

Lecture, informative, considerable, rather, documented, guidelines.

Dear Miss Edwards: The lecture by Mr. Don Kelly yesterday evening was one of the most informative I[1] have ever heard. Mr. Kelly has obviously done considerable research on important environmental[2] issues. Rather than using scare tactics to arouse public interest, he has carefully documented[3] the problems he felt deserve attention.

As a result of his lecture, our organization has decided[4] to work to improve the environment of our area. With the guidelines Mr. Kelly provided, we feel[5] we can be an effective force in our state.

Thank you for your invitation to a very profitable[6] presentation, Miss Edwards. Cordially yours, [127]

TRANSCRIPTION PREVIEW

Spelling. Obviously, tactics, documented, guidelines.
Punctuation. Commas after *public interest* (, introductory); before *Miss Edwards* (, parenthetical).

❡ LETTER 86 ❡ (Related to Lesson 15, Letter 4)

Determined, enthusiasm, reseeding, perpetuation, in the future, let us know.

Dear Mr. Fraser: If the success of a project can be determined by the enthusiasm of its[1] participants, our efforts in reseeding some of the critical grazing lands for our deer herds was a great success.[2]

Our members have thoroughly enjoyed their involvement with your department during the past few months. The cooperation[3] of your range biologist was certainly appreciated.

We hope we have contributed something[4] important to the perpetuation of our wildlife here in our state. If we can be of service again in[5] the future, please let us know. Sincerely yours, [108]

Spelling. Involvement, cooperation, biologist, perpetuation.
Punctuation. Commas after *participants* and *in the future* (, *if* clause).

❏ LETTER 87 ❏ (Related to Lesson 15, Letter 5)

Sponsor, legislation, random, personally, successful.

Dear Mr. Lee: We commend your organization's plans to sponsor legislation to improve the air quality[1] in all public buildings.

The members of our board were in favor of your work. However, a random poll of[2] our members disclosed that a majority are not in favor of becoming actively involved with such a[3] long-term project. I personally hope your efforts are successful.

Please don't hesitate to contact us again[4] in the future if we can be of some service to you. Sincerely yours,   [93]

Spelling. Commend, random, successful, hesitate.
Punctuation. Organization's (singular possessive); hyphenate *long-term* (hyphenated before noun).

❏ LETTER 88

Accident, twice, encourage, specialist, challenge, exploration.

Dear Janice: It is no accident that our firm has been selling twice as many solar heating units to[1] homeowners in this state than in any other state. The legislature here provides a substantial income tax credit[2] to residents who install solar systems.

If we are to increase our sales and meet our long-range goals, we must[3] encourage other states to offer the same kind of incentive to their residents. We would like to hire you as[4] a legislative specialist whose primary responsibility would be to encourage this type of[5] legislation in other states.

If you are interested in such a challenge, call me soon for further exploration[6] of the matter. Cordially yours, [126]

TRANSCRIPTION PREVIEW

Spelling. Solar, homeowners, substantial, incentive.
Punctuation. Hyphenate *long-range* (hyphenated before noun); commas after *goals* and *challenge* (*, if* clause).

❰ LETTER 89

Publication, whereby, although, laboratory, unique, convenience.

Ladies and Gentlemen: In a recent publication I read that your school has developed a process whereby[1] oil may be extracted from oil shale economically. Although many other such plans have surfaced during the[2] past few years, yours appears to be the most feasible.

I have been working with a research laboratory actively[3] involved with this type of extraction. We have made several interesting discoveries. We do not, however,[4] have all the answers to the unique problems we face.

Would you be interested in discussing our findings? Perhaps[5] some of our research will be helpful to your group. We would be happy to talk with you at your convenience.[6] Cordially yours, [122]

TRANSCRIPTION PREVIEW

Spelling. Extracted, laboratory, unique, convenience.
Punctuation. Comma after *years* (, introductory); yours (no apostrophe in possessive pronoun).

❡ LETTER 90

Reclamation, conservation, according, sustain, support, recommendation.

Dear Mr. Morgan: I studied your reclamation proposals and met with our conservation group last evening[1] to discuss the implications.

Our group is unwilling to support your proposal as it now reads. We object[2] to your plan to reduce the water level in several streams. According to the research we have obtained from[3] our team of wildlife specialists and biologists, the remaining flow will not sustain fish life. We believe the[4] water must be maintained at its present level.

If this change in your plans is made, I am sure we will lend our public[5] support to your program. I hope to hear from you soon in regard to this recommendation. Cordially yours,[6] [120]

TRANSCRIPTION PREVIEW

Spelling. Reclamation, conservation, implications, biologists.
Punctuation. Comma after *biologists* (, introductory); after *is made* (, *if* clause).

CHAPTER

MOTOR VEHICLES

LESSON 16

⟮ LETTER 91 ⟮ (Related to Lesson 16, Letter 3)

Suggestion, visited, awaiting, delivery, thank you for your, comfort, convenience.

Dear Mr. Jones: Last Friday, September 20, I took your suggestion and visited my local Davis[1] automobile dealer. The manager, Mr. Mark Garcia, gave me the facts about all seven models of the[2] new Davis cars.

I placed my order with Mr. Garcia for a new Davis, and I am eagerly awaiting[3] delivery sometime next week.

Thank you for your letter inviting me to try the new Davis. I am sure[4] it will provide economy, comfort, and convenience. Yours truly,   [93]

TRANSCRIPTION PREVIEW

Spelling.   Models, sometime (one word), economy, convenience.
Punctuation.   Commas before and after *Mr. Mark Garcia* (, apposition).
Typing Style.   Transcribe: September 20 (figures); seven models (letters).

◖ LETTER 92 ◗ (Related to Lesson 16, Letter 4)

[shorthand symbols]

Reviewed, industry, average, competitor, Cleveland, committed, enjoying.

Dear Ms. Chester: On January 15 I reviewed the past year's financial records of our insurance[1] company. Our operating costs were 10 percent lower than the industry average and 15 percent lower[2] than our nearest competitor here in Cleveland, Ohio.

Our policyholders are committed to the[3] principles of defensive driving; statistics show they have fewer accidents. If you would like to participate[4] in the savings our current members are enjoying, return the enclosed self-addressed card.

If you qualify for[5] our insurance, we would be happy to number you among the more than 100,000 drivers who are paying[6] less for their automobile insurance. Cordially yours,   [131]

TRANSCRIPTION PREVIEW

Spelling.   Financial, statistics, participate, self-addressed.
Punctuation.   Comma after *enjoying* (, *if* clause).
Typing Style.   Transcribe: January 15 (figures); 10 percent, 15 percent, 100,000 (figures).

◖ LETTER 93 ◗ (Related to Lesson 16, Letter 5)

[shorthand symbols]

August, executive, requiring, restraint, history, ahead, contrary.

Mr. White: On August 21 I talked with Mr. William Carson, a government executive, about[1] legislation requiring automobile manufacturers to equip cars with air bags, seat belts, or other[2] restraint devices. He was kind enough to review the history of auto safety laws with me.

Mr. Carson[3] feels that most people who favor the use of air bags are not aware of how much they will add to the cost of[4] a new car. When they realize how much it would cost to purchase air bags, they may decide to use regular seat belts[5] instead.

However, it is my feeling that we should go ahead with research and develop two or three types of[6] air bags. Unless I hear from you to the contrary, I will proceed with your directive. Ellen Agronski   [139]

TRANSCRIPTION PREVIEW

Spelling.   Legislation, restraint, aware, ahead.
Punctuation.   Comma after *However* (, introductory).
Typing Style.   Transcribe: August 21 (figures); two or three (letters).

⊄ LETTER 94

Casualty, depend, whenever, accidents, determined, reviewed, category, premiums, offset, hesitate.

Dear Mr. Harrington: As you know, the rates charged by casualty insurance companies depend on the risks involved.[1] Unfortunately, whenever one of our insured drivers is involved in too many accidents, that person[2] becomes an unusually high risk for the company.

Since January 13 you have had three accidents[3] in which it was determined that you were at fault. We paid out several thousand dollars in claims for these[4] accidents.

We have reviewed your records very carefully, and we feel that we must transfer you to our high-risk[5] category. Your insurance premiums will be increased 5 percent beginning November 10. The increase will[6] help offset the added risk you represent to the company.

If you have questions, please do not hesitate to[7] call us. Yours truly, [144]

TRANSCRIPTION PREVIEW

Spelling. Casualty, risks, carefully, offset.
Punctuation. Commas after *As you know* (, *as* clause); after *Unfortunately* (, introductory).
Typing Style. Transcribe: January 13, November 10 (figures); three accidents (letters); 5 percent (figure).

ℂ LETTER 95

Unhappy, economy, mileage, pointed, conditions, provided.

Dear Ms. Brown: Thank you for your letter of March 21. We are sorry that you are unhappy with the economy[1] of your new Jefferson car. Our records indicate that your mileage is about the same as that experienced[2] by more than 5,000 other Jefferson owners.

As you pointed out, your mileage is below the figure[3] posted on the window sticker of your new car. This figure was based on carefully controlled driving in ideal[4] conditions. We pointed out to you at the time you purchased your car that it was not likely that you could achieve[5] this mileage.

I am sure you can improve your mileage, Ms. Brown, by observing the driving tips outlined in the[6] booklet we provided you.

If we can be of help to you, I hope you will feel free to call on us. Sincerely[7] yours, [141]

TRANSCRIPTION PREVIEW

Spelling. Economy, mileage, ideal, outlined.
Punctuation. Comma after *As you pointed out* (, *as* clause).
Typing Style. Transcribe: March 21, 5,000 (figures).

❅ LETTER 96

(shorthand outline)

Transmission, occasionally, repaired, center, warranty, exchange.

Dear Ms. Franklin: Thank you for your letter of Wednesday, August 2. We were happy to hear from you, but we were sorry[1] to learn that you have had so much difficulty with the transmission in your new car. Occasionally, there[2] is a weakness in a few new parts, and they simply fail to work properly.

That appears to be the problem with[3] your automobile. As you know, we have repaired the transmission three times, but each time a new problem develops.[4]

If you will bring your car to our service center, we will replace the transmission with a new one. Of course, your[5] warranty will cover the cost of this exchange. We will be happy to provide you with one of our demonstration[6] vehicles during the time the repairs are being made. Sincerely yours, [133]

TRANSCRIPTION PREVIEW

Spelling. Transmission, occasionally, develops, exchange.

Punctuation. Commas after *Occasionally* (, introductory); after *service center* (, *if* clause).

Typing Style. Transcribe: August 2 (figure); three times (letters).

LESSON 17

❅ LETTER 97 (Related to Lesson 17, Letter 3)

(shorthand outline)

Provision, installment, license, payment, imposes, credit, union.

Dear Mr. Lane: We have no provision in the law for the payment of personal property taxes on an[1] installment basis. Your automobile tax was due and payable during the month that your car was registered.[2] In fact, we cannot renew the registration on your car or issue you a new license plate without the payment[3] of this tax.

We are sorry that this requirement imposes an economic burden on you. We suggest[4] that you contact a local savings and loan institution, credit union, or bank to arrange a short-term loan.[5]

If you would like to speak with anyone about this matter, I am in my office from 9 a.m. until 5[6] p.m. weekdays. Cordially yours,

[126]

TRANSCRIPTION PREVIEW

Spelling. Installment, license, imposes.
Punctuation. Commas after *In fact* (, introductory); after *institution* and *union* (, series).
Typing Style. Transcribe: 9 a.m. until 5 p.m. (figures).

⁅ LETTER 98 ⁅ (Related to Lesson 17, Letter 4)

International, radial, advise, reputation, therefore, everything.

Dear Ms. Best: Thank you for purchasing a set of International steel-belted radial tires. I am enclosing[1] your warranty; it is good for one year or 10,000 miles.

We advise you to read the warranty carefully,[2] store it in a readily accessible location, and refer to it if you ever have a problem[3] with your International tires.

We are proud of our reputation for standing behind our products. A happy[4] customer will buy from us again and again. Therefore, we will do everything possible to provide the kind[5] of service we think you deserve. Our service department is open from seven in the morning until nine in[6] the evening. You do not need an appointment; just stop in whenever we can be of service to you. Sincerely[7] yours,

[141]

Spelling. Radial, advise, carefully, reputation.
Punctuation. Semicolon after *enclosing your warranty* (; no conjunction).
Typing Style. Transcribe: seven ... nine (letters).

❰ LETTER 99 ❰ (Related to Lesson 17, Letter 5)

Thank you for, checked, trained, remember, appointment, department.

Dear Mr. Benson: Thank you for bringing in your car for an inspection last week. We are certain you will find the[1] car will run better now. We tuned the motor, checked all the electrical wiring, and changed the oil.

Please plan to bring[2] your car in every six months. Our experienced, well-trained staff will keep your car running in perfect condition.[3] Remember, you do not have to have an appointment. Our service department is open from 7 a.m. until[4] 10 p.m. every day. Sincerely yours, [87]

TRANSCRIPTION PREVIEW

Spelling. Inspection, electrical, experienced, appointment.
Punctuation. Comma after *experienced* (, *and* omitted).
Typing Style. Transcribe: 7 a.m. until 10 p.m. (figures).

❰ LETTER 100

Indicate, assumed, references, obtained, previous, delinquent, collateral.

Dear Ms. Elton: Our records indicate that you are more than two months past due on your car payment. At the time we[1] assumed your loan from the Cunningham Motor Company, we checked your references and credit rating thoroughly.[2] The information we obtained on your past credit history showed no previous record of delinquent payments.[3]

Our policy is to repossess the collateral when any account becomes three months past due. We know[4] you would not like to give up your fine, new automobile. To prevent that from happening, please send us your check[5] immediately.

If you are having financial difficulty, please let us know. Our offices are open from[6] nine in the morning until five in the afternoon. Cordially yours, [133]

TRANSCRIPTION PREVIEW

Spelling.   Assumed, delinquent, repossess, collateral.
Punctuation.   Commas after *Company* (, introductory); after *fine* (*, and* omitted).
Typing Style.   Transcribe: nine . . . five (letters).

⟪ LETTER 101

Polls, determine, representatives, image, thoroughly, inspection.

Dear Neighbor: Most polls taken to determine the public's confidence in those engaged in various occupations[1] reveal that car sales representatives are most often low on the list. At Smith Sales and Service we are doing[2] everything possible to change the image.

In the first place, all our personnel are thoroughly trained before[3] they ever sell a car. Second, every car we sell is subjected to a thorough inspection. We provide the[4] prospective customers with a checklist so they know exactly what they are buying.

Try us at Smith Sales and Service[5] when you are in the market for a car. We are open from 8 a.m. until 10 p.m. every day.[6] Cordially yours, [122]

Spelling. Polls, confidence, image, thoroughly.
Punctuation. Public's (singular possessive).
Typing Style. Transcribe: 8 a.m. until 10 p.m. (figures).

❰ LETTER 102

Occupants, vehicle, attorney, situation, difficulties, inconveniences.

Dear Mrs. Farmer: One evening a friend of mine had an automobile accident in a remote location.[1] He went through a stop sign
at an intersection and hit another car. Because the injuries to the
occupants[2] of the other vehicle were severe, he had to post a bond.
The driver of the other car brought a suit[3] against him. Of course,
all of this required the services of his attorney.

Before this situation was resolved,[4] my friend had to pay several
thousand dollars. These financial difficulties could have been eliminated[5] if he had had proper liability insurance.

If you would like to protect yourself from the expenses[6] and
inconveniences of this type of risk, return the enclosed card. One
of our representatives will call[7] for an appointment to explain our
program in detail. We open every morning at 9 a.m. Cordially[8]
yours,   [161]

Spelling. Occupants, resolved, eliminated, liability.
Punctuation. Commas after *resolved* (, introductory).
Typing Style. Transcribe: 9 a.m. (figure).

⫶ LETTER 103 ⫶ (Related to Lesson 18, Letter 3)

Gomez, acquaintances, position, discuss, assistant, associates, recommend.

Dear Janet: When I received your letter on April 3, I immediately called Mr. Bill Gomez, one of[1] my business acquaintances, to see if he might be interested in a position with your firm. Mr. Gomez[2] stated that he would like to discuss the job with you. I gave him your name, address, and telephone number. I am[3] sure that he will call you soon to discuss the opening.

Mr. Gomez is a competent, successful assistant[4] service manager with National Motors here in the East. He has been in the business for ten years and is[5] well liked and respected by his associates.

I recommend him for the position you have available;[6] I am sure he can lead your service department to outstanding achievements in the future. Sincerely yours, [139]

TRANSCRIPTION PREVIEW

Spelling. Acquaintances, discuss, assistant, associates.
Punctuation. Commas before and after *one of my business acquaintances* (, apposition); after *name* and *address* (, series).
Typing Style. Transcribe: National Motors, East (capitalized); service department (not capitalized).

⫶ LETTER 104 ⫶ (Related to Lesson 18, Letter 4)

Edwards, center, Tatum, needed, estimate, completed, businesslike.

Dear Mr. Edwards: On Tuesday, November 3, I brought my car in to the Madison Auto Center for some repair[1] work. Your service manager, Mr. Tatum, explained the work my car needed, gave me an estimate of the[2] charges for both labor and parts, and completed the job on time.

I must say that your professional, businesslike[3] approach was very impressive. As a result, I am more than satisfied with the service I received at[4] the Madison Auto Center.

You may be sure I will bring my automobile to your shop when it again needs repair[5] work. Cordially yours, [104]

TRANSCRIPTION PREVIEW

Spelling. Repair, labor, professional, businesslike.
Punctuation. Commas before and after *November 3* and *Mr. Tatum* (, apposition).
Typing Style. Transcribe: Madison Auto Center (capitalized).

❰ LETTER 105 ❰ (Related to Lesson 18, Letter 5)

Children, eventually, condenser, disconnected, attached, prior.

Dear Mrs. Boyle: A few days ago I was driving in the country with my children. My car began to miss, and[1] eventually the engine stopped running. I raised the hood and noticed almost immediately that the condenser[2] wire had become disconnected. I attached the wire, and the car started instantly.

If this experience[3] had occurred prior to my class in basic auto repairs at East Side High School, I would have had no idea what to[4] do. I am grateful for this fine program. The instructor, Mr. Sweet, did an excellent job. He is both a fine[5] mechanic and an excellent teacher.

I am recommending that several of my friends enroll in the course[6] next term. Cordially yours, [124]

Spelling. Condenser, disconnected, grateful, excellent.
Punctuation. Commas before and after *Mr. Sweet* (, apposition).
Typing Style. Transcribe: East Side High School (capitalized).

❡ LETTER 106

Annual, honors, banquet, history, distinguished, entertainment.

To All Employees: Our annual honors banquet will be held at the Nashville Restaurant on Thursday, the 10th[1] of February, at 7:30 p.m. We hope everyone will make reservations for this meeting by[2] calling Ms. Sue Trent, my executive assistant, before next Friday.

As most of you know, we sold more cars this[3] past year than in any other year of our history. The management of Morgan Motors is proud of this[4] accomplishment. We plan to make several presentations at the banquet to those of you who have distinguished yourselves[5] through your sales achievements.

A fine buffet dinner and outstanding musical entertainment will make this a[6] wonderful, memorable occasion for everyone. Make your reservation soon. Donna Mason   [138]

TRANSCRIPTION PREVIEW

Spelling. Restaurant, distinguished, buffet, memorable.
Punctuation. Commas after *As most of you know* (, *as* clause); after *wonderful* (, *and* omitted).
Typing Style. Transcribe: Nashville Restaurant, Morgan Motors (capitalized).

Awaited, unveiled, improvements, ample, interior, passenger, vehicle.

Dear Customer: The long-awaited day will soon be here. Our new line of National cars and trucks will be unveiled[1] on Thursday, October 21, at all three of our Columbus, Ohio, locations.

We know you will be[2] pleased with the many improvements that have been made in the National vehicles. They are lighter and more[3] economical this year, but they still provide ample space. The interior design of our passenger cars offers[4] more comfort and luxury than any other comparable vehicle on the market today.

We hope you[5] will plan to be among the first to see the new line of National cars and trucks. Sincerely yours,   [117]

TRANSCRIPTION PREVIEW

Spelling.   Unveiled, ample, luxury, comparable.
Punctuation.   Commas before and after *October 21* (, apposition).
Typing Style.   Transcribe: National (capitalized).

◖ LETTER 108

Enviable, experienced, understand, appropriate, program, today.

Dear Ms. Sanders: Southern Driving School has been in business for ten years here in Houston, Texas. Our record during[1] this time is an enviable one. We have taught more than 20,000 people to drive.

Our instructors are trained[2] and experienced. They strive to understand the special problems and needs of each individual student and[3] to design an appropriate instructional program. Our cars are all new, up-to-date models.

If you would like[4] to learn to drive quickly, conveniently, and safely, call the Southern Driving School today; our next session begins[5] on Monday, July 14. Sincerely yours, [108]

TRANSCRIPTION PREVIEW

Spelling. Enviable, design, appropriate, safely.
Punctuation. Commas after *Houston* (, geographical); after *Monday* (, apposition).
Typing Style. Transcribe: Southern Driving School (capitalized).

LESSON 19

⊄ LETTER 109 ⊄ (Related to Lesson 19, Letter 3)

Typical, something, imagine, leased, satisfied, pleasure.

Dear Mr. Bennett: Thank you for inviting me to examine your rental plan at Western Leasing. I was among[1] those typical Americans who thought that leasing automobiles was something only for big businesses.[2]

You can imagine my surprise when I discovered that I could lease and operate a full-size automobile[3] for three years for almost $1,000 less than I could purchase the same vehicle. Needless to say, I leased[4] the car.

I am quite satisfied with the car; it is a pleasure doing business at Western Leasing Company.[5] Sincerely yours, [103]

TRANSCRIPTION PREVIEW

Spelling. Discovered, vehicle, quite, business.
Punctuation. Hyphenate *full-size* (hyphenated before noun).
Typing Style. Transcribe: $1,000 (no decimal).

⟪ LETTER 110 ⟪ (Related to Lesson 19, Letter 4)

[shorthand symbols]

Appreciated, demonstration, disappointed, recall, $800.

Dear Mr. Taylor: We appreciated the opportunity of giving you a demonstration drive in[1] one of our new station wagons. We were, of course, somewhat disappointed that you decided not to make a purchase[2] at the time.

As you may recall, the offer we made you was $800 below the sticker price on[3] the car. We have carefully reviewed our costs on that particular vehicle and are prepared to reduce that[4] figure another $235 if you sign the necessary papers before the 12th of[5] September. This represents a savings of more than $1,000.

Call me at 555-8278[6] if you are still interested in purchasing the station wagon. Sincerely yours,   [135]

TRANSCRIPTION PREVIEW

Spelling.   Demonstration, disappointed, reviewed, represents.
Punctuation.   Commas before and after *of course* (, parenthetical); after *As you may recall* (, *as* clause).
Typing Style.   Transcribe: $800; $235; $1,000 (no decimals).

⟪ LETTER 111 ⟪ (Related to Lesson 19, Letter 5)

[shorthand symbols]

Discuss, impressed, paint, exact, specifications, tentative, behind.

Dear Mr. West: Several weeks ago I visited your shop to discuss my plans for painting my van. I was[1] impressed with the quality of Mr. Don Trenton's work, and he agreed to paint my vehicle according to[2] my exact specifications. The price we agreed on was $500 for the complete job.

Mr. Trenton[3] set a tentative date of August 13 to do the work. He said he would call me to verify the date.[4] It is now September 4. I have called Mr. Trenton three times, but each time he stated that he is behind schedule[5] and will do my work as soon as possible.

If he does not call within five days, I shall be forced to have the[6] job done elsewhere. Yours truly, [125]

TRANSCRIPTION PREVIEW

Spelling.   Specifications, tentative, verify, schedule.
Punctuation.   Commas after *Don Trenton's work* and *three times* (, conjunction).
Typing Style.   Transcribe: $500 (no decimal).

◖ LETTER 112

Parking, frequently, prohibitive, wherever, throughout, suburbs, coordinate.

To the Staff: Parking in the city has become a big problem for many of you. Spaces are frequently[1] unavailable, and cost is becoming prohibitive. Our data shows that our employees spend a total of[2] nearly $8,500 just to park their cars each year. We suggest that you form car pools wherever[3] possible to remedy this situation.

There are several large parking lots located throughout the suburbs.[4] Cars may be parked safely in these lots during the day. If several of you were to meet at one of these parking[5] areas, leave your cars, and proceed into the city in one vehicle, most of your parking problems would be[6] solved.

At our next staff meeting we will allow some time to coordinate the formation of car pools. Jane Street [139]

Spelling.   Prohibitive, suburbs, proceed, coordinate.
Punctuation.   Comma after *unavailable* (, conjunction).
Typing Style.   Transcribe: $8,500 (no decimal).

⟪ LETTER 113

Indicate, salespeople, volume, previous, excited, capable, boosting.

To the Staff: Current sales production figures indicate that our salespeople sold an average of 62[1] new and used cars during the past year. Our total dollar volume for that period was $1 million. This[2] represents a 13 percent increase over the previous year.

All of you appear to be excited with[3] our new line of cars, and we believe we are capable of boosting our sales even further during the coming[4] year.

I am, therefore, increasing the sales quotas for each salesperson by 10 percent. If you feel that this is an[5] unrealistic figure, please see me to discuss your situation immediately. R. D. French   [118]

TRANSCRIPTION PREVIEW

Spelling.   Salespeople, volume, excited, boosting.
Punctuation.   Commas after *line of cars* (, conjunction); before and after *therefore* (, parenthetical).
Typing Style.   Transcribe: $1 million (figure and word).

⟪ LETTER 114

Franklin, hundreds, resisted, along, realize, competent.

Dear Mr. Franklin: We install hundreds of automobile air conditioners each year. Many of these sales are[1] to people who have resisted purchasing air conditioning because they got along without it for so many[2] years. However, when they return to have their units serviced, most of them say they just didn't realize what they[3] had been missing.

We are currently conducting one of our best sales ever on our automobile air conditioners.[4] We can install a new air conditioner in your car for less than $500. Drop in and let[5] one of our competent people tell you how simple and inexpensive it is to drive in cool comfort this year.[6] Cordially yours,   [123]

TRANSCRIPTION PREVIEW

Spelling.   Realize, missing, competent, inexpensive.
Punctuation.   Comma after *However* (, introductory).
Typing Style.   Transcribe: $500 (no decimal).

LESSON 20

◖ LETTER 115 ◖ (Related to Lesson 20, Letter 3)

Purchased, possible, however, appearance, scarcely, thank you for the.

Dear Miss Summers: Three years ago I purchased my first new automobile. I have had great pride in that car, and I[1] have kept it looking as good as possible. Time does, however, take its toll. The car no longer had the bright, fresh[2] appearance it once had.

I took it to King Auto Center at 120 East Main Street last Wednesday as you[3] suggested. I can scarcely believe the difference; my car looks new once again.

Thank you for the fine job; I will see[4] you again in a few months. Cordially yours,   [88]

Spelling.   Great, toll, appearance, cordially.
Punctuation.   Commas before and after *however* (, parenthetical);
semicolons after *the difference* and *the fine job* (; no conjunction).
Typing Style.   Transcribe: 120 East Main Street.

◖ LETTER 116 ◗ (Related to Lesson 20, Letter 4)

Retake, licensing, examination, law, center, necessary.

Dear Mr. Frank: We are sorry that you did not choose to retake
your licensing examination. The law now[1] requires that we suspend your license effective June 25. Please mail your license immediately to the[2] bureau at 400 East 21 Street here in Springfield.

If you decide you want to drive in the future, you[3] may come to
our testing center, reapply for a new license, and take the necessary tests. Sincerely yours,[4]   [80]

Spelling.   Licensing, suspend, effective, reapply.
Punctuation.   Commas after *in the future* (, *if* clause); after *test-
ing center* and *a new license* (, series).
Typing Style.   Transcribe: 400 East 21 Street.

◖ LETTER 117 ◗ (Related to Lesson 20, Letter 5)

Greatly, contributed, added, regulations, decreased, technology.

Dear Mr. Lee: As you no doubt realize, the cost of new cars has increased greatly during the past few years. A number[1] of factors have contributed to this rise in price. These include increased labor costs, higher prices for parts[2] and materials, and the added expense of meeting government regulations.

One factor that adds to the[3] comfort and convenience of your automobile but very little to its cost is the electrical system.[4] Ten years ago the electrical system of your car represented about 18 percent of its total[5] cost. Today that figure has actually decreased to about 15 percent.

The Modern Electronics Company[6] at 1800 East Main Street is proud to have played a major role in the advanced electrical technology[7] that is such an important component of your automobile. Cordially yours, [156]

TRANSCRIPTION PREVIEW

Spelling.   Labor, convenience, actually, technology.
Punctuation.   Commas after *costs* and *materials* (, series).
Typing Style.   Transcribe: 1800 East Main Street.

ℂ LETTER 118

Appreciate, satisfied, indicated, alignment, remedied, refunded.

Dear Mr. Hailey: While I appreciate the efforts of the people who work in your service department in[1] repairing my automobile, I am far from satisfied with their work. My new car, which I purchased from your[2] agency at 200 Elm Street, shakes so badly at high speeds that I can hardly drive it.

When I returned it last[3] month, your service manager indicated that some alignment work was needed. The work was done, but the car seemed[4] to shake worse than ever. I called the manager again yesterday and requested that the car be checked again.[5]

If the problems are not remedied this time, I am afraid I will have to take action to have my money[6] refunded so that I can purchase another car. Cordially yours, [132]

Spelling. Alignment, worse, remedied, refunded.
Punctuation. Comma after *My new car* (, nonrestrictive).
Typing Style. Transcribe: 200 Elm Street.

❡ LETTER 119

Investigating, refurbish, interested, discussing, investment.

Dear James: I have been investigating the possibility of opening a budget automobile leasing[1] company in Medford. I believe there is a market there for the type of operation I would like to[2] run.

My plan is to purchase used cars, refurbish them, and rent them for less than other commercial operators[3] charge. I have discussed my idea with Mr. Max Turner, a business executive in the East who has a[4] similar operation, and he is very optimistic about my plans.

If you would be interested in[5] discussing the investment possibilities of this venture, please write me at 16 East 22 Street here[6] in Phoenix. Sincerely yours,   [125]

TRANSCRIPTION PREVIEW

Spelling. Budget, refurbish, optimistic, venture.
Punctuation. Comma after *venture* (, *if* clause).
Typing Style. Transcribe: 16 East 22 Street.

❡ LETTER 120

Seriously, final, decision, model, appreciate, ideas.

Dear Bill: For several months I have been looking at new cars, and I am seriously considering purchasing[1] a new Lexington from the agency at 200 East Broadway. Before I make a final decision,[2] I would like to have your opinion about the car. I am looking at an eight-cylinder model, but I am[3] afraid that it will give poor gas mileage.

Will you please let me have your opinion on this matter. I will certainly[4] appreciate having your ideas. Sincerely yours, [90]

TRANSCRIPTION PREVIEW

Spelling.   Seriously, cylinder, mileage, appreciate.
Punctuation.   Comma after *model* (, conjunction).
Typing Style.   Transcribe: 200 East Broadway.

PART 2

It is suggested that students transcribe the letters in Part 2 in semiblocked style with standard punctuation. Refer students to the model letter on page 123 of *Gregg Shorthand for Colleges, Transcription, Series 90.*

Beginning with Lesson 29, each lesson contains an office-style dictation letter. The office-style dictation letters in Chapters 6 through 16 illustrate the principles introduced in corresponding chapters in *Gregg Shorthand for Colleges, Transcription.* The problems are reviewed a number of times.

The office-style interpolations are marked in each letter at the point at which they should be dictated. This arrangement makes it possible to use the letters either as an office-style dictation exercise or as a regular timed dictation practice.

Chapter 5
PRINTED MEDIA
Lesson 21   Book titles
Lesson 22   Article titles
Lesson 23   Colon enumeration
Lesson 24   Comma introducing short
 quotation
Lesson 25   Colon introducing long
 quotation

Chapter 6
COMMUNICATIONS
Lesson 26   Capitalization of days,
 seasons, and so on

Chapter 7
HOMES

Chapter 8
AGRICULTURE AND FOOD

CHAPTER PRINTED MEDIA

LESSON 21

ⅭⅠ LETTER 121 ⅭⅠ (Related to Lesson 21, Letter 3)

Suggesting, appreciated, procedures, technical, understandable, libraries.

Ladies and Gentlemen: Your letter suggesting that I purchase a copy of *Your Income Tax Return* was most[1] appreciated. I am teaching income tax procedures to my finance class at Smith Technical College. I[2] bought a copy of your booklet hoping that I might be able to use it as a reference guide in my course.[3]

I am happy to tell you that the approach your authors use in *Your Income Tax Return* is the most precise and[4] understandable I have found. Judging from the reaction of the students who have used it, it is an excellent[5] resource.

Most of my students plan to add your publication to their personal libraries. Cordially yours,[6]   [120]

TRANSCRIPTION PREVIEW

Spelling. Procedures, hoping, precise, libraries.

Punctuation. Comma after *who have used it* (, introductory).

Typing Style. Underscore: *Your Income Tax Return* (underscore booklet title).

◖ LETTER 122 ◗ (Related to Lesson 21, Letter 4)

[shorthand]

Thank you for your order, few days', catalog, interested, budgeting, up-to-date.

Dear Ms. Johnson: Thank you for your order for *Success: Your Ultimate Goal.* It should arrive at your home within a[1] few days' time.

I am taking the personal liberty at this time of sending you our catalog that lists the[2] other financial aids we have available. Whether you are interested in general investments, the stock[3] market, or family budgeting, we can provide you with a variety of up-to-date materials[4] prepared by the most competent research staff in the business.

If you are not completely satisfied with *Success:*[5] *Your Ultimate Goal,* return it within ten days for a full refund. Sincerely yours,

[115]

TRANSCRIPTION PREVIEW

Spelling.   Taking, catalog, budgeting, competent.
Punctuation.   Days' (plural possessive); hyphenate *up-to-date* (hyphenated before noun).
Typing Style.   Underscore: *Success: Your Ultimate Goal* (underscore book title).

◖ LETTER 123 ◗ (Related to Lesson 21, Letter 5)

[shorthand]

Thank you for your, thoughtful, future, complimentary, format, circulate, delivered.

Dear Mr. Lyon: Thank you for your thoughtful letter. We hope you enjoy the future issues of the *Weekly*[1] *Reporter* as much as you did your recent complimentary copy.

Although the *Weekly Reporter* is a small[2] newspaper, we are proud of its well-designed format. We have received several national awards during the[3] past few years. We can publish and circulate our newspaper for only $10 per year because our staff is[4] small and our production costs are low.

You will begin receiving your copy of our newspaper on Monday,[5] November 3. It will be delivered to your door by seven in the morning every Monday. Sincerely yours, [119]

ℂ LETTER 124

Valley, register, conditions, undertake, corporation, Minnesota, Illinois, Ohio.

Dear Mr. Baldwin: Beginning June 1 we plan to start publishing the *Valley Register,* a weekly newspaper[1] in Springfield. The community has not had a local newspaper for more than five years, and we believe[2] conditions are now excellent for us to undertake this venture.

Our corporation is presently publishing[3] weekly newspapers in five other communities in Minnesota, Illinois, and Ohio. We feature[4] local events, sports news, and other items of special interest.

We would like to join the local Chamber of Commerce[5] and become active in your group. We hope to have an opportunity at the next meeting to present our[6] publishing plans to your members. Your interest is, of course, vital to us as we make preparations to begin[7] publication. Cordially yours, [146]

Spelling. Venture, communities, opportunity, preparations.
Punctuation. Commas after *Minnesota* and *Illinois* (, series).
Typing Style. Underscore: *Valley Register* (underscore newspaper title).

❮ LETTER 125

Professions, men and women, occupations, category, evaluate.

Dear Mr. Young: If you had the opportunity, would you change professions? Today men and women throughout the[1] country are seeking new careers.

A recent poll indicated that many employees are dissatisfied with[2] their present occupations. If you are in this category, we suggest that you order our new book, *Today's[3] Career Choices*. This publication is designed to help people of all ages evaluate their interests and[4] aptitudes and learn about new job opportunities. *Today's Career Choices* lists more than 1,000 occupations.[5] It tells you where the jobs are, how to qualify for them, and how to compete successfully for a[6] position.

The book sells for only $20 and is available immediately from the Taylor Press.[7] We hope you will take the time to send for your copy by returning the enclosed self-addressed card. We will bill you[8] later. Sincerely yours,   [164]

TRANSCRIPTION PREVIEW

Spelling. Professions, dissatisfied, designed, aptitudes.
Punctuation. Comma after *If you had the opportunity* (, *if* clause).
Typing Style. Underscore: *Today's Career Choices* (underscore book title).

ℂ LETTER 126

Something, quickly, Seattle, almost, anything, items, convert.

Dear Miss Lee: What do people do when they have something they would like to sell quickly? In Seattle, Washington, they[1] call 555-3215, which is the number of *The Shopping Guide*. They can sell almost anything through this[2] new publication at the lowest possible cost. More people read *The Shopping Guide* than any other weekly[3] newspaper of its kind in the West.

Our rates are low; you can reserve three lines in *The Shopping Guide* for only[4] $4. Your advertisement will be read by more than 10,000 people who are looking for the kind of items[5] you want to sell.

The next time you are in the market to convert some of your property into ready cash, call[6] *The Shopping Guide*. Sincerely yours,

[126]

TRANSCRIPTION PREVIEW

Spelling. Almost, weekly, reserve, convert.
Punctuation. Commas before and after *Washington* (, geographical).
Typing Style. Underscore: *The Shopping Guide* (underscore newspaper title).

LESSON 22

ℂ LETTER 127 ℂ (Related to Lesson 22, Letter 3)

**Article, forum, intensive, limited, contribution,
as soon as possible.**

Dear Ms. Morton: Thank you for your kind invitation to write an article for the *National Forum*.

I am[1] currently involved in an intensive research project on the history of education. Because my time[2] is quite limited, it would be difficult for me to do the research and write the article you suggest. If,[3] on the other hand, you would accept an article on the subject of my current research, I would be very[4] happy to make a contribution.

Would an article entitled "Early Education" be acceptable?[5] If it is, please let me know as soon as possible. Cordially yours, [113]

TRANSCRIPTION PREVIEW

Spelling. Article, current, acceptable.

Punctuation. Commas before and after *on the other hand* (, parenthetical).

Typing Style. Transcribe: "Early Education" (article title in quotation marks).

◖ LETTER 128 ◗ (Related to Lesson 22, Letter 4)

Delighted, grooming, library, references, complete, appreciate.

Dear Dr. Garcia: I was delighted to find a copy of your book, *Personal Grooming*, in our college[1] library. The chapter entitled "Skin Care" was particularly helpful to me in preparing my report.[2]

In addition, several of the references you provided in the bibliography were also[3] available in our library. They provided sufficient material for me to complete my report.

Thank[4] you, Dr. Garcia, for your help; I certainly appreciate it. Sincerely yours,   [96]

TRANSCRIPTION PREVIEW

Spelling. Personal, grooming, library, bibliography.

Punctuation. Commas before and after *Dr. Garcia* (, parenthetical).

Typing Style. Transcribe: "Skin Care" (chapter title in quotation marks).

❲ LETTER 129 ❲ (Related to Lesson 22, Letter 5)

Answers, deductions, entitled, guide, in the future, problems.

Dear Mr. Madison: Thank you very much for your assistance in helping me to find the answers to my questions[1] about business deductions on my income tax. I read the chapter entitled "Business Deductions" from the[2] book, *Income Tax Guide*. In the chapter I found answers to each of the questions that I had.

I plan to keep a copy[3] of the *Income Tax Guide* handy at all times in the future to help me with special tax problems.

Thanks again,[4] Mr. Madison, for your help. Sincerely yours, [89]

TRANSCRIPTION PREVIEW

Spelling. Assistance, answers, future, sincerely.
Punctuation. Comma before *Income Tax Guide* in the first paragraph (, apposition).
Typing Style. Transcribe: "Business Deductions" (chapter title in quotation marks).

❲ LETTER 130

Conscious, conservative, wardrobe, exhibit, describes, include.

Dear Mr. Green: The man in business today is more conscious of clothes than he has ever been before. No longer[1] is he content to have a few conservative suits to form the basis of his wardrobe. His clothes must exhibit[2] a certain flair, color, and style if he is to keep up with current men's fashions.

An article entitled "Today's[3] Man Dresses Up" in the March issue of *The Executive* describes the fashion trends in men's clothing in the[4] kind of detail that we could never include in a brief letter.

A complimentary copy of this publication[5] is on its way to your office. We hope you will consider beginning a regular subscription in[6] the near future. Cordially yours, [126]

TRANSCRIPTION PREVIEW

Spelling. Conscious, conservative, exhibit, complimentary.
Punctuation. Commas after *flair* and *color* (, series).
Typing Style. Transcribe: "Today's Man Dresses Up" (article title in quotation marks).

ℂ LETTER 131

Vocational, aware, thousands, mechanics, domain, counselor's, exist.

Dear Graduate: Our staff at Salem Technical Institute has been visiting high school campuses throughout the[1] East to promote our vocational education programs. We became aware of an important fact through our[2] visits.

Today, thousands of young women are enrolling in classes ranging from drafting to auto mechanics[3] to electronics. No longer are the doors closed in vocational areas once considered to be the[4] exclusive domain of men.

On the other hand, we are finding many men enrolling in courses that have[5] traditionally been taken by women. Men are now preparing to be chefs, flight attendants, and office workers.

In[6] our most recent college catalog, we included a chapter entitled "Making Career Decisions" that deals[7] specifically with the multitude of vocational opportunities available to young men and women.[8] Our catalog is in your counselor's library. Ask for it today and begin making plans for your future[9] education now.

Remember, barriers to vocational choices no longer exist. Sincerely yours,[10] [200]

Spelling. Campuses, enrolling, mechanics, traditionally.

Punctuation. Commas after *Today* and *recent college catalog* (, introductory).

Typing Style. Transcribe: "Making Career Decisions" (chapter title in quotation marks).

❬ LETTER 132

Series, investments, believe, in addition, western, written, proposal.

Dear Mr. Davis: Would you be interested in my writing a regular series of articles on investments[1] for your newspaper? I believe a weekly article under the heading "Investment Corner" would make a[2] valuable contribution to your publication.

As you may know, in addition to my teaching duties here[3] at Western State University, I have written three texts and several articles in the general[4] area of finance and economics.

If you are interested in this proposal, will you please call me at[5] 555-9686 to discuss my plans in greater detail. Cordially yours, [114]

Spelling. Writing, articles, duties, written.

Punctuation. Commas after *As you may know* (, *as* clause); after *in this proposal* (, *if* clause).

Typing Style. Transcribe: "Investment Corner" (section of newspaper in quotation marks).

LESSON 23

❬ LETTER 133 ❬ (Related to Lesson 23, Letter 3)

Completed, requested, optimistic, practical, accompanying.

Dear Mrs. Sweet: I just completed my review of your new magazine, *Family Finance*, as you requested.[1] I am very much impressed with the magazine, and I am optimistic about its chances for success.[2]

Specifically, I observed the following things:

1. The articles are on everyday, practical matters.

2. The[3] type is easy to read.

3. The accompanying illustrations add considerably to the interest of[4] the articles.

I believe you have a winner, Mrs. Sweet. Sincerely yours,   [94]

TRANSCRIPTION PREVIEW

Spelling.   Optimistic, specifically, accompanying, winner.

Punctuation.   Colon after *the following things* (: enumeration).

Typing Style.   Underscore: *Family Finance* (underscore magazine title).

❲ LETTER 134 ❲ (Related to Lesson 23, Letter 4)

Introductory, newsstand, informative, neglected, serious, derive.

Dear Mr. Davis: Enclosed is my check for $12, the price of a three-month introductory subscription[1] to the *Daily Tribune*.

I have occasionally purchased copies of the *Tribune* from the local newsstand. Therefore,[2] I am familiar with it. I particularly like the following sections: the sports section, the world news[3] section, and the fashion section.

Your recent letter outlining the special features of the *Tribune* was very[4] informative, but you neglected to mention an important part of your paper. I am referring to the[5] comic section. Although most newspapers provide a wide range of information for their readers, many people[6] rely on the comic section to provide some daily entertainment.

While I am looking forward to reading[7] the more serious and important sections of the *Tribune*, I am sure I will derive great reading pleasure from[8] your excellent comic section. Cordially yours, [169]

TRANSCRIPTION PREVIEW

Spelling. Newsstand, neglected, comic, derive.
Punctuation. Colon after *the following sections* (: enumeration).
Typing Style. Underscore: *Daily Tribune, Tribune* (underscore newspaper title).

ℂ LETTER 135 ℂ (Related to Lesson 23, Letter 5)

Stopped, magazine, browse, frankly, quality, continued, readership.

Dear Mr. Taylor: Yesterday I stopped at a local magazine shop to buy a few items and to browse through[1] their current publications. I remembered your letter suggesting that I read a copy of the *Financial[2] Digest.* Therefore, I purchased the current issue. Last evening I began reading it at about 8 p.m., and[3] it was nearly 10 p.m. before I stopped.

Quite frankly, Mr. Taylor, the *Financial Digest* is everything[4] you said it was and more. I particularly liked the following features of the magazine: the stock market[5] analysis, the articles on recent business mergers, and the section on foreign business. If the valuable[6] information I gained from the December issue is any indication of the quality of future[7] issues, you can count on my continued readership.

Enclosed is my check for $24, the price of[8] a year's subscription. Please begin it at once. Cordially yours, [171]

TRANSCRIPTION PREVIEW

Spelling. Stopped, browse, valuable, indication.
Punctuation. Colon after *features of the magazine* (: enumeration).
Typing Style. Underscore: *Financial Digest* (underscore magazine title); Transcribe: $24 (no decimal).

◖ LETTER 136

(shorthand outline)

Sorry, relied, competitive, athletics, consistently, resume.

Dear Mr. Collins: We were sorry to learn that you plan to discontinue publishing the *National Sports*[1] *Reporter*. We have relied on your publication throughout the years to bring us information on the most important[2] happenings in the following fields of competitive athletics: baseball, football, and tennis.

We have felt[3] that your editorial board consistently chose the events most people wanted to know more about. You may[4] be sure that we will miss reading the *National Sports Reporter*.

If you should decide to resume publication[5] in the future, please let us know. Cordially yours, [109]

TRANSCRIPTION PREVIEW

Spelling. Relied, competitive, athletics, consistently.
Punctuation. Colon after *athletics* (: enumeration).
Typing Style. Underscore: *National Sports Reporter* (underscore magazine title).

◖ LETTER 137

(shorthand outline)

Requisition, informed, immediately, excellent, behind, industry.

Ladies and Gentlemen: Will you please send us the following books:

1. Five copies of *Power Typing*.
2. Three copies[1] of *Expert Typing*.
3. Six copies of *Secretarial Procedures*.

I have submitted a requisition[2] for these texts, and Miss Janet

Brown, our purchasing agent, informed me that she will prepare the purchase order[3] immediately. We need these texts as soon as possible for several new students who have enrolled in the[4] evening school classes.

We have appreciated your excellent service in the past, and we are reluctant to[5] make a special request at this time. Your help, however, will further convince us that your company stands behind[6] its products with the best service in the industry. Sincerely yours, [133]

TRANSCRIPTION PREVIEW

Spelling. Requisition, immediately, reluctant, its.
Punctuation. Colon after *the following books* (: enumeration).
Typing Style. Underscore: *Power Typing, Expert Typing, Secretarial Procedures* (underscore book title).

◖ LETTER 138

Subscribe, following, they want, challenge, ability, objectives, bookstore.

Dear Neighbor: Most people subscribe to our magazine, *The Young Reader,* for one or more of the following reasons:[1]

1. They want to provide their children with good reading material.

2. They want to challenge their children's ability[2] to make sound judgments.

3. They want to help their children establish good reading habits.

We believe our current[3] readers agree that *The Young Reader* meets these objectives better than any other publication available[4] today.

We would like to invite you to pick up a copy at your local bookstore soon. Determine for[5] yourself whether your own children's education might be strengthened through the interesting, entertaining articles[6] in *The Young Reader.* Sincerely yours, [127]

Spelling. Challenge, habits, bookstore, strengthened.
Punctuation. Colon after *the following reasons* (: enumeration).
Typing Style. Underscore: *The Young Reader* (underscore magazine title).

LESSON 24

❰ LETTER 139 ❰ (Related to Lesson 24, Letter 3)

Thank you for your, publishing, really, unfortunately, definitely, available, receive.

Dear Mrs. Smith: Thank you for your letter telling me about the job opportunities in the publishing field.[1] I have often asked myself the question, "Do I really enjoy the work I am doing?"
Unfortunately, the[2] answer is usually no.
I would definitely like to have more information about the publishing field.[3] Please send whatever information you have available to my home address at 400 East 18 Street.[4] I will be very glad to receive it. Sincerely yours, [90]

TRANSCRIPTION PREVIEW

Spelling. Myself, really, answer, definitely.
Punctuation. Commas after *the question* (, introduce short quotation); Transcribe: "Do I really enjoy the work I am doing?" (? inside final quotation mark).
Typing Style. Transcribe: 400 East 18 Street.

❰ LETTER 140 ❰ (Related to Lesson 24, Letter 4)

Supplementary, colleagues, subsequently, prior, length.

Dear Mr. Williams: I have been looking for an excellent supplementary text for use in my college[1] history course. Recently one of my colleagues loaned me a copy of your publication, *World History.* I[2] examined it carefully and have subsequently decided to order 20 copies as a reference source[3] for my students.

In the text you state, "Price subject to change without prior notice." Please write me immediately[4] and give me the current cost of the book and the length of time required for delivery. When I receive this[5] information, I will submit my order. Cordially yours,

[110]

TRANSCRIPTION PREVIEW

Spelling. Supplementary, colleagues, reference, length.
Punctuation. Comma after *state* (, introduce short quotation); Transcribe: "Price subject to change without prior notice." (. inside final quotation mark).
Typing Style. Underscore: *World History* (underscore book title).

❡ LETTER 141 ❡ (Related to Lesson 24, Letter 5)

Celebrate, accept, extremely, occasion, forward, attending.

Dear Mrs. Tate: Thank you very much for the invitation to attend the party you are having to celebrate[1] the publication of Mary Wilson's article. I am delighted to accept your invitation.

I[2] have received an advance copy of your magazine, *Flower World,* and the article, "Flowers of the South," is[3] extremely well done.

I know Mary will be pleased that you are having a party to celebrate this occasion, and[4] I am certainly looking forward to attending. Sincerely yours,

[93]

TRANSCRIPTION PREVIEW

Spelling. Delighted, accept, occasion, forward.

Punctuation. Transcribe: "Flowers of the South," (, inside final quotation mark).

Typing Style. Underscore: *Flower World* (underscore magazine title).

◖ LETTER 142

Suppliers, although, difficulty, few months, quantity, order.

Mr. Cook: I have followed through on your request to find other suppliers for our paper needs. Although I have[1] some leads that should solve our long-range problems, I am having some difficulty finding a supply for the next few[2] months.

One of my friends who works for a competing company in the West stated recently, "We have a large[3] quantity of paper in our warehouses that we would be willing to sell to you if you cannot find another[4] supplier." Even though we will have to pay a higher price than usual, I believe we should accept the offer.[5] Therefore, I am making the necessary arrangements to order the paper we will require through the next[6] few months.

I will keep you informed of other developments. James Allen

[133]

TRANSCRIPTION PREVIEW

Spelling. Through, quantity, supplier, informed.

Punctuation. Comma after *recently* (, introduce short quotation); period after *find another supplier* (. inside final quotation mark).

Typing Style. Transcribe: West (capitalized).

◖ LETTER 143

Commend, accounting, excellent, helpful, knowledge, certificate.

Dear Miss Singer: May we commend you for enrolling in our correspondence course in accounting. Your materials[1] have been shipped and should arrive at your home in two or three weeks.

This excellent course has helped hundreds of men and[2] women find well-paying jobs in the business world. Just the other day, in fact, a young woman who had completed[3] this course came into my office and said, "This was one of the most helpful, interesting courses I have ever[4] had." She is now working for a large firm and uses her accounting knowledge constantly.

We hope your success with[5] this course has an equally happy ending. When you complete it, you will receive a beautiful, hand-lettered[6] certificate of which you may be justly proud. Cordially yours, [131]

TRANSCRIPTION PREVIEW

Spelling. Commend, correspondence, excellent, helpful.
Punctuation. Comma after *said* (, introduce short quotation); period after *I have ever had* (. inside final quotation mark).
Typing Style. Transcribe: two or three weeks (letters).

❲ LETTER 144

Scheduled, speaker, currently, presentations, speech, expect, crowd.

Dear Member: At our next regularly scheduled luncheon, Mrs. Barbara Adams, the author of a recent article[1] entitled "Looking Upward," will be our guest speaker.

Mrs. Adams is currently on a tour of over[2] 20 cities promoting her forthcoming book. Her presentations have been widely acclaimed for their humor and[3] insight, and we are looking forward to the opportunity of hearing her speech.

Because we expect a large[4] crowd, it is necessary to make reservations for this event. Call our club secretary, Doris Swenson,[5] at 555-8721 for reservations.

We hope you will plan to be with us. Cordially yours, [119]

Spelling. Luncheon, acclaimed, humor, insight.
Punctuation. Transcribe: "Looking Upward," (, inside final quotation mark).
Typing Style. Transcribe: 20 (figures).

LESSON 25

❰ LETTER 145 ❰ (Related to Lesson 25, Letter 3)

Evaluation, already, modification, result, quite, succeed, critique.

Dear Mrs. Bell: Thank you for your letter that you sent when you returned my manuscript, "Outdoor Survival Skills," a[1] few days ago. I appreciate your evaluation of my work and the encouraging comments you made.[2]

Your comments were similar to others that I received. The well-known author, Mr. James Smith, made the following[3] comments about the manuscript: "It is actually quite well done. However, I think it is too long and too detailed[4] for the secondary market. If you were to correct these two problems, I think some company would be glad[5] to publish it."

I am already in the process of revising the manuscript by shortening it and making[6] it less detailed as suggested. I believe that this modification will result in a greatly improved[7] book. I plan to contact another publisher as soon as possible, and I am quite confident that my efforts[8] to have it published will succeed.

Once again, thank you for the time you devoted in giving my manuscript[9] a fair critique. Cordially yours,   [186]

TRANSCRIPTION PREVIEW

Spelling. Evaluation, comments, revising, shortening.
Punctuation. Colon after *about the manuscript* (: introducing long quotation); period after *would be glad to publish it* (. inside final quotation mark).
Typing Style. Transcribe: "Outdoor Survival Skills," (manuscript title in quotation marks).

⊄ LETTER 146 ⊄ (Related to Lesson 25, Letter 4)

[shorthand symbols]

Submitted, preliminary, design, unfortunately, I wanted, situation, unacceptable.

Dear Mr. Brown: Two weeks ago I submitted an order for a full-page advertisement in the *Daily News*.[1] On Friday one of your employees brought the preliminary design of the ad to my office. Unfortunately,[2] the work was not what I wanted.

I called Ms. Mary Johnson of your advertising department and explained[3] the situation. Her considerate reply to my comments showed an unusual degree of understanding.[4] She said: "We are sorry that our design is unacceptable. We did not really understand what you[5] had in mind. We will, of course, redo the ad to your complete satisfaction."

Yesterday I received the revised[6] layout, and it is just exactly what I wanted. I am glad to say that the service I received from Ms. Johnson[7] is everything you said it would be. Sincerely yours,

[150]

TRANSCRIPTION PREVIEW

Spelling.   Submitted, preliminary, unacceptable, complete.
Punctuation.   Colon after *She said* (: introducing long quotation); period after *complete satisfaction* (. inside final quotation mark).
Typing Style.   Underscore: *Daily News* (underscore newspaper title).

⊄ LETTER 147 ⊄ (Related to Lesson 25, Letter 5)

[shorthand symbols]

Edwards, history, complimentary, subscription, entire, continue.

Dear Miss Edwards: Thank you for your interesting letter about the history of the *Medford Register*. I[1] appreciated the complimentary one month's subscription.

I have been reading the paper at home each morning[2] and then taking it to my accounting office for my clients to read. One of my clients recently stated:[3] "I have been reading the *Medford Register* since its first issue. I believe it is the best newspaper in the[4] entire area."

Please continue delivering the *Medford Register* to my residence, and send an[5] additional copy to my office at 375 South Baker Street. Sincerely yours,   [117]

TRANSCRIPTION PREVIEW

Spelling.   History, complimentary, believe, residence.

Punctuation.   Colon after *recently stated* (: introduce long quotation); period after *the entire area* (. inside final quotation mark).

Typing Style.   Underscore: *Medford Register* (underscore newspaper title).

❰ LETTER 148

Guild, we hope you will, prominent, literature, accurate, feature.

Dear Member: The Lexington Library Guild will hold its quarterly meeting on Saturday, May 21, at[1] 2 p.m. at the Baker Hotel. We hope you will meet with us on this occasion.

We plan to review three novels[2] by a prominent Florida author, Mr. James West. In the annual yearbook of *Who's Who in Literature*,[3] the following statements appear concerning him: "James West promises to be one of America's best-known[4] writers in the years to come. He combines the ability to produce large quantities of work with a writing[5] style that is lively, entertaining, and accurate."

Our meeting will feature a personal visit from Mr.[6] West followed by a buffet dinner at 6 p.m. Prior registration is required for this event. Call[7] our secretary today to make arrangements to attend this exciting cultural happening. Yours truly,[8]   [160]

TRANSCRIPTION PREVIEW

Spelling.   Guild, occasion, accurate, buffet.
Punctuation.   Colon after *concerning him* (: introducing long quotation); period after *accurate* (. inside final quotation mark).
Typing Style.   Transcribe: May 21; 6 p.m. (figures); three novels (letters).

◖ LETTER 149

Potential, devoted, hobbies, tentative, proceed, let me, as soon as possible.

Dear Mr. Tate: As you know, for three or four years I have felt that a good market potential exists for a[1] magazine devoted to the hobbies of Americans.

I have gained tentative approval from my publisher[2] to proceed with the project, and I am looking for a person to serve as editor. Would you be interested[3] in the job, Mr. Tate? Please let me know your feelings as soon as possible. Yours truly,   [76]

TRANSCRIPTION PREVIEW

Spelling.   Exists, hobbies, proceed, truly.
Punctuation.   Commas after *As you know* (, *as* clause); after *project* (, conjunction).
Typing Style.   Transcribe: three or four years (letters).

Joined, reason, skeptical, additional, eastern, discounts, convinced.

Dear Miss Lee: If you have never joined a book club, we think we know the reason why. Although the initial offer[1] of most clubs looks attractive, you may have been skeptical when you saw the list prices of the additional books[2] you were required to purchase.

When you join the Eastern Book Club, you may select any three books from our extensive[3] list for only $5. Thereafter, you purchase only the books you want at discounts of 40 percent to[4] 60 percent off the regular retail prices.

Our current members are convinced that we save them money. Let[5] us perform the same valuable service for you. Just return the enclosed card immediately for further[6] information. Yours sincerely,   [125]

TRANSCRIPTION PREVIEW

Spelling.   Initial, skeptical, discounts, valuable.
Punctuation.   Commas after *attractive* (, introductory); after *Eastern Book Club* (, *when* clause).
Typing Style.   Transcribe: Eastern Book Club (capitalized); 40 percent to 60 percent (figures).

CHAPTER

COMMUNICATIONS

LESSON 26

⊄ LETTER 151 ⊄ (Related to Lesson 26, Letter 3)

Analysis, provided, data, capital, recommending, proposal.

Dear Mrs. Fielding: Thank you for the information on the cost analysis of our telephone service that[1] was provided by the Electronic Research Corporation.

In general, this data confirms the feeling[2] that I expressed to you last fall. You will remember that I predicted our rates would have to be increased to[3] recover our capital expenditure for electronic switching equipment.

I caution you, however, on[4] recommending an 18 percent increase to the board at the meeting on Thursday, March 6. I believe that they[5] will reject such a proposal. If you were to suggest that we increase our rates 9 percent this year and 9 percent[6] again next year, the members of the board might approve your recommendation.

You can count on my total support[7] for that proposal. Cordially yours, [147]

Spelling. Analysis, expenditure, recommending, support.

Punctuation. Commas before and after *however* (, parenthetical); after *next year* (, *if* clause).

Typing Style. Transcribe: fall (not capitalized); Thursday, March (capitalized).

❪ LETTER 152 ❪ (Related to Lesson 26, Letter 4)

Compiled, statistics, provided, courteous, revenue, decision.

Dear Miss Mason: We have not compiled statistics on the actual business increases experienced by the[1] companies who advertise in the business section of the *Los Angeles Telephone Directory*. We do[2] know, however, that the number of our customers has increased by an average of 10 percent each year during[3] the past eight-year period.

Figures provided by the local Chamber of Commerce indicate that slightly more[4] than 70 percent of the businesses in Los Angeles County advertise their goods and services in[5] our business section.

Call our office today and let one of our courteous, well-trained representatives help you[6] design an eye-catching ad for inclusion in the spring edition of the directory. We are open Monday[7] through Friday from 9 a.m. until 5 p.m. We think your year-end statement of revenue will show that you[8] made the right decision. Yours truly,   [167]

Spelling. Statistics, design, edition, revenue.

Punctuation. Hyphenate *eight-year, well-trained, eye-catching,* and *year-end* (hyphenated before noun).

Typing Style. Transcribe: spring (not capitalized); Monday, Friday (capitalized).

Telephones, repaired, full, delay, supervisor, memorandum.

Dear Mrs. Oaks: Thank you for the reminder that your telephones have not yet been repaired.

I must accept full blame[1] for the delay. When our crew was unable to make the needed repairs, the supervisor left a memorandum[2] to that effect on my desk. Unfortunately, the memorandum was misplaced. After a thorough search, I[3] found it in my filing cabinet. It was attached to another order for service that also came in on[4] Christmas Day.

Your work order has been prepared and is at the top of our list. Your phones will be in good working order[5] by Tuesday, January 22. Please forgive the delay. Sincerely yours,   [115]

TRANSCRIPTION PREVIEW

Spelling.   Misplaced, thorough, filing, cabinet.
Punctuation.   Commas after *the needed repairs* (, *when* clause); after *Unfortunately* (, introductory).
Typing Style.   Transcribe: Christmas Day, Tuesday, January (capitalized).

❰ LETTER 154

Sanchez, examination, overseas, questionable, circulated, requesting, unauthorized.

Miss Sanchez: A recent examination of our summer telephone bills revealed several overseas[1] calls for which I could not account. The cost of these calls is approximately $300. Last Tuesday my[2] secretary, Mr. Tate, prepared a list of these questionable calls and circulated it throughout the office[3] with a note requesting the calling parties to identify themselves.

None of our employees made any[4] of the calls. I suspect, of course, that some unauthorized person is making overseas calls on our phones. Will you[5] please provide the names and addresses of the persons whose numbers are listed on the enclosed sheet.

We hope that this[6] list will help us solve our problem. Thomas Adamson   [130]

TRANSCRIPTION PREVIEW

Spelling. Revealed, questionable, suspect, whose.
Punctuation. Commas before and after *Mr. Tate* (, apposition); before and after *of course* (, parenthetical).
Typing Style. Transcribe: summer (not capitalized); Tuesday (capitalized).

⟪ LETTER 155

Invitation, seminar, sponsoring, designed, ability, participate, worthwhile.

To the Staff: I received an invitation from the Lexington Company to attend the seminar on[1] effective speaking they are sponsoring in October. This is not a regular public speaking course. It is designed[2] to help office workers improve their communication ability while on the job.

The following topics[3] will be discussed:

1. Saying it right the first time.
2. Using words that count.
3. Speaking effectively.

If[4] possible, we would like every employee to participate in this worthwhile seminar. It will be held on Thursday[5] afternoon, October 12. We will excuse those desiring to attend and pay them in full for the time they[6] attend the seminar.

Please let me know as soon as possible if you would like to participate in this program.[7] Marcia Franklin [144]

TRANSCRIPTION PREVIEW

Spelling. Effective, discussed, worthwhile, desiring.
Punctuation. Colon after *will be discussed* (: enumeration).
Typing Style. Transcribe: October, Thursday (capitalized).

ℂ LETTER 156

Telephone, figure, 10 cents, available, assistance, observe, repeatedly.

To the Staff: When I was reviewing our company telephone bill for the month of September, I was surprised[1] to learn that we had spent more than $100 for information service. At first I did not believe that[2] the figure could be correct. However, the telephone company assured me that we had actually used the[3] services of the information operators more than 1,000 times and that we were charged 10 cents every[4] time.

I realize that we work in a very large city and that telephone books are not available at each[5] telephone extension throughout our building. It would, of course, be a waste of time and money for each of us to[6] go to a centrally located telephone book every time we need a telephone number. Nevertheless,[7] I feel sure that we can cut down on the number of times we need the assistance of the information operator.[8]

In order to do so, I am asking that each of you observe the following rules:

1. Keep a list of[9] frequently called numbers near your telephone.

2. Before you ask the operator for a number, check to see[10] if you have the number on your list.

3. Jot down any numbers that you think you will be calling repeatedly[11] and add them to your list.

If we all follow these few simple guidelines, I am sure we will

be able to reduce[12] our telephone bill substantially. Martin Cunningham   [250]

TRANSCRIPTION PREVIEW

Spelling. Extension, assistance, repeatedly, guidelines.
Punctuation. Comma after *Nevertheless* (, introductory); colon
after *the following rules* (: enumeration).
Typing Style. Transcribe: September (capitalized).

LESSON 27

❨ LETTER 157 ❨ (Related to Lesson 27, Letter 3)

**Analysis, correspondent, predicted, construction, evidently,
enable.**

Dear Miss Green: I have read the complimentary copy of *News
Brief* that you sent me a few weeks ago.

I was[1] particularly interested in the analysis of your veteran
Washington correspondent, James Fox.[2] He accurately predicted
that interest rates would drop slightly in September because the
money supply for[3] residential construction would be expanded.
Evidently, he had given a great deal of thought to this[4] prediction.

My initial reaction to this magazine is positive. I am certain that
the information[5] it contains will enable me to communicate better
with my business associates. Very truly yours,[6]   [120]

TRANSCRIPTION PREVIEW

Spelling. Veteran, construction, given, prediction.
Punctuation. Comma before *James Fox* (, apposition).
Typing Style. Underscore: *News Brief* (underscore magazine
title).

❧ LETTER 158 ❧ (Related to Lesson 27, Letter 4)

[shorthand symbols]

Remarks, metropolitan, written, permission, contact.

Dear Miss Bates: Thank you for your remarks regarding my presentation at the Metropolitan Training Conference[1] in Chicago. I, too, felt that the conference was well planned.

I am very sorry that I do not have a[2] written copy of the speech. Before the luncheon I gave Mr. James Jenson of the First National Bank permission[3] to make a tape recording of the speech. I am sure that if you contact Mr. Jenson, he will be glad to[4] duplicate the tape. His address is 206 State Street in Chicago, Illinois.

If I can be of help to[5] you in any way in the future, I hope you will feel free to call on me. Very sincerely yours, [118]

TRANSCRIPTION PREVIEW

Spelling. Written, luncheon, permission, contact.
Punctuation. Commas before and after *too* (, parenthetical); before *Illinois* (, geographical).
Typing Style. Transcribe: First National Bank (capitalized); 206 State Street.

❧ LETTER 159 ❧ (Related to Lesson 27, Letter 5)

[shorthand symbols]

Completed, communications, realize, associates, gained, self-confidence.

Dear Dr. White: As you know, last week I completed your course in office communications at the Johnson[1] Institute. When I enrolled in the course last fall, I expected to learn a great deal. However, I did not realize[2] just how much I would get from the course.

The quality of my writing has improved, and my associates tell me[3] that I am much more effective as a manager.

I can say honestly, Dr. White, that I enjoyed every[4] one of the lessons and that I gained something from each of them. The course has given me the ability to write[5] clearly and effectively. In addition, it has given me the self-confidence that I need to write convincing[6] business letters.

You may be sure that I will recommend the Johnson Institute to my friends and associates.[7] Thank you for making the course such a worthwhile experience. Very sincerely yours,   [156]

TRANSCRIPTION PREVIEW

Spelling.   Lessons, given, self-confidence, recommend.

Punctuation.   Commas after *As you know* (, *as* clause); after *In addition* (, introductory).

Typing Style.   Transcribe: Johnson Institute (capitalized); fall (not capitalized).

⊄ LETTER 160

Suburban, vicinity, neighborhood, hidden, protected, attractive, dependable.

Dear Mr. Smith: Over the next few months the Suburban Telephone Company will be installing new underground[1] telephone cables in the vicinity of your office building. While we are working, we will have to close[2] several major streets and route traffic through neighborhood streets.

When we finish the work, our telephone lines will be[3] hidden from view and will be protected from the severe winter weather. This will make the neighborhood more attractive[4] and will give you more dependable telephone service.

We are sorry for the inconvenience, but we know[5] that you will be pleased with the final results. Very cordially yours,   [113]

TRANSCRIPTION PREVIEW

Spelling. Underground, vicinity, hidden, severe.

Punctuation. Comma after *When we finish the work* (, *when* clause).

Typing Style. Transcribe: winter (not capitalized).

ℂ LETTER 161

Approximately, basis, station, reduce, expenses, charges.

To the Staff: In checking our telephone bills recently, we noticed that approximately 35 percent[1] of all long-distance calls are made on a person-to-person basis. These calls are considerably more expensive[2] than station-to-station calls.

To reduce our telephone expenses, we recommend that any calls placed during[3] regular working hours be made on a station-to-station basis.

Your strict adherence to this recommendation[4] could substantially lessen our long-distance charges. Ray Mason   [93]

TRANSCRIPTION PREVIEW

Spelling. Approximately, considerably, recommend, lessen.

Punctuation. Comma after *To reduce our telephone expenses* (, introductory).

Typing Style. Transcribe: 35 percent (figures).

ℂ LETTER 162

Request, subdivision, underground, everything, project, patient.

Dear Mr. Reed: We are sorry that we have not been able to honor your request for telephone service at[1] your new suburban home. Mr. Harold Black, the general contractor for your subdivision, placed his order[2] for a main underground line on March 5.

Unfortunately, we are more than three months behind schedule in installing[3] the lines in your area. I am afraid we will not be able to install your telephone before June[4] 5. We will, of course, do everything possible to speed up the project.

We hope you will be patient with us in[5] the meantime. Sincerely yours,   [105]

TRANSCRIPTION PREVIEW

Spelling. Honor, suburban, install, patient.
Punctuation. Commas before and after *of course* (, parenthetical).
Typing Style. Transcribe: March 5, June 5 (figures).

LESSON 28

❆ LETTER 163 ❆ (Related to Lesson 28, Letter 3)

White, everyone, graduate, retained, regularly, registration, benefit.

Dear Mr. White: We are delighted that everyone in your company is interested in the course in speed reading[1] at Reno Business College. The answers to your questions are as follows:

1. The students graduate with an[2] average reading speed of about 1,000 words per minute.

2. The skill is easily retained if students[3] continue to practice regularly.

3. Registration cost for this program is only $15 per student.[4]

We believe that every one of your employees will benefit from the course. Sincerely yours,   [97]

Spelling. Delighted, retained, registration, benefit.
Punctuation. Colon after *as follows* (: enumeration).
Typing Style. Transcribe: Reno Business College (capitalized).

❡ LETTER 164 ❡ (Related to Lesson 28, Letter 4)

Broadcast, western, booth, depends, length, between.

Dear Mr. Gates: We are pleased that you are planning to broadcast your football game with Western State College on October[1] 26.

Broadcasting games away from home is just as easy as it is in your own stadium. Our people[2] will bring a line to the broadcast booth, and you take over from there. Our basic rental fee depends on the length[3] of time the line is needed, the time of the day the line is used, and the broadcast distance involved.

Please call me sometime[4] between nine and five, and I will be happy to spend some time discussing the actual rates with you. Sincerely[5] yours, [101]

TRANSCRIPTION PREVIEW

Spelling. Planning, length, distance, involved.
Punctuation. Comma after *broadcast booth* (, conjunction).
Typing Style. Transcribe: nine and five (letters).

❡ LETTER 165 ❡ (Related to Lesson 28, Letter 5)

System, interesting, communications, activate, automatically, transistor.

Dear Ms. Jackson: We have been using the Jennings Telephone System for some time. It is indeed an interesting[1] device, and I am sure it has the potential to solve many of the communications problems most businesses[2] face.

Unfortunately, our system has worked properly for only a few days since we purchased it. First, the[3] recording device failed to activate automatically. Next, there was a short in the volume switch. Now, one of[4] the transistor units is out of order.

We must insist that you either replace our unit sometime next week[5] or refund our money so that we can be spared further inconvenience. Yours truly,   [115]

TRANSCRIPTION PREVIEW

Spelling.   Device, activate, transistor, insist.
Punctuation.   Comma after *interesting device* (, conjunction).
Typing Style.   Transcribe: Jennings Telephone System (capitalized).

⊄ LETTER 166

Monthly, published, electronic, articles, provided, whether.

Dear Customer: For some time the Davis Company has been sending you a copy of *Telephone Talk* with your[1] monthly telephone bill. We have published this booklet to help you keep up with the rapidly changing field of[2] electronic communications.

We would like to know if you enjoy reading the interesting, informative[3] articles contained in this publication. Will you please take a few minutes to fill out and return the enclosed[4] questionnaire in the self-addressed envelope that is provided. Your answers will tell us whether you like the format[5] and the contents of the booklet. In addition, it will help us to plan future articles.

Thank you for your[6] cooperation; we sincerely appreciate it. Very truly yours,   [133]

Spelling. Electronic, articles, questionnaire, answers.
Punctuation. Semicolon after *Thank you for your cooperation* (; no conjunction).
Typing Style. Transcribe: Davis Company (capitalized); Underscore: *Telephone Talk* (underscore booklet title).

ℂ LETTER 167

Designing, complicated, outcome, directories, judging, complete.

Dear Customer: Designing and putting together a large telephone book is a complicated process. Many[1] important decisions must be made that affect the outcome of the final product.

Because of high costs, the[2] Eastern Telephone Company decided to use less paper last year by reducing the size of print in our[3] directories. Judging from the comment of many of our customers, we made the wrong decision. We apologize[4] for making our directory difficult to read for so many of our customers.

When your new[5] directory is delivered to you sometime next week, we believe you will be happy with the large, easy-to-read[6] type. Your complete satisfaction with our service is of primary importance to us. Sincerely yours, [138]

TRANSCRIPTION PREVIEW

Spelling. Designing, directories, complete, primary.
Punctuation. Hyphenate: *easy-to-read* (hyphenated before noun).
Typing Style. Transcribe: Eastern Telephone Company (capitalized).

ℂ LETTER 168

Recently, southern, residential, throughout, contact, framing, time.

Dear Mr. Strong: We noted recently in *The Southern Reporter* that your firm had applied for 53 permits[1] to build residential housing east of Birmingham. We suggest that you have each of these homes wired for telephone[2] service in every one of the rooms. We will install jacks throughout each home for our low price of only $6[3] each.

Please contact our main office at 555-3219 to place your order. When you have completed[4] the framing on each home, call us and we will wire it within a week's time. Sincerely yours,   [96]

TRANSCRIPTION PREVIEW

Spelling. Southern, build, throughout, framing.
Punctuation. Comma after *the framing on each home* (, *when* clause).
Typing Style. Underscore: *The Southern Reporter* (underscore newspaper title).

LESSON 29

❬ LETTER 169 ❬ (Related to Lesson 29, Letter 3)

Thank you for, Madison, perfectly, courteous, thorough, handling, colleagues.

Gentlemen: Thank you for suggesting that I use a Madison Paging System when I am away from my office.[1] The system has worked perfectly thus far. I am particularly pleased with the fine service your operators[2] provide; I find them courteous and thorough in their handling of my calls.

I am quite certain that several[3] of my colleagues plan to purchase this helpful communications device soon. Thank you for your fine service. Cordially[4] yours,   [81]

Spelling. Courteous, thorough, handling, colleagues.
Punctuation. Semicolon after *provide* (; no conjunction).
Typing Style. Transcribe: Madison Paging System (capitalized).

❆ LETTER 170 ❆ (Related to Lesson 29, Letter 4)

Relatively, certainly, whose, supporters, foreign, quickly,
providing.

Dear Ms. Slater: Your letter on the high quality and relatively low
price of today's telephone service[1] was certainly interesting. I am
sure the person whose story you related is currently one of the best[2]
supporters of the telephone service in America.

I had no idea, of course, that using the telephone[3] in a foreign
country could be such a problem. When you stop to think of it,
being able to call someone[4] 2,000 miles away almost as quickly as
you can your next-door neighbor is amazing.

I appreciate[5] your efforts in providing me with another point of
view. Sincerely yours,   [114]

Spelling. Whose, foreign, almost, neighbor.
Punctuation. Hyphenate *next-door* (hyphenated before noun).
Typing Style. Transcribe: 2,000 (figures).

❆ LETTER 171 ❆ (Related to Lesson 29, Letter 5)

Efficiency, answering, impressed, eager, returned, encourage,
future.

Dear Mr. Barnes: When you called the Phillips Communication Service to assess the efficiency with which our[1] answering service operates, you seemed impressed with our service. We believed you were eager to have us handle[2] your calls for you. Thus far, however, you have not returned the application form we mailed to you.

We know that[3] professional people are always quite busy. If you have simply not had the time to fill out the form, we encourage[4] you to do so now while the matter is on your mind.

We hope to hear from you in the near future, Mr. Barnes.[5] Very cordially yours,   [104]

TRANSCRIPTION PREVIEW

Spelling. Efficiency, quite, encourage, future.
Punctuation. Commas before and after *however* (, parenthetical).
Typing Style. Transcribe: Phillips Communication Service (capitalized).

◖ LETTER 172

Thank you for your, distance, August, improperly, found, defective, automatic.

Dear Mrs. Lake: Thank you for your letter concerning the long-distance charges on your telephone bill for the month[1] of August. We are sorry that several calls were improperly charged to you.

I checked into the problem[2] personally, Mrs. Lake, and found that the trouble was caused by a defective electronic switch in one of our[3] automatic posting machines. The calls have been removed from your bill, and a correct statement is enclosed.

We will[4] do everything in our power to be sure that such an error does not happen again. Thank you for your patience.[5] Very sincerely yours,   [104]

Spelling.   Sorry, improperly, personally, switch.
Punctuation.   Commas before and after *Mrs. Lake* (, parenthetical).
Typing Style.   Transcribe: August (capitalized).

⟨ LETTER 173

Months ago, pleasant, at that time, into, area, construction.

Dear Mr. Moore: Three months ago I moved to my new home in Pleasant Valley, which is about 100 miles from[1] Providence. At that time the telephone company said there would be a one-month wait before my telephone could[2] be installed. The problem was that there were no lines into the area.

After one month, there was no evidence[3] that new work was being done on the construction of the lines. About two months ago the work was started, but little[4] has been done since then.

Will you please inform me about the status of this project. I need telephone service[5] now. Cordially yours,   [104]

Spelling.   Pleasant, installed, area, evidence.
Punctuation.   Period after *status of this project* (. courteous request).
Typing Style.   Transcribe: Pleasant Valley, Providence (capitalized).

⟨ LETTER 174 ⟨ (Office Style)

Communications, understood, whose, interested, encountered, available.

Dear Mrs. Overmeyer: An article in the January issue of *The Office Today* pointed out[1] that only about 35 percent of the oral communications in the average office are clearly[2] understood. This means, of course, that 65 percent of our oral communications are not clear to those whose[3] job performance may depend on what we say.

We have prepared a short film

Take out *short*.

entitled *Using the Right Words*, which you[4] might be interested in showing to your office staff. The film points out the common communication problems[5] frequently encountered

Delete *frequently*.

in offices and offers concrete steps to solve them. The film is available free of charge;[6] you pay only a small shipping fee.

This is just one of the many services available from the National[7] Business Publications Company. Order today while the best booking dates are still available. Yours very[8] truly, [162]

LESSON 30

◖ LETTER 175 ◖ (Related to Lesson 30, Letter 3)

Procedures, offices, acquainting, ourselves, functions, misunderstandings, appreciate.

Dear Ms. White: Thank you for hosting our business procedures class last Friday during our tour of your offices. Even[1] though we had spent some time in class acquainting ourselves with the functions of the stock market, we still had a great[2] deal to learn. The visit cleared up a number of misunderstandings we had about the operation of the[3] stock market.

We appreciate your acquainting us not only with the fascinating aspects of the investment[4] business but also with the role electronic communication plays in helping to turn the wheels of[5] America's economy. Sincerely yours, [108]

Spelling. Though, acquainting, misunderstandings, fascinating.

Punctuation. Comma after *functions of the stock market* (, introductory).

Typing Style. Transcribe: America's (capitalized; singular possessive).

❰ LETTER 176 ❰ (Related to Lesson 30, Letter 4)

Discussing, Miami, mentioned, equipment, posed, mistake.

Dear Mrs. Lopez: Last week I had the opportunity of discussing telephone services with one of[1] my friends who was here in Miami, Florida, on business. When I mentioned that the Southern Telephone Company[2] was installing electronic switching equipment, my friend posed the following interesting questions:

1. Is[3] the company making a mistake to invest so much money in new equipment at this time?

2. How much will[4] the new equipment save the average customer?

3. Will the length of time taken to complete a call be decreased?[5]

Unfortunately, these questions were not covered in your booklet, *Electronic Switching: What It Means to You.* I[6] hope you will send me the answers as soon as possible; it will help to clear up several misunderstandings.[7] Sincerely yours, [143]

Spelling. Discussing, mentioned, mistake, misunderstandings.

Punctuation. Colon after *the following interesting questions* (: enumeration).

Typing Style. Underscore: *Electronic Switching: What It Means to You* (underscore booklet title).

[shorthand symbols]

Few days ago, occupying, comply, installed, outstanding, disconnected.

Dear Mr. Stern: We received your check a few days ago for $10.60, the cost of your last month's basic[1] telephone service for the apartment you rent to college students. You did not, however, include the charges[2] for the long-distance calls that were placed from your telephone.

I understand these calls were placed by students occupying[3] the apartment; however, you are responsible for them. These charges amount to $32[4] for the month.

In order to comply with the agreement we signed when your telephone was installed, you must pay this[5] outstanding balance before Friday, April 3. Unless the bill is paid in full, your telephone service will be[6] disconnected. Don't make this mistake, Mr. Stern; send us your check immediately. Sincerely yours, [138]

TRANSCRIPTION PREVIEW

Spelling. Received, agreement, disconnected, mistake.
Punctuation. Comma after *Friday* (, apposition).
Typing Style. Transcribe: $32 (no decimal).

◖ **LETTER 178**

[shorthand symbols]

Acquaintance, large, receptionist, frustration, techniques, self-teaching, self-addressed.

Dear Mrs. Smith: A few days ago, I called a business acquaintance who works for a large firm in Albany. The[1] receptionist said her employer was busy and asked if I wanted to hold. I made the mistake of saying[2] yes. Approximately three minutes later I was still on hold, and I hung up in frustration.

Perhaps you have[3] had a similar experience; most business executives have. How to handle calls that are put on hold is[4] just one of the many telephone techniques discussed in our new training manual *Telephone Tips*. This publication[5] is a self-teaching course in proper telephone usage.

If you would like a complimentary copy[6] for your employees, please return the enclosed self-addressed card. Sincerely yours,

[134]

❡ LETTER 179

Someone, total, attention, enthusiasm, yourself, listener, concentration.

Dear Miss Adams: When someone talks to you, do you give that person your total attention, or do you let your mind[1] wander? Do you reflect the enthusiasm others project when they speak with you? In short, do you consider[2] yourself a good listener? Good listeners are indeed unusual because most people lack the necessary[3] skills and concentration.

On Thursday evening at 8 o'clock in the Municipal Building at 410 Third[4] Avenue, O'Brien Human Relations Institute is sponsoring a program devoted entirely to[5] the art of listening. There is no admission charge. We recommend that you and your employees make plans to be there.[6] It could have a very good effect on the way your company does business.

You will be making no mistake by[7] investing an evening in this manner. We hope to see you there. Sincerely yours, [154]

TRANSCRIPTION PREVIEW

Spelling. Enthusiasm, listener, concentration, admission.

Punctuation. Comma after *When someone talks to you* (, *when* clause); after *your total attention* (, conjunction).

Typing Style. Transcribe: 8 o'clock (figure); 410 Third Avenue.

❡ LETTER 180 ❡ (Office Style)

Opportunity, to present, February, relationships, excellent, appropriate.

Dear Mrs. Benson: On Thursday, December 4, I had the opportunity of hearing your address before[1] the American Banking Institute in Dallas, Texas.

Make that just *Dallas.*

Would you be willing to present the same material[2] to our insurance sales force on February 13 in Denver, Colorado?

Your suggestions for[3] improving interpersonal relationships through better communication skills are excellent, and they would be[4] quite appropriate for the 300 salespeople we expect at our conference.

Will you please let me know as[5] soon as possible if you will be able to be with us.

Delete *as soon as possible.*

Cordially yours, [114]

CHAPTER

HOMES

LESSON 31

◖ LETTER 181 ◖ (Related to Lesson 31, Letter 3)

Discussing, gardening, landscaping, handling, maintenance, objectionable.

Dear Mrs. Brown: Thank you for discussing my gardening and landscaping needs with me last week. I have considered[1] carefully the bid you gave me for handling my yard maintenance. At this time, however, my budget will not allow[2] the luxury of turning over the work at my residence to your organization.

I usually enjoy[3] taking care of my own yard. The one task I find objectionable, however, is mowing the lawn. Your bid[4] included a figure of $45 a month to mow my lawn once each week. If you are interested in[5] accepting only this part of my yard care, please let me know.

I look forward to hearing from you. Cordially yours,[6]   [120]

TRANSCRIPTION PREVIEW

Spelling. Landscaping, carefully, handling, luxury.

Punctuation. Commas before and after both *howevers* (, parenthetical).

Typing Style. Transcribe: $45 (no decimal).

❲ LETTER 182 ❳ (Related to Lesson 31, Letter 4)

[shorthand symbols]

Evaluated, requirements, residence, shrubs, residents, acceptable.

Dear Mr. Stern: We have carefully evaluated the landscaping and gardening requirements at your residence[1] at 347 West 23 Street. To keep the grounds around your residence in beautiful, well-groomed[2] condition, we will perform the following services:

1. Water your lawn twice a week and mow it every ten[3] days.
2. Trim your shrubs early in the spring and once again in the summer.
3. Plant your garden areas and weed[4] them when necessary.

Our bid for all these services is $600, which is much less than most commercially[5] operated nurseries charge. To prove this to yourself, just compare what the other residents of your[6] area are paying for similar services.

Please let us know as soon as possible if our terms are[7] acceptable. Cordially yours,   [145]

TRANSCRIPTION PREVIEW

Spelling.   Gardening, beautiful, nurseries, acceptable.
Punctuation.   Hyphenate *well-groomed* (hyphenated before noun);
no hyphen after *commercially* (no hyphen after *-ly*).
Typing Style.   Transcribe: 347 West 23 Street.

❲ LETTER 183 ❳ (Related to Lesson 31, Letter 5)

[shorthand symbols]

Examined, impressed, maintenance, insects, attacking, commended.

Dear Ms. Roberts: Enclosed is my check for $9.50 to cover the cost of *Total Lawn and Garden*[1] *Care.* I have examined the book carefully, and I am very much impressed with the practical approach it takes[2] to handling the various aspects of yard care and maintenance. I particularly enjoyed reading the chapter[3] entitled "Insects That Destroy Your Lawn."

A few days ago I went to a local garden shop and purchased[4] the spray your book recommended for the insects that are attacking my roses and trees at my residence. Within[5] three days after I applied the spray, I could find no trace of insect life. Several of the residents of[6] the neighborhood have commented, "Your trees and shrubs have never looked better."

Your staff is to be commended for putting[7] together such a well-planned, effective publication. Cordially yours,   [154]

TRANSCRIPTION PREVIEW

Spelling.   Carefully, practical, maintenance, publication.

Punctuation.   Comma after *have commented* (, introduce short quotation); period after *better* (. inside final quotation mark).

Typing Style.   Transcribe: $9.50; Underscore: *Total Lawn and Garden Care* (underscore book title).

❨ LETTER 184

Watering, diminished, providing, driest, infest, acquainted.

Dear Mr. Jackson: When the fall months arrive and the need for watering and mowing our lawns has diminished, most[1] of the residents of this area are ready for a well-earned rest. We caution you, however, about the[2] importance of providing proper care for your lawn during the fall months.

Here in the West the fall is one of the[3] driest times of the year, and plants continue to require water. In addition, harmful insects may still infest[4] our plants if we fail to protect them.

The next time you are in Madison, stop in and get acquainted with our fine[5] staff at the Village Green Garden Shop. We are

located at 13 Fourth Avenue. We will be happy to share[6] our knowledge with you and provide the products necessary to help you get
your yard ready for the winter months[7] ahead. Sincerely yours, [144]

TRANSCRIPTION PREVIEW

Spelling. Diminished, driest, acquainted, knowledge.
Punctuation. Commas before and after *however* (, parenthetical).
Typing Style. Transcribe: fall, winter (not capitalized); West
(capitalized).

◖ LETTER 185

**Subdivision, surprised, occurred, enjoy, anywhere, alternative,
isn't.**

Dear Mrs. Roberts: As I was driving through a local subdivision
recently, I was surprised at the number[1] of residents who were
working in their yards.

The thought occurred to me that there are many people who
enjoy[2] working in their yards. They would rather be there than
anywhere else. Others, however, toil in their yards because the[3]
work simply has to be done, and they do not want to pay someone
else to do it. They may not like the job, but there[4] seems to be no
alternative.

If you are interested in saving time and effort in the care of
your yard, we[5] suggest that you become acquainted with the many
timesaving commercial products that are available at[6] the Lexington Outdoor Shop. The Lexington line of products is sold with a
money-back guarantee. When we sell[7] you something, we will
provide complete, easy-to-follow instructions on its use.

Isn't it time you let us help[8] you with your lawn and garden
chores? Sincerely yours,   [169]

Spelling. Surprised, thought, occurred, alternative.
Punctuation. Commas after *recently* (, *as* clause); after *something* (, *when* clause).
Typing Style. Transcribe: Lexington Outdoor Shop (capitalized).

❲ LETTER 186 ❲ (Office Style)

Yards, dangerous, disposing, trimmings, beautifully, appointment.

Dear Mr. Powers: One of the most difficult tasks residents face in keeping their yards well groomed is that of trimming[1] their trees. In the first place, it is physically difficult to trim branches and limbs from the tops of large trees. In[2] the second place, it is dangerous work. Finally, there is the difficult problem of disposing of the excess[3] trimmings.

Delete *difficult.*

The Butler Garden Shop has been keeping the trees in Troy in good shape for years. A call to our office[4] before the end of March guarantees that your trees will be trimmed and beautifully shaped within two weeks. The average cost[5] for this service is less than $100.

Take out *average.*

Call today for an appointment before our busy season arrives.[6] Yours very truly, [124]

LESSON 32

❲ LETTER 187 ❲ (Related to Lesson 32, Letter 3)

Questions, months ago, yes, consequently, critical, in the future.

Dear Mr. Lang: The questions you included in your letter two months ago were certainly well timed. I answered[1] yes to three of four questions you asked.

Consequently, I went to Allen Brothers in the Valley View Shopping[2] Mall and purchased the weather stripping that you recommended. I easily installed it around my doors and windows.[3] This simple operation made a critical difference in the cost of heating my home during the winter[4] months.

Thank you for taking the time to offer me some good advice; you may be sure that I will come to Allen[5] Brothers regularly in the future. Sincerely yours, [110]

TRANSCRIPTION PREVIEW

Spelling. Questions, stripping, recommended, critical.
Punctuation. Semicolon after *good advice* (; no conjunction).
Typing Style. Transcribe: Valley View Shopping Mall (capitalized); winter (not capitalized).

⟨ LETTER 188 ⟨ (Related to Lesson 32, Letter 4)

Interested, ceramic, Springfield, preliminary, inexpensive, obstacle.

Mr. Watson: I was interested in your memorandum exploring the possibility of constructing[1] a ceramic tile manufacturing plant here in Springfield. Of course, I would like to see your preliminary[2] figures.

We must answer the following critical questions:
1. Could a convenient, inexpensive site be purchased?[3]
2. Would obtaining financing be an obstacle?
3. Will the rate of construction remain stable in the[4] next decade?

I will be in Springfield next week on another matter. Please plan to meet me at the Hotel Baker[5] on Thursday, November 13, at three in the afternoon. Barbara P. Tate [114]

Spelling. Ceramic, critical, financing, obstacle.

Punctuation. Colon after *the following critical questions* (: enumeration).

Typing Style. Transcribe: three in the afternoon (letters).

❡ LETTER 189 ❡ (Related to Lesson 32, Letter 5)

Discussing, periodical, although, maintenance, appearance, constructed.

Dear Mr. Miller: Thank you for your recent visit to our store; we appreciate the opportunity of[1] discussing your home plans with you.

Enclosed is a copy of an article from a recent periodical,[2] *Homes Today*. The article describes in detail all the features of the materials we sell. Although these[3] materials do not require maintenance, we understand you will not use them on your home unless you like their[4] appearance.

Enclosed is a map of your area showing the location of 15 homes where our materials[5] have been used. Take a short drive to see for yourself the beautiful homes that have been constructed with our siding.

We[6] hope to see you in our store again soon. Cordially yours,

[130]

TRANSCRIPTION PREVIEW

Spelling. Discussing, periodical, although, maintenance.

Punctuation. Semicolon after *visit to our store* (; no conjunction).

Typing Style. Underscore: *Homes Today* (underscore magazine title).

Manual, periodical, charges, remodel, eager.

Ladies and Gentlemen: Please send me a copy of your manual, *Making Your Own Home Repairs*, that I saw[1] advertised in a recent periodical. Enclosed is a money order for $9.50 to cover[2] the cost of the manual and the shipping charges.

For my bonus selection, I would like a copy of[3] your publication, *Homes Today*. I am planning to remodel an old home that I purchased recently, and these[4] books will help me a great deal.

I hope you will fill my order promptly; I am eager to begin work. Sincerely[5] yours,   [101]

TRANSCRIPTION PREVIEW

Spelling.   Manual, shipping, planning, promptly.
Punctuation.   Semicolon after *promptly* (; no conjunction).
Typing Style.   Underscore: *Making Your Own Home Repairs*, *Homes Today* (underscore book titles).

◑ LETTER 191

Figures, appraising, interesting, slightly, physical, indefinitely.

Dear Mr. Yates: A local real estate broker, Miss Maria Lopez, gave me the figures she and her associates[1] use in appraising the value of a home. It is interesting to note that the use of brick siding can[2] add as much as $10,000 to the value of a home. However, the cost of using brick is only[3] slightly more than the cost of other exteriors.

Lexington Company brick comes in three beautiful colors.[4] It adds to the physical attractiveness of your home and it requires no maintenance. In addition, it will[5] last indefinitely.

Before you make your final building plans, come into our showroom and see our attractive[6] display samples. Sincerely yours, [126]

TRANSCRIPTION PREVIEW

Spelling. Appraising, slightly, physical, indefinitely.

Punctuation. Commas after *However* and *In addition* (, introductory).

Typing Style. Transcribe: Lexington Company (capitalized); three beautiful colors (letters).

❡ LETTER 192 ❡ (Office Style)

Homeowner, critical, exposed, concrete, deteriorate, replacement.

Dear Homeowner: If your walks, driveways, and patios are more than eight years old, their surfaces are probably showing[1] critical signs of wear. In our harsh, changing climate, exposed concrete surfaces deteriorate in a[2] few years' time. The physical appearance is unattractive, and broken concrete can cause accidents. If this has[3] happened to your concrete areas, we encourage you to call one of our representatives for details on[4] our new concrete restoration process.

In the past, little could be done to repair concrete. The usual[5] solution to the problem was to replace it. This solution, of course, is quite expensive.

Delete *quite.*

With our new process, your[6] walks, driveways, and patios will be as good as new and at a fraction of replacement cost.

Call us anytime[7] during business hours for additional information on this money-saving new process.

Take out *anytime.*

Yours very truly,[8]   [160]

❮ LETTER 193 ❯ (Related to Lesson 33, Letter 3)

[shorthand symbols]

Completed, furniture, building, Denver, quite, proud.

Dear Mr. Smith: As you know, I have just completed the short course in furniture building and repair offered at[1] Denver Community College. I had a great deal to learn, and I found the course to be a worthwhile, rewarding[2] experience.

I am quite proud of the table and chairs that I built; I use them every day. In addition, I[3] know I can use the skills I gained throughout my lifetime.

Thank you for being such a good teacher, Mr. Smith. Yours very[4] truly, [82]

TRANSCRIPTION PREVIEW

Spelling.   Offered, quite, proud, built.
Punctuation.   Semicolon after *that I built* (; no conjunction).
Typing Style.   Transcribe: Denver Community College (capitalized).

❮ LETTER 194 ❯ (Related to Lesson 33, Letter 4)

[shorthand symbols]

Unable, chandeliers, disappointed, foreign, schedule, electric company's.

Dear Mrs. Boyd: I am sorry you have been unable to get the two chandeliers I ordered last April. We[1] had looked in several stores before deciding on those particular fixtures, and we are disappointed that[2] foreign labor difficulties have made them unavailable.

Because of the strict time schedule we are following[3] in the construction of our house, it is necessary for us to order our living room fixtures elsewhere.[4] As you may remember, we chose the National Electric Company's chandeliers as our second choice, but your[5] store does not carry that line. Will you please return our $100 deposit to us as soon as possible.[6]

We appreciate your concern and promptness in dealing with this matter; we will certainly order other[7] items from your store in the future. Sincerely yours, [149]

TRANSCRIPTION PREVIEW

Spelling. Chandeliers, disappointed, foreign, elsewhere.

Punctuation. Comma after *in the construction of our house* (, introductory); semicolon after *with this matter* (; no conjunction).

Typing Style. Transcribe: April (capitalized); $100 (no decimal).

ℂ LETTER 195 ℂ (Related to Lesson 33, Letter 5)

Expect, salespeople, necessary, delivered, equitable.

Dear Miss Evans: When you buy carpeting, you expect to get more than just a high-quality product. You want[1] excellent service as well.

You want to deal with salespeople whose attitude reflects a genuine concern for you[2] and your ideas. You want to have the option of buying on convenient credit terms when necessary. You want[3] your carpet delivered and installed on a certain day. If the quality of the carpet or the installation[4] work is not completely satisfactory, you want an immediate, equitable adjustment.

Our goal[5] at Adams Carpet Company is to assure your satisfaction; we want you to do business with us again[6] in the future.

We hope you will stop in at our store soon, Miss Evans. Sincerely yours, [135]

Spelling. Excellent, completely, equitable, satisfaction.
Punctuation. Semicolon after *your satisfaction* (; no conjunction); comma before *Miss Evans* (, parenthetical).
Typing Style. Transcribe: Adams Carpet Company (capitalized).

ℂ LETTER 196

Beautifully, stylish, coordinated, accessories, interiors, featured, prominence.

Dear Miss Taylor: A beautifully decorated home means more than having fine carpets, stylish furniture, and[1] coordinated draperies. The picture is simply not complete without beautiful pictures and other accessories[2] to provide the finishing touches.

Southern Interiors of Mobile has won three national awards[3] for originality and design in interior decoration. Our displays have been featured in seven[4] national publications in the past year alone.

Despite our prominence in the interior decoration[5] field, our services cost much less than you might think. Call us the next time you need pictures or accessories[6] that will transform your home into a showcase. Sincerely yours, [131]

TRANSCRIPTION PREVIEW

Spelling. Stylish, accessories, touches, prominence.
Punctuation. Commas after *carpets* and *furniture* (, series).
Typing Style. Transcribe: Southern Interiors of Mobile (*of* not capitalized).

ℂ LETTER 197

Introducing, New York City, acclaimed, interior, Broadway, intelligent.

Dear Mrs. Yates: We would like to have the opportunity of introducing you to Miss Mary Bishop, a[1] new member of our New York City staff.

Mary comes to us from a widely acclaimed interior decorating[2] firm in Chicago, Illinois. We have planned to have Mary remain in our Broadway store during the week of[3] March 14 so that our preferred customers will have the opportunity to meet her.

We think you will agree[4] with us that Miss Bishop is a delightful, intelligent, and highly talented person. We feel her expertise[5] as a decorator will be shown clearly through her displays that will be exhibited throughout our store.

Your[6] visit will entitle you to a $25 coupon, which can be used as cash toward the purchase of any[7] merchandise valued at $100 or more in any department in our store. We hope you will take[8] advantage of this splendid opportunity, Mrs. Yates. Sincerely yours,   [174]

TRANSCRIPTION PREVIEW

Spelling.   Preferred, intelligent, decorator, exhibited.
Punctuation.   Commas after *delightful* and *intelligent* (, series).
Typing Style.   Transcribe: $25; $100 (no decimals).

❮ LETTER 198   (Office Style)

Paneling, neighborhood, February, attribute, wallpaper.

Dear Mr. Bates: We are opening a new branch of Atlanta Custom Paper and Paneling in your neighborhood[1] on Monday, February 16.

Delete *Monday.*

Our organization is one of the largest, most successful companies[2] in the South. We attribute our success to the large variety of stock that we carry. Our wallpaper[3] selection ranges from simple prints to luxurious flocks and foils. Our paneling is available in a[4] wide variety of sizes, colors, and styles. Our prices begin at just $2 for a single

Take out single.

roll of[5] wallpaper and just $10 for a sheet of wood paneling.

We hope you will join us at the grand opening[6] of our new store. Come early; we will be looking forward to seeing you. Cordially yours,   [136]

LESSON 34

❰ LETTER 199 ❰ (Related to Lesson 34, Letter 3)

Invitation, subdivision, today's, solar, researching, showcase, demonstrate.

Dear Mr. Harrington: Thank you for your invitation to attend this year's Parade of Homes at the Valley View[1] subdivision. Considering today's energy picture, it seems only fitting that the top award went to[2] the Ryan Company's home, which was heated and cooled with solar energy.

My firm, the Best Heating Company,[3] has spent several years researching solar heating systems, and we think that next year's Parade of Homes would be an[4] appropriate showcase to display the products that we are presently developing. Will you please send me any[5] information you may have on renting space at next year's Parade of Homes. We would need a rather large area[6] to demonstrate exactly how our various systems operate.

We have to hear from you soon; we are eager[7] to begin making our plans. Yours very truly,   [150]

TRANSCRIPTION PREVIEW

Spelling.   Year's, today's, fitting, exactly.
Punctuation.   Comma after *energy picture* (, introductory); period after *next year's Parade of Homes* (. courteous request).
Typing Style.   Transcribe: Parade of Homes (*of* not capitalized); Valley View (capitalized).

◖ LETTER 200 ◖ (Related to Lesson 34, Letter 4)

Rather, selection, expensive, respiratory, electric heat, considering, backup.

Dear Mr. Stern: Your request for information on home heating systems is a rather difficult one to answer[1] in just a few words. I would like to offer some ideas, however, that you may find helpful in making your[2] selection.

Gas and hot water systems are presently among the least expensive to install and operate.[3] They dry out the air, however, and may cause some problems if a family member has any respiratory[4] ailments.

Electric heat is the cleanest heat presently available. In addition, it is absolutely[5] quiet. The disadvantage is that its cost of operation is presently the highest of the systems[6] you are considering. You could pay as much as $100 or $200 per month for[7] electricity during the winter.

Solar heating systems have not proved to be economical in this particular[8] area. A backup system must also be installed, which makes it quite expensive.

When you are in town,[9] please stop in to see me. I will be glad to provide any additional information on heating systems[10] that I have available. Sincerely yours,   [208]

TRANSCRIPTION PREVIEW

Spelling. Answer, respiratory, absolutely, backup.

Punctuation. Commas before and after both *howevers* (, parenthetical); after *When you are in town* (, *when* clause).

Typing Style. Transcribe: $100; $200 (no decimals); winter (not capitalized).

◖ LETTER 201 ◖ (Related to Lesson 34, Letter 5)

Discuss, ideas, described, library, referred, excellent.

Dear Don: Would it be possible for us to get together on Tuesday, August 13, in your office to discuss[1] your ideas on solar heating systems? I, too, am excited about the plans you described in your letter.[2] I even went to my local library, where I read the *Great American Homes* article you referred to.[3]

Mr. Brown's design is excellent. There are some unanswered questions, of course. I believe, however, that we should[4] investigate the possibility of incorporating some of his ideas in your new home.

Please let me[5] know as soon as possible if you will be able to meet with me on the suggested date. Sincerely yours,   [119]

TRANSCRIPTION PREVIEW

Spelling. Discuss, described, referred, excellent.

Punctuation. Commas before and after *too* and *however* (, parenthetical).

Typing Style. Underscore: *Great American Homes* (underscore magazine title).

❰ LETTER 202

Adopted, electrical, probably, upgrading, surprised, obligation.

Dear Mr. Tracy: On January 10, 1975, the State Building Commission adopted the[1] present electrical code. Prior to that time, most homes were built with electrical systems that are inadequate[2] for today's needs. Because your home was constructed in 1973, you probably know exactly[3] what we are talking about.

Our staff here at the Troy Electric Company, the largest, best-known electric[4] company in the East, would like to give you an estimate of the cost of upgrading your electrical system.[5] We think you will be pleasantly surprised at how much we can do to add to the convenience, comfort, and safety[6] of your home for such a small investment.

Of course, there will be no cost or obligation on your part for this[7] initial estimate. Sincerely yours,   [147]

Spelling.   Adopted, inadequate, upgrading, safety.

Punctuation.   Commas after *convenience* and *comfort* (, series); after *largest* (, *and* omitted).

Typing Style.   Transcribe: State Building Commission, East (capitalized).

ℂ LETTER 203

Unusual, reduced, fuel, determining, adequate, apparent, excessive.

Dear Mr. Stevens: The Pittsburgh Insulation Company is really in the business of saving money for[1] our customers. Although this statement may sound unusual, it is actually true. By adding insulation[2] to your home, you will save money every year through reduced fuel bills.

There is a simple method of determining[3] if a house has adequate insulation. When it snows during the late fall and winter months, heat loss for a[4] particular home is apparent by the length of time snow remains on the roof. If heat loss through the roof is excessive,[5] snow melts quickly, and your heating bills are likely high.

The next time we have a storm, see just how long it takes the[6] snow on your roof to melt. If you feel that you have a problem, please call us at 555-3356. We would[7] like to help you start saving money as soon as possible. Cordially yours,   [154]

TRANSCRIPTION PREVIEW

Spelling.   Really, adequate, excessive, likely.

Punctuation.   Comma after *The next time we have a storm* (, introductory).

Typing Style.   Transcribe: Pittsburgh Insulation Company (capitalized).

◖ LETTER 204 ◖ (Office Style)

Diminishing, indicate, decrease, contractors, notify, wisdom.

Dear Customer: Everyone is concerned about our country's rapidly diminishing fuel supplies. We all want[1] to do our part in conserving energy, but we do not always know exactly what action we should take.

Our[2] records indicate that you are using about 60 percent more natural gas than the average customer[3] in this area. The Central Gas Company would like to help you decrease

> Make that *cut;* no, leave it *decrease.*

your monthly gas bills.

If you would like[4] to save energy and reduce your fuel bills at the same time, we have a suggestion for you. Contact several[5] reputable home insulation contractors and get cost estimates for increasing the amount of insulation[6] in your home. When you have made a choice, notify our main office in Kansas City, Missouri. We will[7] pay for the additional insulation and add it to your monthly gas bills over the next three years.

Join the[8] thousands of natural gas users who have seen the wisdom of this proposal and accepted our offer. Call[9] us soon for further

> Make that *more;* no, leave it *further.*

details. Sincerely yours,   [188]

LESSON 35

◖ LETTER 205 ◖ (Related to Lesson 35, Letter 3)

Diagram, incorporate, yard, physical, playroom, outdoor.

Dear Mr. Fraser: Enclosed is a diagram of the changes we would like to incorporate in our house and[1] yard design to provide for the physical and recreational needs of our family.

As you will notice,[2] we are considering building a small addition to the east side of our house that would house a playroom for the[3] children. We would like to add a swimming pool as well as some outdoor furniture in the backyard. Naturally, we[4] do not want to displace any of the large trees.

Will you please analyze these plans and give us some idea of the[5] cost of the additions we are suggesting. Sincerely yours,   [111]

TRANSCRIPTION PREVIEW

Spelling.   Design, physical, analyze, displace.
Punctuation.   Comma after *As you will notice* (, *as* clause); period after the last sentence (. courteous request).
Typing Style.   Transcribe: east (not capitalized).

❬ LETTER 206 ❬ (Related to Lesson 35, Letter 4)

Inquiry, tennis, property, estimate, concrete, as soon as possible.

Dear Mr. Norris: Thank you for your letter of inquiry concerning the possibility of constructing[1] a tennis court on your property. I apologize for not answering your letter sooner, but I have been[2] out of town on a business trip. Before we can give you an estimate, we must have some additional information.[3] Please answer the following questions in as much detail as possible:

1. Can we get our heavy-duty[4] equipment into your backyard?
2. Will any trees have to be displaced?
3. Do you want your tennis court equipped[5] with night lights?
4. What type of fencing would you like?
5. Do you want a concrete or clay surface?

Now is an[6] excellent time to get started on this project. Our people are not as busy in the fall as they will be in the[7] spring. Will

you please send us the information we need as soon as possible.
Sincerely yours, [157]

TRANSCRIPTION PREVIEW

Spelling.   Possibility, apologize, additional, fencing.
Punctuation.   Hyphenate *heavy-duty* (hyphenated before noun).
Typing Style.   Transcribe: fall, spring (not capitalized).

❡ LETTER 207 ❡ (Related to Lesson 35, Letter 5)

Stereo, installed, rightfully, conclude, completed, speakers.

Dear Mrs. Lloyd: The other day my wife said to me, "Why did we wait so long to have a National stereo[1] system installed in our home?"

From that comment you may rightfully conclude that we are certainly not disappointed[2] with our new stereo system. It has provided many hours of pleasure for the entire family, and[3] we know it will continue to do so for many years to come. We are glad that we did not compromise by[4] purchasing a lower-priced model.

We were delighted that the work was completed on time, and your people required[5] only three hours' time to complete the installation. The system was so expertly installed that the National[6] speakers actually add to the looks of our house.

Thanks, Mrs. Lloyd, for a job well done. Sincerely yours,   [138]

TRANSCRIPTION PREVIEW

Spelling.   Wait, compromise, delighted, hours'.
Punctuation.   Comma after *said to me* (, introduce short quotation); question mark after *in our home* (? inside final quotation mark).
Typing Style.   Transcribe: National (capitalized).

(LETTER 208

[shorthand symbols]

Basically, addition, parcel, borrow, beautiful, functional, designers.

Dear Mr. Jefferson: If you would like to have a larger home, I am sure you realize that basically you have[1] only two options. You can sell your house and purchase a larger one, or you can build an addition to your present[2] house.

Shopping for a new home today can be very discouraging; prices are extremely high. Building an[3] addition to your present home could save you money because you do not have to purchase another parcel of[4] land at today's highly inflated prices. You can also keep your existing low-interest mortgage and simply[5] borrow enough to construct the addition.

If the idea of adding a room or two to your present home appeals[6] to you, the staff at Davis Building Supply Company would like to show you how we can add a beautiful,[7] functional addition for a very reasonable price. Call us at 555-5629 for an[8] appointment with one of our skilled designers. Sincerely yours, [170]

TRANSCRIPTION PREVIEW

Spelling.   Options, discouraging, existing, reasonable.
Punctuation.   No hyphen after *highly* (no hyphen after -*ly*); hyphenate *low interest* (hyphenated before noun).
Typing Style.   Transcribe: Davis Building Supply Company (capitalized).

(LETTER 209

[shorthand symbols]

Rapidly, doubling, realize, practical, efficiently, cozy, dealer.

Dear Homeowner: Considering the rapidly increasing cost of home heating fuels, it is no wonder that sales[1] of our wood-burning stoves are doubling each year. Because you are a homeowner, you realize that you must keep your[2] expenses at a minimum.

The Thomas stove burns ordinary wood and will pay for itself in fuel savings in[3] just a few years. In fact, many of our customers have discovered that they can save as much as $100[4] on their fuel bills in just one winter.

The Thomas stove is a beautiful, practical addition to any[5] home. It operates so efficiently that a few pieces of wood will burn all evening. It will keep your house warm[6] and cozy even on the coldest nights.

Before next winter arrives, drop in to see your local Thomas dealer[7] and let one of our representatives discuss the merits of our efficient wood-burning stoves with you. Yours truly,[8]   [160]

TRANSCRIPTION PREVIEW

Spelling.   Doubling, discovered, practical, efficiently.

Punctuation.   Commas after *In fact* and *Before next winter arrives* (, introductory).

Typing Style.   Transcribe: winter (not capitalized).

❏ LETTER 210 ❏ (Office Style)

Awoke, unpleasant, discovered, ceiling, assessment, installed.

Dear Mr. Lee: This morning I awoke to a very unpleasant circumstance. I discovered that during the[1] night my roof had begun to leak. The ceiling and one wall in my living room are badly damaged, and some of the[2] carpeting is soaked. It will be several days before a damage assessment

Make that *estimate;* no, leave it *assessment.*

can be made.

I read the warranty[3] that you issued at the time you installed the roofing material on my house, and I am sure that the cost[4] of the repair work is covered.

Will you please make arrangements to take care of these repairs in the next few days.[5]

Change that to *immediately;* no, leave it as it was.

Cordially yours, [102]

CHAPTER **8**

AGRICULTURE AND FOOD

LESSON 36

❰ LETTER 211 ❰ (Related to Lesson 36, Letter 3)

[shorthand]

Responding, inquiry, extremely, culinary, popular, elementary.

Dear Dr. Moore: Thank you for responding to my letter of inquiry about Ms. Mary Cunningham. I am[1] happy to tell you that we hired Ms. Cunningham this fall and that she has become an extremely valuable member[2] of the faculty here at the Virginia School of Culinary Arts. She is one of the most popular[3] teachers on our faculty, and she gets along well with everyone.

As you stated, she is quite adept at[4] adjusting to various situations. She teaches both day and evening classes in elementary and advanced[5] food preparation. She has made a number of suggestions concerning new courses that we should offer, and[6] we are considering adopting her recommendations.

If you know of any other teachers as well[7] qualified as Ms. Cunningham, I hope you will refer them to us. Cordially yours,

[154]

Spelling. Faculty, culinary, adept, elementary.
Punctuation. Commas after *on our faculty* and after *we should offer* (, conjunction).
Typing Style. Transcribe: Virginia School of Culinary Arts (*of* not capitalized).

❰ LETTER 212 ❰ (Related to Lesson 36, Letter 4)

Acknowledging, annual, I do not have, could be done, forward, attending.

Dear Ms. White: Thank you for acknowledging the suggestions that I made to improve the annual cooking course sponsored[1] by the National Department Store.

I am sorry that you cannot adopt the suggestions that I made, but[2] I am happy that you will be able to adapt some of them to fit your particular needs. At the present[3] time I do not have any further recommendations to make. I will, of course, get in touch with you should I think[4] of anything else that could be done to improve the cooking course.

I am looking forward to attending the course[5] again next summer. Cordially yours,   [107]

TRANSCRIPTION PREVIEW

Spelling. Sponsored, adopt, particular, forward.
Punctuation. Commas before and after *of course* (, parenthetical).
Typing Style. Transcribe: National Department Store (capitalized).

❰ LETTER 213 ❰ Related to Lesson 36, Letter 5)

Efficiency, markings, imprinted, definitely, average, between.

Dear Miss Rodriguez: Thank you very much for your letter telling me of the efficiency made possible by[1] the magnetic markings that are imprinted on many of the containers in my food store.

I am definitely[2] interested in adding to the efficiency of my operations and particularly in speeding[3] up the time at the checkout counter. On an average Friday or Saturday it takes half an hour for a customer[4] to check out once his or her goods have been selected.

If the program can help me operate more efficiently[5] and profitably, I will definitely adopt it. Will you please ask one of your representatives to[6] come to my store any weekday between the hours of nine and five. Very sincerely yours, [136]

TRANSCRIPTION PREVIEW

Spelling. Efficiency, imprinted, speeding, profitably.
Punctuation. Comma after *profitably* (, *if* clause); period after last sentence (. courteous request).
Typing Style. Transcribe: Friday, Saturday (capitalized).

ℭ LETTER 214

Complimentary, Jefferson, successful, chef, praise, efforts.

Dear Mr. Olson: Thank you for your complimentary letter on our food services here at The Jefferson[1] Cafeteria. We are pleased that you enjoyed your meal; we look forward to your return visit.

We believe the[2] key to any successful cafeteria operation is the chef, who is responsible for hiring[3] the staff, planning the menus, and supervising the preparation of the food. Our chef, Ms. Maria Lopez,[4] has been with us for the past six years. She is adept in each one of these important areas.

You may be sure[5] that we will pass along to her your words of praise for her efforts. Cordially yours, [114]

Spelling.   Enjoyed, forward, chef, praise.

Punctuation.   Commas after *is the chef* (, nonrestrictive); after *staff* and *menus* (, series).

Typing Style.   Transcribe: The Jefferson Cafeteria (*The* capitalized).

❡ LETTER 215

Annoyed, groceries, neighborhood, installed, electronic, scanner.

Dear Customer: If you have ever felt annoyed at the time it takes to get your groceries through the checkout[1] register of your neighborhood food store, you owe it to yourself to shop at Eastern Supermarket. We have just installed[2] a new electronic system that cuts your checkout time in half.

Most of the items in our store are stamped with[3] a special machine. The product is simply placed under an electronic scanner. The scanner is connected[4] to a computer that is attached to the register. Each item that you purchase is listed, and the correct[5] price is printed automatically on the register tape. The clerk then places the items directly into[6] shopping bags, and you are ready to go.

We hope you will let us give you a personal demonstration of this[7] exciting, innovative service in the near future. Sincerely yours,   [153]

Spelling.   Neighborhood, stamped, scanner, demonstration.

Punctuation.   Commas after *food store* (, *if* clause); after *is listed* and *shopping bags* (, conjunction).

Typing Style.   Transcribe: Eastern Supermarket (capitalized).

◖ LETTER 216 ◖ (Office Style)

(shorthand outline)

Handling, seminar, science, prospective, employees, benefit.

Dear Mr. Tracy: Our next food handling seminar

Make that class; *no, leave it* seminar.

will be held on Monday, June 14, in the conference room[1] of the Science Building on the Lincoln College campus. The two-hour seminar will begin at 6 p.m., and[2] there will be a short break after the first hour.

If you have new or prospective employees who would benefit from[3] participating in this seminar, send in their registration forms now.

Make that as soon as possible.

The fee for the seminar is still[4] only $15. Sincerely yours,   [87]

LESSON 37

◖ LETTER 217 ◖ (Related to Lesson 37, Letter 3)

(shorthand outline)

Attracting, candidates, successful, program, locality.

Dear Mr. Chan: Our efforts in attracting candidates for your training program have not been too successful. Those[1] who inquire about this program want to know your beginning pay level.

Your present entry-level wage is[2] considered much too low by most applicants. Many jobs that require little or no experience are available[3] in our locality, and the wages for these jobs are considerably higher than what you are offering.[4]

If you would be willing to increase the beginning salary by at least 50 cents per hour, I am sure[5] we would succeed in finding enough candidates for your needs. Cordially yours, [114]

TRANSCRIPTION PREVIEW

Spelling. Candidates, successful, beginning, succeed.
Punctuation. Hyphenate *entry-level* (hyphenated before noun).
Typing Style. Transcribe: 50 cents (figures and word).

◖ LETTER 218 ◖ (Related to Lesson 37, Letter 4)

Accepted, afraid, position, until, circumstances, accede.

Dear Dr. Washington: Thank you very much for your letter of July 23. I was, of course, very happy[1] to have been accepted as a graduate student and as a part-time member of the faculty at Southern[2] State College.

I am afraid, however, that I will not be able to begin my graduate work this fall.[3] My employer, Mr. Frank Jones, had a heart attack last week and will be out of the office for at least four months.[4] He has asked that I remain in my position until he is well enough to return to work. Under the[5] circumstances, I feel that I must accede to his request.

I sincerely hope that I will be able to begin[6] my graduate work in January. Will you please let me know if the teaching assistantship will be available[7] at that time. Thank you very much for your consideration. Sincerely yours, [154]

TRANSCRIPTION PREVIEW

Spelling. Graduate, accede, request, assistantship.
Punctuation. Period after *at that time* (. courteous request).
Typing Style. Transcribe: Southern State College (capitalized); four months (letters).

Package, design, exceeded, corresponding, promotional, evaluate.

Dear Miss Green: We are quite pleased with the work your firm did on the new package design for Powers Frozen Dinners. As[1] you know, we converted to the new package on October 1. Our sales during the past three months have exceeded[2] the sales for the corresponding period of last year by more than 20 percent.

We will soon begin a[3] nationwide promotional campaign, which we are confident will enable us to increase our sales even more. We[4] would like to have you meet with us on February 25 and 26 at the Portland Hotel in[5] Atlanta, Georgia, to evaluate our plans.

Will you please let us know if you can be with us on those dates. Cordially[6] yours,   [121]

TRANSCRIPTION PREVIEW

Spelling.   Frozen, exceeded, enable, evaluate.
Punctuation.   Comma after *As you know* (, *as* clause); period after the last sentence (. courteous request).
Typing Style.   Transcribe: Powers Frozen Dinners (capitalized); 20 percent (figures and word).

❮ LETTER 220

Everyone, cookers, minimum, electricity, basis, satisfied.

Dear Miss Edwards: These days it seems that almost everyone is turning to slow cookers to prepare food. Slow cookers[1] use a minimum amount of electricity, preserve the flavor of foods, and are convenient to use.

The[2] National Press Corporation has just published a 150-page book of special recipes called *The[3] Delights of Slow Cooking*. This book has received outstanding reviews in most of America's major newspapers,[4] and it is immediately available on a ten-day trial basis.

Return the enclosed coupon for your[5] copy of *The Delights of Slow Cooking*. If you like the book, keep it and send us your check for $9.95.[6] If you are not completely satisfied, return it after the trial period; there will be no obligation,[7] of course. Sincerely yours, [146]

TRANSCRIPTION PREVIEW

Spelling. Minimum, recipes, America's, trial.
Punctuation. Commas after *electricity* and *foods* (, series).
Typing Style. Underscore: *The Delights of Slow Cooking* (underscore book title).

❨ LETTER 221

Kitchen, requested, remained, unchanged, promptly.

Dear Ms. Mason: We are sorry that we cannot deliver your order of food and kitchen supplies next week as[1] you requested. Our records indicate that your present balance of $500 has remained unchanged on[2] our books for more than two months.

Our contract states: "No orders will be filled when the customer's existing balance exceeds[3] $200. Furthermore, a past-due account will be assessed an interest charge of 2 percent each month,[4] and the customer will pay all costs involved in making collection."

We are eager to continue providing[5] you with the Western Farms products that you need. Please send us your check today; we will fill your order promptly when we[6] receive it. Cordially yours, [125]

Spelling. Customer's, exceeds, assessed, promptly.

Punctuation. Colon after *Our contract states* (: introduce long quotation); period after *collection* (. inside final quotation mark).

Typing Style. Transcribe: $200 (no decimal); 2 percent (figure and word).

❪ LETTER 222 ❪ (Office Style)

Representative, attend, interested, innovative, assignment, few days.

Dear Mr. Trent: Would you be willing to serve as our representative at the National Food Convention in[1] Philadelphia, Pennsylvania, next summer? We understand that

> Make that *We heard that;* no, leave it *We understand that.*

you are planning to attend that event, and[2] we would like you to represent our organization.

We are, of course, interested in any innovative[3] marketing ideas and newly developed strategies that may be presented at the show, and your appraisal[4] of them would be of great importance to us. We will pay all your expenses plus a fee of $300[5] if you accept the assignment.

May we hear from you immediately.

> No, make that *within the next few days.*

Sincerely yours,   [116]

LESSON 38

❪ LETTER 223 ❪ (Related to Lesson 38, Letter 3)

Recent, dairy, containers, disposed, handles, suppliers, liters.

Dear Mrs. Smith: When we received your recent letter, we went right to our dairy cases to check the dates on our milk[1] containers. We found that approximately 20 percent of the milk in our cases was too old. We promptly[2] disposed of the old milk and immediately called the firm that handles our dairy account.

Most of our suppliers[3] operate on a contract basis with our store. Our agreement with the dairy specifically requires that[4] they stock our cases with fresh products every day. If they do not, the contract may be revoked. We brought this matter[5] to their attention, and we guarantee that you will not find any old milk in our dairy cases again.

Please[6] accept the enclosed coupon for three free liters of milk as our gift. Thank you for your understanding, Mrs. Smith.[7] Sincerely yours,   [143]

TRANSCRIPTION PREVIEW

Spelling. Dairy, disposed, handles, liters.
Punctuation. Commas after *your recent letter* (, *when* clause); after *for your understanding* (, parenthetical).
Typing Style. Transcribe: 20 percent (figures and word); three free liters (letters).

❰ LETTER 224 ❰ (Related to Lesson 38, Letter 4)

Examination, reference, shelf, illustrated, requisition.

Gentlemen: Enclosed is my check for $24.95 in payment for my copy of *New Ways*[1] *To Prepare Food.*

When the examination copy arrived, I placed it on the reference shelf of our food resource[2] center. During the past three weeks, it has been used every day.

Several students have commented on the value[3] of the book in their studies. One student said: "This is the most beautifully illustrated cookbook I have ever[4] seen. Its topical index makes it easy and convenient to use as a resource aid. Maybe we should use this[5] book as our regular text."

I have placed an order with our department head for three additional copies. When[6] my requisition is approved, you will receive the order. Cordially yours, [134]

TRANSCRIPTION PREVIEW

Spelling. Reference, every day, topical, requisition.
Punctuation. No hyphen after *beautifully* (no hyphen after *-ly*).
Typing Style. Underscore: *New Ways To Prepare Food* (underscore book title).

ℂ LETTER 225 ℂ (Related to Lesson 38, Letter 5)

Cited, inability, citizens, overextended, priority, mention.

Dear Ms. Cunningham: Our board of directors discussed the problem you cited in your recent letter concerning[1] the inability of some of our senior citizens to come to our center to participate in the[2] programs. Everyone liked your suggestion; we should purchase a bus as soon as possible. It is imperative[3] that we reach a greater percentage of our eligible population on an everyday basis.[4]

Unfortunately, our present budget is somewhat overextended, and there does not seem to be any way we can[5] purchase a bus this year. However, we are giving this matter high priority in next year's budget.

Will you[6] please mention this in your next issue of *Senior Citizen News*. Thanks for your concern, Ms. Cunningham. Sincerely[7] yours, [141]

TRANSCRIPTION PREVIEW

Spelling. Discussed, inability, imperative, overextended.
Punctuation. Comma after *However* (, introductory); period after *Senior Citizen News* (. courteous request).
Typing Style. Underscore: *Senior Citizen News* (underscore newspaper title).

Gardens, vegetables, throughout, greenhouse, sunny, yard.

Dear Mr. Mason: Many people love the late summer and early fall of the year best because they can go to[1] their gardens and pick fresh vegetables right off the vines. You can enjoy that special experience throughout the[2] year with the Garden King greenhouse.

The Garden King greenhouse may be located in any sunny place in your yard,[3] and it can be assembled in just an hour or two. The maintenance costs are low; in fact, the savings on your food[4] bill will more than pay for the electricity required to operate it.

Our greenhouses come in five sizes;[5] each is on display at the Lexington Nursery located at 375 North 21 Street here[6] in Dover, Delaware.

We hope you will come in to see us soon. Cordially yours,   [134]

TRANSCRIPTION PREVIEW

Spelling.   Vegetables, greenhouse, sunny, display.
Punctuation.   Comma after *in your yard* (, conjunction); semi-colon after *five sizes* (; no conjunction).
Typing Style.   Transcribe: summer, fall (not capitalized); 375 North 21 Street.

◖ **LETTER 227**

To participate, certainly, consultant, unfortunately, assignment.

Dear Ms. White: Thank you for your invitation to participate in the National Department Store's cooking course[1] again next summer. I certainly enjoyed serving as a consultant during the course last year, and I wish that[2] it were possible for me to work with you again next year. Unfortunately, I have already accepted[3] another assignment for the entire summer. Therefore, I will not be able to accept your offer.

I hope,[4] Ms. White, that you will ask me to work with you again in the future. Please write to me at 402 East 21[5] Street in Los Angeles, California, anytime in the future. Cordially yours,

[116]

TRANSCRIPTION PREVIEW

Spelling. Enjoyed, consultant, accepted, entire.
Punctuation. Comma after *Therefore* (, introductory).
Typing Style. Transcribe: summer (not capitalized); 402 East 21 Street.

❡ LETTER 228 ❡ (Office Style)

Purchased, restaurant, property, permit, inspector.

Dear Mr. Gold: Several months ago I purchased a piece of land at 502 East Elm Drive. I bought the land[1]

Make that *property.*

in order to build a first-class restaurant. Officials of the city government assured me at the time that[2] the property could be used for commercial purposes.

Last week I applied for a building permit from the city[3] building inspector, and I was told that the property could be used only for residential purposes.[4]

Will you please look into this matter yourself, Mr. Gold, and tell me what the problem is. I have made a substantial[5] investment,

Make that a *large investment;* no, leave it *substantial investment.*

and I do not want to lose it. I am sure you can understand my position. Very truly[6] yours,

[121]

◖ **LETTER 229** ◖ **(Related to Lesson 39, Letter 3)**

Ruling, experiencing, orchards, permit, hundreds, certain.

Dear Miss Franklin: A recent ruling by the state government should help to provide some relief for the problems you[1] are experiencing in finding part-time employees to work in your orchards. Until recently, all employees[2] had to be at least 18 years of age. The new ruling will permit employers to hire part-time employees[3] who are 16 years old.

Historically, fruit growers have had difficulty in finding enough employees. Finding[4] a suitable labor supply has become increasingly difficult in recent years. Now, however, there[5] are hundreds of young people who will be out of school for the summer and available for work.

We are certain[6] you will be able to find the help you need for your orchards. Sincerely yours, [134]

TRANSCRIPTION PREVIEW

Spelling. Government, experiencing, historically, suitable.
Punctuation. Hyphenate *part-time* (hyphenated before noun).
Typing Style. Transcribe: summer (not capitalized).

◖ **LETTER 230** ◖ **(Related to Lesson 39, Letter 4)**

Outlining, benefits, cooperative, almanac, article, entitled.

Dear Mrs. Brown: Thank you for your letter outlining some of the benefits of becoming associated[1] with your cooperative.

After reading your letter, I read a few articles in the *American Farming*[2] *Almanac*, which I had retained in my library through the years. In one article entitled "New Choices for[3] Today's Progressive Farmer," the author explored the growing benefits of the cooperative movement in farming.[4]

I was quite surprised to discover, Mrs. Brown, that you were the author of that article. I must confess[5] that I was impressed. My completed application for membership in the cooperative is enclosed.

I hope[6] to hear from you soon with regard to my membership request. Sincerely yours, [134]

TRANSCRIPTION PREVIEW

Spelling.   Cooperative, benefits, article, regard.
Punctuation.   Commas before *which I had retained* (, nonrestrictive); before and after *Mrs. Brown* (, parenthetical).
Typing Style.   Underscore: *American Farming Almanac* (underscore magazine title); Transcribe: "New Choices for Today's Progressive Farmer," (quote title of article).

ℂ LETTER 231 ℂ (Related to Lesson 39, Letter 5)

Judge, livestock, accepted, several months ago, successful, event.

Dear Mr. Sanders: Thank you for your recent letter offering me an opportunity to serve as a judge[1] at the Utah Livestock Show on July 15, 16, and 17. Unfortunately, I accepted a[2] request several months ago to meet with the county agents in Nebraska on those dates. Therefore, I will be[3] unavailable.

I suggest that you contact Mr. Don Harrington, a former student of mine at Western[4] State College. Don is one of the finest livestock specialists in our area, and he has had considerable[5] experience judging livestock contests. If you wish, you may contact Don at 924 East 21[6] Street in Boise, Idaho. His telephone number is 555-5367.

Best wishes for a most[7] successful event, Mr. Sanders. Yours truly, [149]

Spelling. Livestock, unavailable, judging, successful.
Punctuation. Commas after *Unfortunately* and *Therefore* (, introductory).
Typing Style. Transcribe: Utah Livestock Show, Western State College (capitalized); 924 East 21 Street.

❨ LETTER 232

Chemicals, pose, survival, destroy, pesticides, practical.

Dear Mr. Simmons: Despite the large number of chemicals that have been used to control destructive insects during[1] the past ten years, these pests still pose the greatest threat to the survival of the world's farms. An article in a[2] recent issue of the *British Farm Journal* stated that insects probably destroy more than 30 percent of[3] the world's food.

Although chemical pesticides are not the only means of controlling destructive insects, they are[4] presently the most important and are often the only practical method of control.

To help you win the[5] ever-raging war against insects, we have stocked our shelves with every useful chemical you might need. In addition,[6] our staff can provide information on the most effective use of our products.

We hope you will call on us[7] soon for assistance in helping you increase your crop yield. Yours truly,   [153]

TRANSCRIPTION PREVIEW

Spelling. Chemicals, controlling, assistance, yield.
Punctuation. Hyphenate *ever-raging* (hyphenated before noun).
Typing Style. Underscore: *British Farm Journal* (underscore magazine title).

ℂ LETTER 233

[shorthand outline]

Thousands, inadequate, underground, virtually, agricultural.

Dear Mr. Morgan: As you know, thousands of acres of land in our area are not being used because of[1] inadequate water supplies. Food production in this area could be greatly increased if water resources[2] were available.

I understand that the National Company has recently discovered a huge supply[3] of underground water in the region. They believe this water could be pumped economically to land that[4] is now virtually worthless.

The water rights to this property are currently for sale. Would you be interested[5] in working with me in forming a corporation to raise funds to purchase these water rights and the adjacent[6] property? If you are, please let me know as soon as possible. I would like to discuss this exciting[7] agricultural project with you. Sincerely yours, [148]

TRANSCRIPTION PREVIEW

Spelling.   Inadequate, discovered, virtually, discuss.
Punctuation.   Comma after _If you are_ (, _if_ clause).
Typing Style.   Transcribe: National Company (capitalized).

ℂ LETTER 234 ℂ (Office Style)

[shorthand outline]

Annual, privilege, selected, approximately, acceptable.

Dear Mr. Stone: Thank you for your recent letter asking me to speak at the annual meeting of the National[1] Farming Association. I am very happy to accept. I consider it a privilege and an honor[2]

Make that *an honor and a privilege.*

to have been selected as the main speaker for this very important meeting.

I will plan to speak on the[3] subject of government regulations that affect farming. I will be prepared to speak for approximately[4] one hour and will answer any questions that members of the audience may have after the talk.

Will you please let[5] me know if this topic is acceptable. Thank you sincerely

Change that to *once again.*

for the opportunity of speaking to your[6] group. Very cordially yours,   [125]

LESSON 40

❲ LETTER 235 ❲ (Related to Lesson 40, Letter 3)

Announcing, intention, discontinue, irregular, ventures, associate.

Dear Mr. Trent: Your letter announcing your intention to discontinue your canning business in Ocean City[1] came as a surprise to me. I thought you planned to operate your cannery for several more years. However,[2] I can easily understand your desire to be relieved of the burdens of the irregular hours and[3] demanding work schedule.

Unfortunately, I have become involved in several other ventures, and my time[4] and capital are now heavily committed. My business associate, Mr. Lee Chan, would like to discuss[5] the matter with you, however. He plans to be in Ocean City on January 12. If that date is[6] convenient for you, he will examine your plant and equipment and discuss the financial arrangements with you.

If[7] you are unavailable at that time, please let me know. Yours truly,   [153]

Spelling. Intention, convenient, financial, arrangements.
Punctuation. Commas before and after *Mr. Lee Chan* (, apposition).
Typing Style. Transcribe: January 12.

◖ LETTER 236 ◗ (Related to Lesson 40, Letter 4)

Pinpointed, persistent, commodity, observe, exceeded, extraordinary.

Dear Mrs. Nettles: Your letter pinpointed a persistent problem food growers experience. Shoppers are more[1] aware of changes in food prices than in any other commodity they buy. This is because they purchase[2] food more frequently than anything else. This provides them with a regular, continuing opportunity[3] to observe rising prices.

Last year the cost of marketing food actually exceeded the cost of growing it.[4] That unfortunate factor has produced the extraordinary rise in food prices to which consumers are now[5] reacting. The fact that food is still a better buy in America than almost anywhere else in the world[6] seems almost irrelevant to shoppers whose food dollars are buying less and less.

Our local association[7] is considering several options to counter this unfounded criticism. Would you like to present some[8] of your ideas at our next meeting in April? Cordially yours,   [172]

Spelling. Persistent, commodity, exceeded, irrelevant.
Punctuation. Comma after *regular* (, *and* omitted).
Typing Style. Transcribe: April (capitalized).

◖ LETTER 237 ◖ (Related to Lesson 40, Letter 5)

Remember, tractor, operated, transmission, center, irreparable.

Dear Mr. Taylor: As you will remember, last year I purchased a King tractor from your company. During the[1] first three or four months the tractor operated very well, and I was quite happy with its performance.[2]

Unfortunately, after I had used it for about six months, the transmission failed to work properly. I returned it[3] to your service center, and one of your people worked on it for two days. I was assured that it would run properly[4] in the future.

The tractor did operate satisfactorily for a few months, but then the transmission[5] started giving trouble again. I called your service center, and Mr. James Lee, your representative, came to my[6] farm. Mr. Lee feels that the motor and the transmission have been damaged. He feels that the damage is irreparable.[7]

I am sure you can understand my feelings, Mr. Taylor. The guarantee period for the tractor has[8] expired, but I feel that it was totally misrepresented to me at the time of the purchase. Will you please[9] let me hear from you as soon as possible as to how we can settle this matter. Yours truly,   [197]

TRANSCRIPTION PREVIEW

Spelling.   Tractor, irreparable, totally, misrepresented.
Punctuation.   Commas after *for a few months* (, conjunction); before and after *your representative* (, apposition).
Typing Style.   Transcribe: King (capitalized).

◖ LETTER 238

Several months, increasingly, sympathetic, statistics, legislation.

Dear Mrs. Royal: During the past several months I have become increasingly aware of the concern farmers[1] everywhere are feeling for the rapid growth in property taxes. I am, of course, sympathetic to your[2] cause.

Statistics indicate that farm property taxes have increased 20 percent faster in our state than have[3] residential property taxes during the past three years. As a result, I have already prepared three major[4] pieces of tax legislation that I intend to introduce at the next session of the legislature.[5] Nearly all of the representatives from rural counties support these bills; I believe their chances for passage[6] are good.

I will be happy to discuss the matter at length with you at your convenience. Yours truly,   [138]

TRANSCRIPTION PREVIEW

Spelling.   Sympathetic, statistics, residential, already.
Punctuation.   Semicolon after *these bills*, (; no conjunction).
Typing Style.   Transcribe: 20 percent (figures and word).

❡ LETTER 239

Weeks ago, severe, beautiful, lightning, uprooted.

Dear Mr. Mason: As you will remember, two weeks ago we had a severe storm here in the Tulsa, Oklahoma,[1] area. At that time I lost two beautiful old trees. One was hit by lightning, and the other was[2] uprooted by high winds. These trees were well over 100 years old, and they are irreplaceable.

Under the terms[3] of my insurance contract with your company, I should receive up to $1,000 for each of the trees.[4] Will you please stop by my property at 802 Route 23 at your convenience. I would like to receive[5] the final settlement as soon as possible. Very cordially yours,   [113]

Spelling.   Severe, irreplaceable, settlement.
Punctuation.   Comma after *with your company* (, introductory);
period after *at your convenience* (. courteous request).
Typing Style.   Transcribe: 802 Route 23.

⊄ LETTER 240 ⊄ (Office Style)

Elementary, accept, modern, preparing, crops.

Dear Mr. Lee: Thank you very much for your invitation for my elementary school class to spend Saturday,[1] October 3, at your farm near Springfield. We are, of course, very delighted to accept.

Delete *very.*

All the students are[2] excited about coming to the farm to see how an up-to-date, modern farm

Make that *a modern, up-to-date farm.*

actually operates. Each of[3] the students is preparing a report about the various crops that are grown in this area. I am sure[4] that the students will be ready to ask many questions during their visit.

We are all looking forward to seeing[5] you on October 3. We should arrive about 10 a.m. Very sincerely yours,   [116]

PART

It is suggested that students transcribe the letters in this part in full block style with open punctuation. Refer students to the model letter on page 220 of *Gregg Shorthand for Colleges, Transcription, Series 90*.

Chapter 9
FINANCE
Lesson 41   Capitalization
   of general classifications,
   names, and titles

Chapter 10
CREDIT

Chapter 11
SALES

Chapter 12
TRAVEL AND
TRANSPORTATION

LESSON 41

❲ LETTER 241 ❲ (Related to Lesson 41, Letter 3)

Inquiring, Europe, immediately, authorized, notify, transaction.

Dear Ms. Brown: Thank you for your letter inquiring about the way in which you can cash your personal checks overseas.[1] Should you need extra money during your travel in Europe, all you need do is contact one of the European[2] branch offices of the American National Bank.

The branch managers there will help you immediately.[3] They are authorized to issue to you the amount of money you need and then notify us of the[4] transaction. We will deduct that amount from your checking account here. There will be no added charge for this service.

We[5] hope you will have an enjoyable vacation, Ms. Brown. Cordially yours,   [113]

TRANSCRIPTION PREVIEW

> **Spelling.** Inquiring, European, authorized, enjoyable.
> **Punctuation.** Commas after *Europe* (, introductory); before *Ms. Brown* (, parenthetical).
> **Typing Style.** Transcribe: Ms. Brown, American National Bank (capitalized); managers (not capitalized).

ℂ LETTER 242 ℂ (Related to Lesson 41, Letter 4)

[shorthand notation]

Attention, investing, daughter, Broadway, residence, higher.

Dear Mr. Larson: Thank you for calling to my attention the fact that the interest rates have been increased on time[1] certificates. I have been out of town for the past two weeks and had not yet learned of this change at the Second[2] National Bank.

My wife and I were just talking about investing $5,000 in a time certificate.[3] We are interested in one that will mature in five years, when our daughter Sally will start college.

We have just moved[4] to the east side of town, and the Broadway branch is near our new residence. Therefore, we will make our deposit[5] there rather than go to the main branch, which is a great distance away.

We will be looking forward to receiving[6] the silver serving plate as well as a higher rate of interest on our deposit. Thank you for calling this matter[7] to my attention, Mr. Larson. Sincerely yours,

[150]

TRANSCRIPTION PREVIEW

Spelling. Certificates, mature, daughter, college.
Punctuation. Comma after *in five years* (, nonrestrictive).
Typing Style. Transcribe: Second National Bank, Broadway (capitalized); branch (not capitalized).

ℂ LETTER 243 ℂ (Related to Lesson 41, Letter 5)

[shorthand notation]

Combination, retirement, participate, monthly, automatically, deposited.

Dear Professor O'Brien: Thank you for the interest that the group of professors has shown in the Oregon Funding[1] Association. Yes, we do offer a combination savings and retirement plan. This plan requires that[2] at least 15 persons participate. Each must make an initial deposit of no less than $1,000;[3] the monthly deposit thereafter must be no less than $50.

Each month our investment managers[4] will buy shares of stocks with the funds deposited. We will, of course, try to obtain the greatest value for our[5] investors. It is possible to have the desired amount automatically withheld from your paycheck and deposited[6] with us.

If you or your committee members have any questions, Professor O'Brien, I would be happy[7] to speak with you and discuss them further. Cordially yours,   [151]

TRANSCRIPTION PREVIEW

Spelling.   Participate, thereafter, withheld, speak.
Punctuation.   Commas before and after *of course* (, parenthetical).
Typing Style.   Transcribe: $1,000; $50 (no decimals).

❰ LETTER 244

Yourself, wondering, necessary, Christmas, designating, determine.

Dear Mrs. Johnson: Do you find yourself wondering how you will have the necessary funds to pay for all the[1] Christmas gifts you want to purchase for your family and friends?

Our suggestion to our valued customers is that[2] you open a Christmas account with our bank. You may do so by depositing as little as $5 and[3] designating this amount as the opening of your Christmas account.

After that, you determine how much money[4] you want to deposit each week or each month and authorize us to transfer that amount automatically[5] from your checking account to your Christmas account. It is as simple as that. When December arrives, you will have[6] extra cash for all your Christmas shopping.

Do not delay; come in today and open your Christmas account. Yours very[7] truly, [141]

TRANSCRIPTION PREVIEW

Spelling. Friends, designating, authorize, automatically.

Punctuation. Comma after *arrives* (, *when* clause); semicolon after *delay* (; no conjunction).

Typing Style. Transcribe: Christmas (capitalized); account (not capitalized).

❰ LETTER 245

Requested, carefully, aware, utmost, accurate, agent.

Dear Miss West: Enclosed is the supply of checks that you recently requested from the General National Bank.[1] Please examine the checks carefully before you use any of them.

Check your name, your address, and your account number.[2] As you are well aware, accuracy is of utmost importance in the banking business. We want to be[3] sure that all of the materials supplied to you are accurate in every way.

If you should find an error[4] in this supply of checks, notify our customer relations agent immediately. We will have the checks[5] reprinted promptly. Thank you for banking at General National Bank. Sincerely yours, [116]

TRANSCRIPTION PREVIEW

Spelling. Examine, carefully, address, accurate.

Punctuation. Commas after *name* and *address* (, series); after *well aware* (, *as* clause).

Typing Style. Transcribe: General National Bank (capitalized).

❡ LETTER 246 ❡ (Office Style)

[shorthand outline]

Shares, purchase, already, trend, pleasure.

Dear Ms. Best: Enclosed is your stock certificate for the 100 shares of Rand Motor Company stock you purchased.[1] As you will recall, we talked about the many advantages of this purchase last month. Already the stock[2] has started climbing; it rose 50 cents in value during the past month, and the trend should continue.

If you decide[3] to buy any other bonds or stocks, please contact me.

Make that *stocks or bonds.*

I will be happy to purchase the stock for you at the[4] least expense to you.

Please keep your Rand stock certificate in a safe place; a safe deposit box is best. It has[5] been a pleasure to work with you, Ms. Best. Sincerely yours, [110]

LESSON 42

❡ LETTER 247 ❡ (Related to Lesson 42, Letter 3)

[shorthand outline]

Correspondence, reached, organized, acknowledge, likely, signature.

Dear Mr. Smith: Your correspondence file and completed loan application reached my desk today. It is a pleasure[1] to work with a company that is so well organized and that has such a fine credit record.

We are pleased[2] to acknowledge your request and to grant your loan. It is likely that we will have all the papers ready for your[3] signature by the end of next week.

Thank you for selecting the Management Funding Corporation, Mr. Smith.[4] Sincerely yours, [83]

TRANSCRIPTION PREVIEW

Spelling. Acknowledge, request, likely, sincerely.
Punctuation. Comma before *Mr. Smith* (, parenthetical).
Typing Style. Transcribe: Management Funding Corporation (capitalized).

❰ LETTER 248 ❱ (Related to Lesson 42, Letter 4)

Commercial, associations, influenced, processing, fortunately, feature, penalty.

Dear Ms. Jason: As you requested, I have made a thorough check on a number of commercial banks, savings and[1] loan associations, and other lending institutions. As you know, all of them are governed by law as to[2] the maximum interest rates they can charge. However, some charge significantly more than others. Therefore, your choice[3] of a loan company should be influenced by several items:

1. The actual interest charged.
2. Quickness[4] in processing loans.
3. Repayment plans.

Fortunately, all the lending agencies I checked meet your minimum[5] specifications. Your best choice would likely be the Guaranty Trust Company. They offer low-interest loans to[6] qualified borrowers. They can process your loan easily and quickly. Another good feature of their service[7] is that you can repay our loan early without suffering a penalty.

If you decide you want to borrow[8] from this company, will you please call me as soon as possible. I will arrange an appointment for us to meet[9] with Mr. Dover, the credit manager. Yours truly, [190]

Spelling. Commercial, institutions, fortunately, truly.
Punctuation. Commas after *As you requested* and *As you know* (, *as* clause).
Typing Style. Transcribe: Guaranty Trust Company (capitalized); credit manager (not capitalized).

❘ LETTER 249 ❘ (Related to Lesson 42, Letter 5)

Welcome, remodel, inventory, unable, circulars.

Dear Mr. Martin: Welcome to the Tacoma area. Thank you very much for the personal letter you[1] sent to us; we received it yesterday.

We plan to remodel our present building and to increase our inventory[2] within the next year. We were glad to know that you make loans specifically for these purposes.

Unfortunately,[3] I will be unable to attend your introductory session next week; I will be out of town on[4] business. Do you have any brochures or circulars that explain your business services in detail? If you do,[5] please ask your assistant to mail copies to me at your convenience. Very truly yours,   [116]

TRANSCRIPTION PREVIEW

Spelling. Welcome, remodel, specifically, introductory.
Punctuation. Comma after *Unfortunately* (, introductory); semicolon after *next week* (; no conjunction).
Typing Style. Transcribe: assistant (not capitalized).

❘ LETTER 250

Frequently, realize, arrangements, 9 p.m., determined.

Dear Miss Miller: Because you travel frequently, you realize the importance of making good travel arrangements.[1] Southern Airlines, which recently began servicing this area, is able to help you with all your travel[2] arrangements.

Our company has several especially designed plans for travelers. If you board a flight after[3] 9 p.m., you will get a 30 percent discount. If you pay for your ticket at least a month before you[4] depart, you can travel at half the regular price.

Southern Airlines accepts all major credit cards and personal[5] checks as payment. If you find it more convenient, we will arrange for you to pay for your ticket in two or[6] three monthly installments.

We are determined to do all in our power to make your travels more convenient and[7] enjoyable. The next time you plan a trip, please be sure to contact us or your local travel agent; we are[8] looking forward to serving you. Cordially yours, [169]

TRANSCRIPTION PREVIEW

Spelling. Arrangements, accepts, personal, determined.
Punctuation. Semicolon after *local travel agent* (; no conjunction).
Typing Style. Transcribe: Southern Airlines (capitalized).

◖ LETTER 251

Disabled, competent, productive, attendance, handicapped.

Dear Mr. Davis: Did you know that there are thousands of disabled people living in the United States? These[1] people are often competent, capable workers. However, they sometimes have difficulty finding suitable[2] positions because prospective employers hesitate to hire them.

Statistics prove that many disabled[3] people are often better, more productive workers than those who suffer no disability. In addition,[4] they generally have extremely good attendance records.

If you have any job openings that could be filled[5] by a physically handicapped person, take this opportunity to hire a competent, dedicated person.[6] You will be doing yourself and your company a favor, Mr. Davis. Yours truly, [137]

TRANSCRIPTION PREVIEW

Spelling. Disabled, capable, prospective, handicapped.
Punctuation. Comma after *better* (, *and* omitted).
Typing Style. Transcribe: company (not capitalized).

ℂ LETTER 252 ℂ (Office Style)

Interested, establish, financial, principal, discount.

Dear Mrs. Peters: We were sincerely happy to learn that you are interested in stocking our products in your[1] store. We will establish a line of credit for you if you will merely do the following three things:

1. Send us[2] a copy of your latest financial statement.

2. Supply us with the name of your bank and your account number.[3]

Oh, reverse items *1* and *2*.

3. Give us a list of the principal dealers with whom you presently do business.

Change *dealers* to *suppliers*.

Once your account is established[4] with us, we will offer you a 2 percent discount on all your purchases. We look forward to working with[5] you. Yours very truly, [104]

LESSON 43

ℂ LETTER 253 ℂ (Related to Lesson 43, Letter 3)

Cunningham, misplace, mailed, distribution, earnings, contributed.

Dear Mr. Long: Enclosed is your copy of the *Cunningham Company Annual Report*. You did not misplace[1] your copy; the reports are just now being mailed. The paper shortage has affected our publication and[2] distribution dates.

We, too, are excited about the progress our company has made. In fact, this year we achieved[3] the highest level of performance of any year in our history. We topped the $1 billion mark in[4] sales for the first time, and we established all-time highs in earnings.

A combination of factors contributed[5] to our outstanding performance. The demand for our industrial products has been unprecedented. In[6] addition, the continuing and well-planned capital investments we made over the past several years put us[7] in a good position to meet the surge in demand.

We look forward to even greater progress in the future.[8] Cordially yours,   [163]

TRANSCRIPTION PREVIEW

Spelling.   Misplace, achieved, unprecedented, capital.
Punctuation.   Commas before and after *too* (, parenthetical);
   hyphenate *all-time* and *well-planned* (hyphenated before noun).
Typing Style.   Transcribe: $1 billion (figure and word).

❮ LETTER 254 ❮ (Related to Lesson 43, Letter 4)

Regarding, annuity, statistics, options, available, before.

Dear Mr. King: I have asked Mrs. Mary Baker, one of our officers, to gather all of the data[1] regarding your annuity contract. She will have your file and all the statistics ready when you are in San[2] Francisco on February 7. She has outlined the options you have available for collection and will[3] be happy to explain each one and its tax advantage to you.

Please call Mrs. Baker at 555-7109[4] before February 7 to let her know when you will be in the office. Sincerely yours,   [99]

TRANSCRIPTION PREVIEW

Spelling.   Regarding, ready, explain, sincerely.
Punctuation.   Commas before and after *one of our officers* (, apposition).
Typing Style.   Transcribe: February 7 (figure).

❡ LETTER 255 ❡ (Related to Lesson 43, Letter 5)

Explaining, situation, quite, I am sure, advisors, in the future.

Mr. Keith: Thank you for your memo explaining the situation regarding the sale of the stocks we held in[1] the City Insurance Company. Your report was quite disturbing to me, and I am sure it was disturbing[2] to the other members of the board.

Because we did not ask our financial advisors to sell the stock on Thursday,[3] December 13, as we should have, we suffered a substantial financial loss. As you stated, the[4] responsibility is ours, not theirs.

I am sure that you will take all necessary steps to see that such a delay[5] does not happen in the future. James Tate   [108]

TRANSCRIPTION PREVIEW

Spelling.   Quite, advisors, ours, theirs.
Punctuation.   Commas before and after *December 13* (, apposition).
Typing Style.   Transcribe: City Insurance Company (capitalized); board (not capitalized).

❡ LETTER 256

Merged, combined, efficient, certificates, inquiries, materialize.

Dear Ms. Lee: We are pleased to inform you that two of the companies in which you own stock have merged. Jones and Company[1] and Smith Investment Company will operate under the name of National Investment Company[2] effective January 31. This new firm will offer you the combined strength of two extremely successful[3] financial organizations. The new company will continue to offer each customer the most efficient,[4] finest services possible.

Because you have stock in both companies, you will be interested in reading[5] the enclosed brochure outlining the ways in which new stock certificates will be issued. If you have any questions[6] about the merger, please call us at 555-7201; we will be very happy to answer[7] any inquiries.

We are sure, Ms. Lee, you will be happy with the merger and the greater returns that are likely[8] to materialize. Sincerely yours, [168]

TRANSCRIPTION PREVIEW

Spelling. Strength, extremely, efficient, inquiries.
Punctuation. Commas after *efficient* (, *and* omitted); before and after *Ms. Lee* (, parenthetical).
Typing Style. Transcribe: Jones and Company (*and* not capitalized); January 31 (figures).

ℂ LETTER 257

Effective, accumulate, prefer, return, announce, change.

Dear Mrs. Edison: Effective July 1 the Federal Savings and Loan Association will credit[1] interest earned on your savings account every three months. If you want to have your interest accumulate in your account[2] every quarter, you do not need to notify us.

If you prefer, you can have your interest check mailed directly[3] to you every quarter. To have this done, simply fill out the enclosed form and return it to us.

Federal[4] Savings and Loan is happy to announce this change in our service; we hope you will be pleased too. Sincerely yours, [99]

Spelling. Accumulate, quarter, directly, enclosed.
Punctuation. Semicolon after *our service* (; no conjunction).
Typing Style. Transcribe: Federal Savings and Loan Association
(*and* not capitalized).

❰ LETTER 258 ❰ (Office Style)

Storm, surprise, shock, gardens, hillsides, adjusters.

Dear Customer: The very severe summer storm

Take out *very.*

was a total surprise to all of us here in the Springfield,[1] Montana, area. The storm came so fast and with such force that it was difficult to see buildings that were located[2] only a short distance away. It was a shock to all of us to watch gardens and trees wash down the hillsides.[3]

Make that *trees and gardens.*

It will take a long time for our insurance adjusters to assess the property damage to determine the[4] payments due homeowners. If you are in need of immediate cash to start repairs, call us today. Otherwise,[5] we will process your claim as soon as possible. Sincerely yours, [112]

LESSON 44

❰ LETTER 259 ❰ (Related to Lesson 44, Letter 3)

Requested, initial, municipal, penalty, commission, prospectus.

Dear Mr. Williams: By now I hope you have received all the information you requested on our fund and that[1] you have had a chance to study the financial report. The funds are exempt from federal taxes, but they are[2] not exempt from state or local taxes.

The initial required investment in our municipal fund is[3] $2,500; you can make subsequent investments of $100 or more at any time. You[4] may redeem your bond at any time with no penalty. There is no commission charge when you invest, no monthly[5] maintenance charge, and no charge when you redeem your shares.

An application blank is attached to our *Prospectus*, which[6] is enclosed. When we receive your initial investment and your completed application blank, we will forward[7] to you the legal papers for your signature. Please call us at 555-8209 if you have further[8] questions. Sincerely yours, [164]

TRANSCRIPTION PREVIEW

Spelling. Financial, subsequent, penalty, commission.
Punctuation. Semicolon after *$2,500* (; no conjunction).
Typing Style. Underscore: *Prospectus* (underscore publication title).

❬ LETTER 260 ❬ (Related to Lesson 44, Letter 4)

Shareholder, additional, reinvested, quarterly, status.

Dear Mr. Williams: I am delighted to welcome you as a new shareholder in the Municipal Bond Fund.[1] Enclosed is a summary of how your $5,000 was invested. Keep in mind that you can make additional[2] investments at any time in amounts of $100 or more. The necessary forms for the[3] additional investments are enclosed.

Dividends are usually declared on an annual basis. They are[4] reinvested in your account unless you elect to receive them in cash. Each month you will get a regular[5] report on the fund, and you will receive quarterly status reports of your account. We will also send your tax[6] information at the end of the year.

We know you will be happy with your investment, Mr. Williams.
Sincerely[7] yours,   [141]

❮ **LETTER 261** ❮ (Related to Lesson 44, Letter 5)

Misunderstanding, application, invested, varies, further, hesitate.

Dear Mr. Jackson: I am very sorry that there has been a misunderstanding about your investment. When[1] you sent in your application blank and your first payment, you indicated that you wanted to have 50 percent[2] of your money invested in stock and 50 percent invested in interest-bearing notes. That is why two[3] different earnings were reported on your statement.

As you know, the value of common stocks varies with the status[4] of the market. However, the interest paid on notes remains the same. When you invest half of your money in[5] each fund, you have the advantages of both types of investments.

If you have further questions or if you want to[6] change your investment plan, please do not hesitate to contact us. Cordially yours,   [134]

ℂ LETTER 262

Requested, separately, registered, acknowledge, negotiable, consequently.

Dear Mr. Gates: As you requested, we are returning to you the seven bonds we have been holding for you; they[1] are being mailed to you separately by registered mail. Please acknowledge receipt of the bonds by signing the return[2] receipt that the letter carrier will have.

Please bear in mind that these bonds are negotiable. Consequently,[3] they should be kept in a safe place; a safe deposit box is preferable.

If we can be of further service[4] to you, please let us know. Yours sincerely, [87]

TRANSCRIPTION PREVIEW

Spelling. Separately, signing, bear, preferable.
Punctuation. Semicolons after *holding for you* and *a safe place* (; no conjunction); comma after *Consequently* (, introductory).
Typing Style. Transcribe: seven bonds (letters).

ℂ LETTER 263

Account, savings, bank, available, assistant, forward.

Gentlemen: In July I will be moving to Great Falls, and I would like to open a checking account and a[1] savings account with your bank. In addition, I will need a safe deposit box if there is one available.[2]

For the past six years I have lived in Billings and have had an account with the First National Bank there. You may write[3] to Mr. James Parks, who is an executive assistant at the First National Bank in Billings, for a credit[4] reference if you wish.

I am looking forward to living in Great Falls, and I will stop in to see you on[5] my next trip to the city. Sincerely yours, [108]

TRANSCRIPTION PREVIEW

Spelling. Deposit, assistant, credit, forward.
Punctuation. Comma after *In addition* (, introductory).
Typing Style. Transcribe: executive assistant (not capitalized).

⊄ LETTER 264 ⊄ (Office Style)

Springville, pooled, privately, tremendous, interested, speak.

Dear Neighbor: As you may have read, several of us in Springville have pooled our efforts and resources and have bought[1] land on which we will build a privately operated and owned bank.

Make that *owned and operated bank.*

The bank will be known as the Springville Community[2] Bank.
We believe there is a tremendous need for such a bank,

Change that to *a great need.*

and we are looking for other people who[3] have the same belief. We hope to raise $1 million in capital for the new operation. We are now[4] offering 1,000 shares of stock to the public.

If you are interested in such an investment, please contact[5] me at 555-4211. I would be happy to speak with you about our plans and goals. Sincerely yours,[6] [120]

LESSON 45

❡ LETTER 265 ❡ (Related to Lesson 45, Letter 3)

[shorthand symbols]

Received, request, cancel, properly, appreciate, reconsider.

Dear Mr. Simms: We have received your request to cancel your International credit card. You did not mention[1] if you are canceling because of something we did or did not do. If you had a problem that we did not handle[2] properly, we would appreciate your telling us about it. We will, of course, try to resolve it to your[3] satisfaction.

We hope you will reconsider your decision to cancel your credit card. Simply fill out and[4] return the enclosed card if you would like to keep your card. Cordially yours, [93]

TRANSCRIPTION PREVIEW

Spelling.   Mention, canceling, satisfaction, reconsider.
Punctuation.   Comma after *properly* (, *if* clause).
Typing Style.   Transcribe: International (capitalized); credit card (not capitalized).

❡ LETTER 266 ❡ (Related to Lesson 45, Letter 4)

[shorthand symbols]

Forgive, catch, developed, references, meantime, handling.

Dear Mr. Washington: Please forgive the delay in acknowledging your request for a loan from the Interstate[1] Bank. I have been away from the city for the past week, and I have not been able to catch up on the backlog[2] of work that developed while I was gone.

We are now checking your credit references, and you should hear from us[3] within the next few days. In the meantime, we hope you will forgive us for not handling your credit application[4] in a more efficient manner. Sincerely yours, [89]

TRANSCRIPTION PREVIEW

Spelling. Forgive, backlog, references, meantime.
Punctuation. Comma after *In the meantime* (, introductory).
Typing Style. Transcribe: Interstate Bank (capitalized).

◖ LETTER 267 ◖ (Related to Lesson 45, Letter 5)

Tired, postage, October, identification, creditor, remarkable.

Dear Customer: Are you tired of writing checks at the end of the month to pay your bills? Are you tired of paying postage[1] to mail these checks? Would you like to pay your bills by phone? Now you can.

Starting in October the Interstate Bank will[2] allow you to pay your bills by phone instead of by check. All you need to do is:

1. Call the 800 telephone[3] number listed on the enclosed identification card; this will put you in contact with the phone center.[4]

2. Tell the telephone agent how much money you want sent to each creditor.

3. Sit back and relax.

Our highly[5] trained people using the latest electronic equipment will do the rest.

This plan has advantages for[6] all of us. You do not have to write and mail checks to pay your bills. Your creditors do not have to worry about[7] receiving your checks on time. Interstate Bank will not have to worry about processing the checks.

If you would like more[8] information about this remarkable new method of paying your bills, just call our bank. We will be glad to[9] hear from you. Sincerely yours, [185]

Spelling. Identification, contact, electronic, creditors.

Punctuation. Colon after *All you need to do is* (: enumeration); no hyphen after *highly* (no hyphen after *-ly*).

Typing Style. Start each numbered paragraph on a separate line.

ℂ LETTER 268

Window, conduct, realized, convenience, withdraw, satisfactory.

Dear Miss Harris: The drive-up window at the City Bank of Portland is now open from 8 a.m. during the[1] week. The drive-up window makes it possible for you to conduct your banking business before regular banking[2] hours.

We realized that many business executives could not get to the bank during the regular banking hours;[3] therefore, we have extended the hours at the drive-up window service as another convenience. Now you can handle[4] more of your banking business without interfering with your regular work schedule.

Without leaving your car,[5] you will be able to deposit or withdraw money, make a loan payment, and conduct many other transactions[6] that you usually do inside the bank.

We invite you, Miss Harris, to try our new service. We are sure you[7] will find it satisfactory and most convenient. Yours truly, [152]

TRANSCRIPTION PREVIEW

Spelling. During, deposit, withdraw, usually.

Punctuation. Commas after *withdraw money* and *make a loan payment* (, series).

Typing Style. Transcribe: 8 a.m. (figure).

ℂ LETTER 269

Equity, family, assist, suitable, specialists, security.

Dear Mr. Bates: If you are tired of paying rent and not building any equity in a home of your own, now[1] is the time to think about purchasing a home for you and your family. Our bank will be glad to assist you[2] in buying a home that will be suitable for your family.

Our loan officers are specialists in arranging[3] home loans that will fit your income. In fact, they can arrange your loan so that you will be able to meet your monthly[4] payments without any difficulty. If you wish, they can arrange your loan to include the price of your taxes[5] and insurance as well. This allows you to make only a single payment per month rather than three[6] individual payments.

Come in soon and talk with one of our loan officers about how easy it is to obtain[7] a home loan. It takes only a few minutes of your time but can give you the security you are looking for.[8] Very truly yours, [164]

TRANSCRIPTION PREVIEW

Spelling. Tired, equity, suitable, specialists.
Punctuation. Comma after *a home of your own* (*, if* clause).
Typing Style. Transcribe: loan officers (not capitalized).

❴ LETTER 270 ❴ (Office Style)

Financial, future, appointment, family, obligate, hesitation.

Dear Mr. Byers: We are glad to have the opportunity to help you with your financial plans for the future.[1] One of our financial counselors, Ms. Jane Smith, will call you for an appointment within the next two weeks.

Change that to *within the next week or two.*

Ms.[2] Smith will discuss with you ways in which our investment service can help you provide your family with income long[3] after you have retired.

Make that *with a steady income.*

She will ask questions that will help us design a plan tailored to your specific needs.

This[4] meeting will not obligate you in any way. Ms. Smith and the rest of our staff are eager to devise an income[5] plan that will allow you to retire without hesitation and without any financial burdens or worries.[6] Cordially yours, [124]

LESSON 46

❮ LETTER 271 ❮ (Related to Lesson 46, Letter 3)

Pleasure, visited, counseling, thoroughly, appreciated, principally.

Dear Mr. Dix: It was a pleasure meeting you last week when I visited your new credit counseling office[1] here in Chicago. I am thoroughly convinced that the service you are providing is a valuable one indeed.[2]

When I was in your office, there were 15 or 20 people waiting to see one of your financial[3] counselors. This in itself tells me that the service you provide is valued and appreciated.

I understand[4] that the office is staffed principally by retired business executives who serve on a voluntary basis.[5] I will be retiring in several months, and I would like to become one of your part-time workers. If you would[6] like me to work two or three days each week, I will be more than happy to do so.

You may contact me at[7] 555-8109 Monday through Friday. I will be looking forward to hearing from you soon, Mr. Dix. Very[8] cordially yours, [163]

Spelling. Counseling, thoroughly, principally, contact.

Punctuation. Comma after *in several months* (, conjunction).

Typing Style. Transcribe: 15 or 20 people (figures); two or three days (letters).

❨ LETTER 272 ❨ (Related to Lesson 46, Letter 4)

Congratulating, major, you can be sure, established, answer, requires.

Dear Mr. Quinn: Thank you very much for your nice letter congratulating me on my graduation from Western[1] State College. Thank you also for adding a credit line of $1,000 to my regular checking[2] account at the First National Bank. I am planning to make several major purchases in the next month or[3] so, and you can be sure that I will make use of the credit line that you have established for me.

In addition,[4] I plan to purchase a car sometime during the year. Will you please answer the following questions for me:

1. What[5] is the amount of down payment that your bank requires for a car costing about $6,000?

2. How long[6] can I take to pay the principal and the interest?

3. What is the rate of interest charged?

I will appreciate[7] receiving answers to these questions, Mr. Quinn. Very sincerely yours, [153]

Spelling. Planning, major, answer, principal.

Punctuation. Colon after *answer the followng questions for me* (: enumeration).

Typing Style. Transcribe: Western State College, First National Bank (capitalized).

Apologies, mistake, inconvenience, customers, objective, patience.

Dear Mr. Smith: Please accept our apologies for sending Frank R. Smith's bills to you by mistake. We are sincerely[1] sorry for any inconvenience we have caused you.

We are not trying to make excuses, but we are in[2] the process of installing a new computer to handle all our billing. Unfortunately, several errors[3] such as the one you have experienced have occurred. We should have all the problems worked out by the end of[4] September, and we promise that you won't receive incorrect bills in the future.

It is our principal goal here at[5] the Acme Gas Company to give the best service to each of our customers, and we know the new computer[6] will help us to achieve our objective.

Thank you, Mr. Smith, for your patience and understanding. Yours very truly,[7]   [140]

TRANSCRIPTION PREVIEW

Spelling.   Apologies, mistake, principal, achieve.
Punctuation.   Commas after *to make excuses* (, conjunction); before and after *Mr. Smith* (, parenthetical).
Typing Style.   Transcribe: Acme Gas Company (capitalized).·

(LETTER 274

Corporate, aware, requested, honoring, participating, mailed.

Dear Mr. Burton: We are pleased to tell you that your corporate application for a General credit card[1] has been approved. We welcome you into the large family of General credit card holders. You are aware,[2] of course, that the General credit card is designed principally for companies and organizations that have[3] many representatives traveling for them. Presently we have nearly 1 million men and women using[4] General credit cards.

We are enclosing the 15 credit cards that you requested. You and your representatives[5] may use your General card in the United States, Canada, and Mexico. The card is also[6] accepted in 25 other countries.

Ask your representatives to carry their General credit card with[7] them at all times. Many organizations will grant a special discount to your representatives when they present[8] their card. The General credit card tells the honoring organization that the Wheeler Publishing[9] Company is an organization of principle and integrity. Your people will never have trouble[10] obtaining credit at any participating hotel, airline, or other institution.

Fifteen copies of[11] our national directory will be mailed to you in a few weeks. We are confident that you and your employees[12] will enjoy the convenience of the General credit card. Yours truly, [254]

TRANSCRIPTION PREVIEW

Spelling. Representatives, traveling, accepted, integrity.
Punctuation. Commas after *United States* and *Canada;* after *hotel* and *airline* (, series).
Typing Style. Transcribe: 1 million (figure and word).

❡ LETTER 275

Southern, credit, reference, determine, extend, unblemished.

Ladies and Gentlemen: The Southern Supply Company has applied to us for credit and has listed you as[1] a credit reference. Will you please answer the questions listed on the enclosed form.

We would appreciate your[2] frank, honest answers; they will help us determine how much credit we should extend to this company.

We follow[3] the principle of extending credit to all potential customers if they have unblemished credit records.[4]

A stamped, self-addressed envelope is enclosed for your convenience in returning the credit form to us. Thank you[5] for your cooperation. Cordially yours, [108]

TRANSCRIPTION PREVIEW

Spelling.   Principle, unblemished, convenience, cooperation.
Punctuation.   Commas after *frank;* after *stamped* (*, and* omitted).
Typing Style.   Transcribe: Southern Supply Company (capitalized).

❰ LETTER 276 ❰   (Office Style)

Bennington, loan, elementary, somewhere, certificate.

Dear Mr. Thomas: In September I will return to Bennington College to begin working on a master's[1] degree, and I would like to apply for a loan from your bank.

Make that *an educational loan.*

As you know, I have been teaching in South Side[2] Elementary School here in Atlanta, Georgia, for the past three years. I want to become principal of an[3] elementary school somewhere in the city, and I must have an administrator's certificate in order to[4] do so. If all goes as planned, I should finish my work at Bennington College in one year.

Let's make that *only one year.*

I would like to borrow[5] $6,000 from your bank and repay the principal and the interest over a three-year period. Will[6] you please let me know if your bank is interested in helping me.

Thank you for your consideration. Sincerely[7] yours, [141]

LESSON 47

℀ LETTER 277 ℀ (Related to Lesson 47, Letter 3)

[shorthand]

Clarification, denied, extremely, until, totaling.

Dear Mr. Mathis: Thank you for your letter asking for clarification of why your two loan applications[1] with the United Mutual Bank were denied.

We are extremely sorry that you left our bank with the[2] understanding that the applications were approved. It is a principle of our organization that we never[3] approve a loan application for a new customer until we have made a thorough credit check. We[4] certainly should have made this clear to you when you were in the bank.

When we checked your credit records, we found that you had[5] credit accounts with two major department stores. One account had never been used, but the other account was canceled[6] because an outstanding balance of $300 was never paid. Under the circumstances, we feel[7] that it would be unwise to approve loans totaling $15,000 at this time.

We hope that you will be[8] able to clear your credit rating in the near future, Mr. Mathis, and that we will be able to serve you.[9] Yours truly, [182]

TRANSCRIPTION PREVIEW

Spelling.   Principle, thorough, canceled, totaling.
Punctuation.   Commas before and after *Mr. Mathis* (, parenthetical).
Typing Style.   Transcribe: $300; $15,000 (no decimal).

℀ LETTER 278 ℀ (Related to Lesson 47, Letter 4)

[shorthand]

Borrowing, college, excellent, purposes, withdraw, complete.

Dear Mr. McCoy: Your father was right; there is nothing wrong with borrowing money if you have a good reason.[1] We certainly agree that financing your son's college education is an excellent reason for taking[2] out a loan.

United Mutual Bank makes many loans for educational purposes. We have three basic[3] plans. They are as follows:

1. One-year loans issued in the fall to be repaid monthly during the course of the year.[4]

2. An approved credit line from which you may withdraw funds at any time.

3. Four-year loans to be repaid starting[5] four years from the date the loan is approved.

A complete explanation of each of the plans is included in the[6] enclosed booklet. We believe that you will agree that United Mutual Bank offers unexcelled convenience[7] and service. When you have had an opportunity to study the booklet, please call one of our representatives[8] at 555-8081. Very sincerely yours,   [171]

TRANSCRIPTION PREVIEW

Spelling. Financing, college, excellent, unexcelled.
Punctuation. Semicolon after *Your father was right* (; no conjunction).
Typing Style. Transcribe: United Mutual Bank (capitalized); fall (not capitalized).

❮ LETTER 279 ❮ (Related to Lesson 47, Letter 5)

Overdue, balance, deliberately, forwarded, you can be sure.

Dear Miss Marsh: Thank you for your letter of Tuesday, April 5. You are certainly right; I have not paid my overdue[1] balance of $100. My check for this amount is enclosed.

I want to dispel any notion that[2] I deliberately avoid paying my bills. I have been out of the city for the past three months, and my mail[3] was not forwarded to me. Unfortunately, I simply forgot that I had not paid my bill from your company.[4]

I certainly do not want to have my charge account with your store canceled. I have found your store to be a[5] convenient, pleasant place to do much of my shopping. You can be sure that I will take care of my credit obligations[6] on a regular basis in the future, Miss Marsh. Sincerely yours,   [133]

TRANSCRIPTION PREVIEW

Spelling. Dispel, deliberately, forwarded, canceled.
Punctuation. Comma after *convenient* (, *and* omitted).
Typing Style. Transcribe: April 5; $100 (no decimal).

ℂ LETTER 280

Cog rto 4 Lro nel

Application, signature, opportunities, virtually, restaurants.

Dear Mrs. Morris: Your application for a National credit card has been approved; the card is enclosed. Please[1] sign it in the signature block on the back.

This card affords you many opportunities. When you are traveling,[2] you may charge your airline tickets on virtually every national and international airline. Your card[3] may be used in many of the finest hotels, motels, and restaurants throughout the world. More than 100 car[4] rental agencies also honor the National credit card.

Welcome to the world of National credit[5] services; we know you will enjoy the many conveniences that are now available to you. Sincerely yours,[6]   [120]

TRANSCRIPTION PREVIEW

Spelling. Virtually, restaurants, honor, welcome.
Punctuation. Semicolon after *has been approved* (; no conjunction).
Typing Style. Transcribe: 100 (figures).

¶ LETTER 281

Accommodations, services, foreign, luncheon, correct.

Dear Mrs. Thomas: It is a pleasure to enclose your new National credit card. Now you can enjoy the[1] accommodations and services of many of the world's finest hotels, airlines, and restaurants. Whether you are[2] traveling in a foreign country or just enjoying luncheon with business associates, you will find the[3] National credit card a great convenience.

Please check your card to be sure that your name and address are correct; notify[4] us immediately if we need to make any changes. Yours sincerely, [94]

TRANSCRIPTION PREVIEW

Spelling. Accommodations, world's, traveling, foreign.
Punctuation. Comma after *business associates* (, introductory).
Typing Style. Transcribe: National (capitalized); credit card (not capitalized).

¶ LETTER 282 ¶ (Office Style)

Account, up to date, apologize, emergency, personal.

Dear Mr. Smith: Enclosed is my check for $130. This brings my account up to date.

Make that *my account with your company.*

I apologize[1] for being late with my payment; I know it is three weeks late.

Change that to *overdue.*

I was called to Paris on an emergency[2] audit for my firm about a month ago. Because I left in such a hurry, I did not have time to take[3] care of my personal matters.

You can be sure that my payments will not be late in the future. I certainly[4] do realize the importance of a good credit reputation. Yours very truly,   [95]

LESSON 48

❡ LETTER 283 ❡ (Related to Lesson 48, Letter 3)

Trouble, international, contacted, discovered, typically, accepted.

Dear Mr. Dawson: We are very sorry about the trouble that you experienced at the International[1] Hotel in St. Louis, Missouri. We contacted the hotel manager, Mr. Joseph Tate, when we received[2] your letter. He told us that they do accept the General credit card.

Mr. Tate investigated the[3] matter and discovered that a clerk who had worked for the hotel for only three days either did not know that the[4] hotel typically accepted the General credit card or had forgotten this fact. You were the first one to[5] bring this matter to our attention.

Won't you let us have another chance, Mr. Dawson? We are returning your[6] card to you. If you still wish to close your account, either dispose of the card or mail it back to us. Sincerely[7] yours,
                                                                          [141]

TRANSCRIPTION PREVIEW

Spelling. Discovered, either, accepted, dispose.
Punctuation. Comma after *close your account* (, *if* clause).
Typing Style. Transcribe: International Hotel (capitalized).

❡ LETTER 284 ❡ (Related to Lesson 48, Letter 4)

Thank you for your, throughout, several hundred dollars, major, visit, financial.

Dear Mr. Mason: Thank you for your recent letter in which you requested information about your source of[1] money as you travel throughout England and Spain.

Because you plan to be out of the country for at least six months,[2] we suggest that you take with you several hundred dollars in cash and several hundred dollars in traveler's[3] checks. In addition, we suggest that you let us arrange a line of credit for you at banks in three or four[4] of the major cities that you will visit. We will be happy to do this for you.

If you will come by the bank[5] a month or so before you leave, we will be able to take care of these financial matters for you. Cordially[6] yours, [121]

TRANSCRIPTION PREVIEW

Spelling. Source, throughout, dollars, financial.
Punctuation. Comma after *before you leave* (, *if* clause).
Typing Style. Transcribe: six months (letters).

❡ LETTER 285 ❡ (Related to Lesson 48, Letter 5)

Announced, discount, identification, substantial, unfortunately.

To the Staff: Several months ago we announced that the regular company discount on rented cars would be[1] made available to all employees for their personal use. At that time we sent to each of you an[2] identification card that entitles you to a substantial discount when you rent a car from one of the five major[3] rental companies.

Unfortunately, there has been some confusion about the use of the card. On numerous[4] occasions the bills for personal car rentals have been mailed directly to the company. We have had to[5] trace the charges and refer them to the proper persons for payment. This has taken a great deal of time and effort.[6]

In the future will you please be sure that you either pay cash when you rent a car or charge the bill on your[7] personal credit card. We want to continue this service to our employees, but we cannot do so if we[8] continue to have personal bills sent to our company accounting offices. Fred Smith   [176]

TRANSCRIPTION PREVIEW

Spelling.   Identification, major, numerous, occasions.
Punctuation.   Period after *personal credit card* (. courteous request).
Typing Style.   Transcribe: five major rental companies (letters).

ℂ LETTER 286

American, charge, destroy, easier, valued, to make.

Dear Miss Evans: Your new American Department Store personal charge card is enclosed. It replaces your old[1] American charge card, which you should destroy.

Your name, address, and account number are embossed on the new card. Please[2] check your new card to be sure that all the information is correct. If it is correct, sign your name in the space[3] provided on the back of the card.

Your shopping with us will be made easier and more pleasant through the use of[4] this new card. The card will identify you as a valued customer in any of our stores throughout the[5] United States. All you need to do to make a purchase is present your new card to the salesclerk.

Thank you for shopping[6] at American Department Stores and for using your charge card. Sincerely yours, [134]

TRANSCRIPTION PREVIEW

Spelling. Personal, destroy, embossed, salesclerk.
Punctuation. Commas after *name* and *address* (, series).
Typing Style. Transcribe: American Department Store (capitalized).

(LETTER 287

Inquiry, possibility, tenants, blank, routine, reputable.

Dear Mr. Edwards: We were pleased to receive your inquiry about the possibility of your living at[1] the Western Apartments. New tenants are always welcome.

We are enclosing a credit form and an information[2] blank that we ask you to complete so that we may make a routine credit check. As you know, the managers of[3] all reputable apartment complexes use similar forms to obtain information about prospective[4] tenants.

The forms will take less than a half hour for you to complete. Please bring the completed forms with you when you come[5] to see the model apartment. Any information that you supply on these forms will be kept confidential,[6] of course. Cordially yours, [124]

TRANSCRIPTION PREVIEW

Spelling. Tenants, complete, reputable, confidential.
Punctuation. Comma before *of course* (, parenthetical).
Typing Style. Transcribe: Western Apartments (capitalized).

⟪ LETTER 288 ⟪ (Office Style)

[shorthand symbols]

Thank you for, current, possible, telephone, cooperation, up to date.

Dear Mrs. Gray: Thank you for sending us your current home address. We try to keep our files

Make that *all our files.*

as current as possible[1] so that we can give you better service when you are in need of it. Please let us have your business address as[2] well as the telephone numbers at both your office and home.

Change that to *home and office.*

Thanks for your cooperation in helping us keep[3] our records up to date. Cordially yours,   [67]

LESSON 49

⟪ LETTER 289 ⟪ (Related to Lesson 49, Letter 3)

[shorthand symbols]

Application, realize, properly, notify, debts.

Ladies and Gentlemen: Enclosed is my completed application form for a United Bank credit card. I[1] did not realize it was so easy to apply for a credit card.

I think I answered all the questions properly.[2] If you need further information, please notify me immediately. The mortgage on my house will be[3] paid in two years, and my car payments will be completed next February. Those are my only long-term debts.

Even[4] though I am proud of how well I have managed my money, I am looking forward to having a United[5] Bank credit card. I hope it does not take too long to clear my application and issue my card. Cordially yours,[6] [120]

TRANSCRIPTION PREVIEW

    Spelling. Further, mortgage, February, debts.
    Punctuation. Hyphenate *long-term* (hyphenated before noun).
    Typing Style. Transcribe: United Bank (capitalized).

❡ LETTER 290 ❡ (Related to Lesson 49, Letter 4)

Thank you very much, services, genuinely, thoughtfulness, arranged, thanks.

Dear Mrs. Morgan: Thank you very much for your nice letter offering the services of the Eastern State Bank[1] in helping me to get my new furniture business under way. I genuinely appreciate your thoughtfulness[2] in writing to me.

For many years I have been using the First National Bank of Troy for both personal[3] and business matters, and I have arranged for that bank to help me with the various expenses involved in[4] opening my new store.

If at sometime in the future I need the services of a bank that is located closer[5] to my store, I will certainly call on you. Thanks for your offer of assistance. Very sincerely yours, [119]

TRANSCRIPTION PREVIEW

    Spelling. Thoughtfulness, various, sometime, assistance.
    Punctuation. Comma after *personal and business matters* (, conjunction).
    Typing Style. Transcribe: First National Bank of Troy (*of* not capitalized).

❲ LETTER 291 ❲ (Related to Lesson 49, Letter 5)

[shorthand symbols]

Return, interested, processing, tenant, anticipating.

Dear Mr. Gates: Enclosed is the card you asked me to return if I was interested in learning more about the[1] services of the Boston Credit Bureau. I certainly am interested because the processing of tenant[2] applications takes a great deal of my time.

Will you please ask a representative of your organization[3] to contact me as soon as possible. I am anticipating a vacancy within the next few weeks. It[4] would be a genuine welcome to have someone else do the credit checking for me. Sincerely yours, [98]

TRANSCRIPTION PREVIEW

Spelling. Bureau, tenant, anticipating, vacancy.
Punctuation. Period after *as soon as possible* (. courteous request).
Typing Style. Transcribe: Boston Credit Bureau (capitalized).

❲ LETTER 292

[shorthand symbols]

Friendly, reminder, mortgage, have not yet, everyone.

Dear Mr. Peterson: This is just a friendly reminder that your mortgage payments for the past two months have not[1] yet reached the First National Bank.

Everyone overlooks an overdue payment on occasion. If you merely[2] forgot to make these payments, please send us your check by return mail. On the other hand, if you are having some[3] financial difficulty, please send us notification as soon as possible. We will do everything in our[4] power to help you.

Please accept our thanks and disregard this letter if you have already mailed your check. Sincerely[5] yours, [101]

TRANSCRIPTION PREVIEW

    Spelling.   Friendly, mortgage, overdue, merely.
    Punctuation.   Commas after *forgot to make these payments* and *some financial difficulty* (*, if* clause).
    Typing Style.   Transcribe: First National Bank (capitalized).

❡ LETTER 293

Believes, being able, purchases, always, deplete, return.

Dear Mr. Smith: Are you one who believes in paying cash for everything you buy? Many people think that paying[1] cash is the best, easiest way to do business.

Being able to pay cash for all your purchases is a[2] remarkable achievement, but it is not always the wisest way to buy. For example, if a person paid cash[3] for a new house, it could easily deplete his or her entire savings.

It is a very good idea to[4] establish a good credit rating even if you do not need to borrow money now. There will probably be a[5] time when you will need to borrow a substantial amount of money.

Start building a solid credit record today.[6] Return the enclosed application for a Miller credit card; you will be making no mistake. Cordially[7] yours, [141]

TRANSCRIPTION PREVIEW

    Spelling.   Believes, achievement, always, deplete.
    Punctuation.   Comma after *best* (*, and* omitted).
    Typing Style.   Transcribe: Miller (capitalized).

❧ LETTER 294 ❧ (Office Style)

Recall, annual, conference, accommodate, let me.

Mr. Dennis: You will recall that several weeks ago I asked you to begin plans for the annual sales[1] conference of Cunningham and Company. In today's mail I received your preliminary report. I want[2] you to know, Mr. Dennis, that I am very well pleased with the progress you have made in setting up this meeting.[3]

There are several things that I would like you to keep in mind as you continue with the preparations for this[4] very important meeting:

1. We must meet in a hotel that can easily accommodate our 500[5] sales representatives.

2. We will need a meeting room that can be used for general meetings.

3. We will need[6] to have most meals catered.

Please let me know if you can find a hotel that has the facilities we require. Mildred[7] O'Connor   [143]

> Let's add a fourth item to the list: *We will need to be located within easy commuting distance of a major air terminal.*

LESSON 50

❧ LETTER 295 ❧ (Related to Lesson 50, Letter 3)

Enlightening, informative, multiple, classroom, involved.

Dear Mr. Worth: Thank you very much for sending me a copy of the booklet, *Understanding Credit.* I find[1] it to be an enlightening, informative book, and I would like to have 50 additional copies to give[2] to students in my finance class at Baker High School here in Cleveland, Ohio.

If it is possible for you[3] to send multiple copies of this booklet for classroom use, I would appreciate receiving them before classes[4] begin in the fall. If there is a charge involved in printing and mailing these additional copies, please send[5] the bill directly to me. Very sincerely yours, [110]

TRANSCRIPTION PREVIEW

Spelling. Enlightening, informative, additional, finance.
Punctuation. Commas after *for classroom use* and *these additional copies* (, *if* clause).
Typing Style. Underscore: *Understanding Credit* (underscore booklet title).

❡ LETTER 296 ❡ (Related to Lesson 50, Letter 4)

So much, offered, confused, several thousand dollars, bracket, municipal.

Dear Ms. White: Thanks so much for sending me information about the new savings plans offered by the Central Savings[1] and Loan Association. I have read the information carefully, but I am still somewhat confused.

In[2] the spring I will have several thousand dollars to invest, and I definitely want to put the money where[3] it will earn the highest rate of interest possible. However, I am in a fairly high tax bracket, and I[4] will have to pay income taxes on any interest that I receive.

Do you think that I should place my extra money[5] in a savings account, or do you think it would be a better idea to invest in municipal bonds?[6]

Please let me have your frank opinion, Ms. White. A stamped, self-addressed envelope is enclosed for your convenience.[7] Sincerely yours, [142]

Spelling. Offered, carefully, fairly, bracket.

Punctuation. Commas after *tax bracket* (, conjunction); after *stamped* (, *and* omitted).

Typing Style. Transcribe: Central Savings and Loan Association (*and* not capitalized); spring (not capitalized).

❰ LETTER 297 ❰ (Related to Lesson 50, Letter 5)

Memorandum, agree, multitude, major, profitably.

Mr. Norris: This is to acknowledge receipt of your memorandum of Tuesday, December 23.

I[1] agree with you, Mr. Norris, that our organization is facing a multitude of problems. However,[2] we are taking many major steps to ensure that we will be operating profitably in the years ahead.[3]

We have set as a goal to reduce our accounts receivable to $100,000 within six[4] months. In addition, the head of our marketing staff has initiated steps to increase sales by 10 percent[5] during the coming year.

At 9 a.m. on Monday, January 5, we will hold a staff meeting in our Pittsburgh,[6] Pennsylvania, office to determine what other steps can be taken to improve our financial status.[7] M. C. Pryor   [143]

Spelling. Acknowledge, multitude, major, profitably.

Punctuation. Commas before and after *January 5* (, apposition); before and after *Pennsylvania* (, geographical).

Typing Style. Transcribe: 9 a.m. (figure).

❰ LETTER 298

Cunningham, following, telephone, routine, within.

Dear Friend: Let me take this opportunity to invite you to enjoy the many conveniences of a[1] Cunningham Department Store charge account.

When you have a charge account at our store, you are billed once a month for all of[2] your purchases. There is no service charge if your bill is paid in full by the 10th of the following month.

You will[3] also derive a multitude of other advantages. They include such items as the following:

1. You[4] will get advance notices of sales.

2. You may shop in person, by mail, or by telephone.

3. You do not have[5] to bring cash with you; all you need is your charge card.

It is easy to open a charge account at the Cunningham[6] Department Store. Just fill out the enclosed form and return it to us. We will make a routine credit check, and you[7] should have your credit card within two weeks' time. Cordially yours,   [151]

TRANSCRIPTION PREVIEW

Spelling.   Billed, routine, weeks', cordially.
Punctuation.   Colon after *as the following* (: enumeration).
Typing Style.   Transcribe: 10th (figures and letters).

❡ LETTER 299

Automobile, sprained, imagine, partial, patience.

Dear Miss Mendez: On Saturday, November 21, I was traveling west on Lexington Avenue in[1] uptown Detroit, and I was involved in a very serious automobile accident. I suffered multiple[2] fractures to my left arm, and my back is badly sprained.

As you can imagine, the accident has placed a severe[3] strain on my budget. I understand that my monthly payment of $100 for furniture that I[4] bought from your store last December is now past due. I am enclosing a check for $25 in partial[5] payment. Under the circumstances, I hope that you will accept it and my promise that

I will pay the full balance[6] of my account just as soon as I am able to return to work.

Thank you for your patience and understanding,[7] Miss Mendez. Sincerely yours, [146]

TRANSCRIPTION PREVIEW

Spelling. Traveling, multiple, fractures, imagine.
Punctuation. Do not hyphenate *past due* (no noun, no hyphen).
Typing Style. Transcribe: west (not capitalized); $100; $25 (no decimals).

◖ LETTER 300 ◖ (Office Style)

Multinational, community, employees, you will find.

Dear Mr. Mason: Did you know that Hastings Enterprises is a large, multinational organization?[1] Most people don't realize this fact because we try to be a real part of each community we serve.

The employees[2] of each of our offices are members of local service organizations and often spend many hours[3] working on projects in the public interest.

> Insert the following sentence before the last one: *Each of our offices is managed by a person who takes part in local civic, cultural, and charitable activities.*

We do not have to teach our employees to do these things. We just make[4] sure that anyone we hire for one of the positions in our organization already has the personal[5] qualities that will make him or her a valuable, contributing member of the community as well[6] as our organization.

> Make that *company;* no, leave it *organization.*

It is no accident that people think of Hastings Enterprises as a small[7] organization; we plan it that way. We want to assure you that you will find the same type of friendly, cooperative[8] people in each of our offices throughout the world. Sincerely yours, [173]

CHAPTER

SALES

LESSON 51

⊄ LETTER 301 ⊄ (Related to Lesson 51, Letter 3)

Describing, fuel, system, deductible, decision, whether.

Gentlemen: Your interesting letter describing the Fuel Saver arrived in today's mail. I am definitely[1] interested in doing anything possible to save fuel. With the ever-increasing cost of fuel today, it[2] just doesn't make sense to waste oil.

Will you please answer the following questions for me:

1. What is the total cost[3] of the system described in your letter?

2. Is the cost of such a device deductible for income tax[4] purposes?

3. Do you have a financing plan available?

When I receive the answers to these questions, I will[5] make a decision about whether or not to install a Fuel Saver. I will be looking forward to hearing[6] from you. Sincerely yours,   [124]

❡ LETTER 302 ❡ (Related to Lesson 51, Letter 4)

Device, installed, furnace, minor, satisfactorily, removed, reimburse.

Dear Mr. Davis: Thank you very much for telling us about the trouble you had with the fuel-saving device[1] that my organization installed in your furnace last month. I am very sorry that the device did not work[2] properly.

As you know, Mr. William White, our service representative, made several minor adjustments[3] to the system yesterday. He believes that it is working satisfactorily now. In this day of high fuel[4] costs, it definitely makes sense to use a device such as the one we installed. I hope you will find that it is[5] working to your complete satisfaction and that you will not ask to have it removed.

We were wrong in telling you[6] to call the gas company when you noticed the scent of gas in your home; we should have sent someone to your home[7] immediately. I apologize sincerely for the inconvenience we have caused you, Mr. Davis. Enclosed[8] is a check for $20 to reimburse you for the charge that was made by the gas company.

If you have[9] any further trouble with your furnace, please call me personally. Very cordially yours,   [197]

❡ LETTER 303 ❡ (Related to Lesson 51, Letter 5)

Government, savings, actually, power, every dollar, whatever.

Dear Mrs. Yates: Thank you for your letter about the advantages of investing in government bonds. I am[1] quite disturbed about the high rate of inflation today, and I am definitely looking for a safe long-term[2] investment.

Last year I put $1,000 in a savings account at 7 percent interest.

I had to[3] pay income taxes on the 7 percent interest, of course. The rate of inflation was nearly 10 percent last[4] year. The result, therefore, was that I actually lost a few cents in purchasing power on every dollar I[5] had saved.

It does not make sense to leave my hard-earned money in an account in which I will actually lose purchasing[6] power in the long run. Will you please send me whatever information you have available about[7] government bonds. If you wish, you may call me at 555-8996. Cordially yours, [156]

❘ LETTER 304

Credentials, outstanding, uptown, interview, graduated.

Dear Mr. Dennis: Thank you for your letter of application and your data sheet. Your credentials are outstanding.[1]

We will soon have a sales opening in the men's clothing department of our uptown store. We would be happy[2] to interview you for the position on Thursday, March 17, at 10 a.m. if this is convenient for[3] you.

We understand that you will not want full-time employment until after you have graduated in June. This[4] decision shows much common sense on your part; your education is of utmost importance. If you are hired by[5] our organization, we will be happy to have you work on a part-time basis until your graduation.[6]

We are looking forward to seeing you soon. Sincerely yours, [131]

❘ LETTER 305

Reminder, subscription, articles, ensure, abundance, newsstand.

Dear Mr. Taylor: This is just a friendly reminder to let you know that your subscription to *Gardening Today*[1] will expire with the March issue. This is the season that you will probably be most interested in reading[2] the interesting, up-to-date articles about flowers, trees, and shrubs.

Now is the time that you should be giving your[3] garden the special attention that will ensure that you will have an abundance of flowers and a lush garden[4] during the summer and early fall months.

Don't miss an issue of *Gardening Today*. If you send your renewal[5] today, you will be paying only 75 cents for each issue during the coming year. This represents a[6] savings of more than 50 percent of the newsstand price. Just fill out, sign, and return the enclosed card. You need not[7] send in any money now; we will bill you later. Sincerely yours, [152]

❡ LETTER 306 ❡ (Office Style)

Thank you for, explain, women's, children's, sensible.

Dear Mr. Yale: It was certainly nice to meet you on your visit to Springfield last week. Thank you for taking the[1] time to come to our store to explain the new line of women's and children's clothing that your company manufactures.[2] I know that our sales representatives will be able to do a better job because of the sensible,[3] thorough explanation you gave.

Please stop in our store whenever you are in the area. Yours truly, [78]

> Insert this before the last sentence: *Our complete staff enjoyed meeting you, Mr. Yale, and we hope you will visit us often.*

❬ LETTER 307 ❬ (Related to Lesson 52, Letter 3)

Allotted, mailed, customers, omitted, additional, gratitude.

Dear Mr. Rogers: As you know, we were allotted 1,000 copies of the book, *The Challenge of Running*, that[1] was recently published by your company. Thank you for sending the copies to us; we were very glad to receive[2] them.

When we first received notification that you would supply us with copies of the first printing of the[3] book, we mailed letters to our regular customers stating that we would reserve a copy for each of them.[4] Unfortunately, we inadvertently omitted more than 100 names from our mailing list.

We were able[5] to fill most of the orders. However, we need an additional 50 copies of the book for people whose[6] names were omitted from the original mailing. Would it be possible, Mr. Rogers, for you to send us[7] 50 additional copies of the first printing? We need them in order to keep the goodwill of some of our[8] best customers.

If you can help us in this matter, you will have our gratitude. Sincerely yours,   [177]

❬ LETTER 308 ❬ (Related to Lesson 52, Letter 4)

Virginia, suitable, satisfactorily, specifications, adjustments, permitted.

Dear Mr. Harris: Thank you for notifying us that you will be moving to Virginia in the near future.[1] We will be more than happy to help you and your family find suitable living accommodations in the[2] Richmond area.

There are many houses on the market that should meet your needs satisfactorily. However,[3] 30 new homes will be built in a new subdivision just west of the city. These houses should be completed[4] by the middle of July, and most of them meet your specifications.

There are several major advantages[5] in purchasing a new house. They are as follows:

1. You will be able to make minor adjustments in[6] the floor plans before actual construction begins.

2. You will be able to select the interior and[7] exterior colors.

3. You will be able to choose the carpeting and other floor coverings that you like.[8]

The floor plans for several of the models are enclosed. If you like any of them, please let me know. I will then[9] find out the exact dates that we will be permitted to take you through the model houses.

We are delighted to[10] have the opportunity to serve you, and we are looking forward to meeting you and your family. Sincerely[11] yours,
[221]

❲ LETTER 309 ❲ (Related to Lesson 52, Letter 5)

Disappointed, you ordered, credited, misrepresented, garment, description.

Dear Ms. Bates: We are very sorry that you were disappointed in the jacket that you ordered from our store. It[1] arrived in our receiving department today. We immediately credited your account for $95,[2] which included the cost of the jacket and the postage.

We were disturbed that you felt that the jacket was[3] misrepresented in our catalog. Unfortunately, the color of the jacket is not the exact shade[4] shown in the illustration. We usually have some difficulty in matching the color of the ink in the[5] catalog with the color of the actual garment. However, we feel that the description is accurate.

You[6] have been a customer of ours for many years, Ms. Bates, and we want to keep your goodwill. Please help us to do so[7] by permitting us to serve you again in the near future. Very sincerely yours,   [155]

ℂ LETTER 310

Management, holiday, greetings, patronage, limited, ticketed.

Dear Mrs. Washington: The management of the Madison Gift Shop wants to take this opportunity to send[1] you very special holiday greetings and to thank you for the business that you have given us during the past[2] year. Because of the continued patronage you and our other regular charge customers have given us, we[3] have been able to give you high-quality service at low, economical prices.

As you know, each year we[4] hold a very special sale in January. Our next sale begins on Wednesday, January 2, and will last[5] for two full weeks. The sale will not be limited to special goods; several items in our entire store will be[6] on sale at 50 percent off the ticketed prices.

The sale will be announced in the Sunday, December[7] 28, edition of the local newspapers. Before we open the sale to the general public, however,[8] we will have two special days for our regular charge customers. On Friday and Saturday, December[9] 26 and 27, you will be able to select any item in our store and pay only 50[10] percent of the regular price.

Make your plans now, Mrs. Washington, to come to the Madison Gift Shop on[11] December 26 or 27. Our doors will be open at 9 a.m., and you will be able to make[12] great savings on any item in our store. Sincerely yours,   [251]

ℂ LETTER 311

Announced, customers, prior, permitted, will you please.

Mr. Jones: As you know, our regular winter sale begins on Wednesday, January 2, at 9 a.m. The[1] sale will be announced to the general public on the weekend after Christmas.

This year we will have two special[2] days for our regular charge customers. On the Friday and Saturday prior to the regular sale, our charge[3] customers will be permitted to make purchases and pay half the ticketed prices. All they will have to do[4] to take advantage of the special prices is present their charge card to the sales representative.

Will you please[5] be sure that each of the sales representatives in your department knows about the two special days for our charge[6] customers. Jane White [124]

⊂ LETTER 312 ⊂ (Office Style)

Permitting, reference, trainee, marketing, posted.

Dear Professor Mason: Thank you very much for permitting me to use your name as a reference when I applied[1] for a position with Lexington and Company. I am happy to tell you that I was hired as a sales[2] management trainee. I will begin work on Monday, January 5.

Delete that last sentence.

I remembered the many principles[3] that I learned in your course in marketing at State College. I know that I will certainly use many of your[4] suggestions in the days ahead.

I will be glad to keep you posted on my progress at Lexington and Company.[5] When you are in the area, I hope you will stop in to see me. Very cordially yours, [117]

Add the following sentences after the first paragraph: *I am sure that your recommendation had a great deal to do with my obtaining the position. I sincerely appreciate your thoughtfulness and your help.*

LESSON 53

❆ LETTER 313 ❆ (Related to Lesson 53, Letter 3)

Invited, 5 p.m., allowed, you will be able, crowds,
you should be able, family.

Dear Mr. Morgan: Because you are a special charge customer of
our store, you are invited to attend a[1] special sale that we will be
conducting on Monday evening, June 4, in our main store.

On that day we will close our[2] doors to the general public at
5 p.m. We will reopen at 6 p.m., but only those customers[3] who
bring the special enclosed invitation will be allowed to pass
through our doors. You will be able to take[4] advantage of the
many special buys without having to worry about the large crowds
that usually attend public[5] sales.

You should be able to make substantial savings on everything
you need for your home, your family, and[6] yourself. Don't you
think you ought to be with us Monday evening, Mr. Morgan? We
will be looking forward to seeing[7] you then. Sincerely yours,   [145]

❆ LETTER 314 ❆ (Related to Lesson 53, Letter 4)

Desk, apologize, frankly, dismayed, mix-up, guarantee.

Dear Mr. West: Thank you for your letter of July 21. It arrived
on my desk this morning. I apologize[1] sincerely for the inconvenience you have been caused during the past year.

Frankly, I am as dismayed about[2] the problem as you are. We
actually mailed your order the day after you were in our store.
Unfortunately,[3] it was sent to another customer. The mix-up occurred in our own shipping department.

Based on the service[4] you have received from us recently, I could not blame you if you decided to take your business to another[5] company. However, I hope you will give us another chance. We have the towels you ordered in stock, and they[6] are packed and ready for delivery. If you will call us at 555-9632, we will have them sent[7] to you immediately. We guarantee you will get the right ones this time. You should have them within three days' time.[8] Cordially yours, [163]

ℂ LETTER 315 ℂ (Related to Lesson 53, Letter 5)

To join, philatelic, stamps, answered, printed, base.

Dear Ms. Malone: Thank you very much for your invitation to join the National Philatelic Society.[1] As you stated in your letter, I am interested in collecting stamps. In fact, I have been collecting stamps[2] for more than five years. I now have a collection of more than 5,000 stamps that were issued in various countries[3] throughout the world.

There are three questions, therefore, that I would like to have answered before I decide whether or not[4] to join your organization. The questions are as follows:

1. How many issues of the magazine, *Stamp[5] Collecting*, are printed each year?

2. How will I know when there is a new issue of a stamp that I might like to purchase?[6]

3. What other services does your organization provide to its members?

I will base my judgment on[7] your answers to these questions, Ms. Malone. Sincerely yours, [150]

ℂ LETTER 316

Announce, officially, located, attractive, capable, courteous, register.

Dear Mrs. Lopez: We are pleased to announce that we will officially open the Ryan's Children's Shop on Wednesday,[1] August 13. The shop is located at 9001 Park Avenue here in Akron, Ohio.

Our[2] new shop will be one of the most attractive, exciting, and well-stocked stores in this part of the country. We will carry[3] all the right kinds of clothing for your children. We will have light clothing for spring and summer and warm clothing for[4] fall and winter.

Our capable, courteous employees will be on hand from nine in the morning until eight[5] in the evening to help with your needs. Plan to visit us at our grand opening and register for the many free[6] gifts that we will be giving away. You will be delighted with our staff, our service, and our clothing. Yours very[7] truly,   [141]

❡ LETTER 317

Insulation, you ordered, recently, stapled, one of the, authorized, assured.

Dear Mr. Wilson: The insulation you ordered recently has been shipped and ought to be at your residence[1] by September 20. If you plan to install this insulation yourself, you will find a complete set of[2] instructions in the envelope that is stapled to one of the packages.

We suggest, however, that you let our[3] authorized dealer in Shreveport, Louisiana, install the insulation for you. By doing so, you will[4] be assured that the insulation is installed properly.

Our dealer in Shreveport is the Young Company, which[5] is located at 140 North 27 Street. You may call them at 555-4433 to make[6] arrangements for immediate installation. Yours very truly,

[132]

❡ LETTER 318 ❡ (Office Style)

We have not, mailed, popular, subscription, expire, will you please.

Dear Professor Chang: We have not mailed the last two editions of our popular weekly magazine, *News Report*,[1] to you. We wrote you several times in the past few months explaining that your subscription would expire with the June[2] issue. However, we never received a reply.

Will you please do us a favor? We would like to have an answer[3] to the following questions:

1. Did we do something to offend you?
2. Were we late in sending the magazine[4] to you?
3. Is there some other reason why you did not choose to renew your subscription?

> Delete *choose to.*

As you know, *News Report*[5] is written for the reader who does not have much time to keep up with world events. It is light, informative[6] reading that is based on the major news stories of the past week.

If you will give us the answers to these questions,[7] you will have our gratitude. Sincerely yours,   [148]

> Add this question after the second one: *3. Are you dissatisfied with the way our magazine is written and edited?*

LESSON 54

ℂ LETTER 319 ℂ (Related to Lesson 54, Letter 3)

Shocked, leather, you ordered, apologize, notices, via, reported.

Dear Mr. Johnson: We were shocked to receive your letter of August 15 informing us that you still have not[1] received the 24 sets of leather luggage that you ordered from us on June 15. We apologize[2] sincerely for not acknowledging your letter of inquiry. On checking our shipping notices, we found that the[3] luggage was sent to you on June 24 via Baker Trucking Company.

We checked with the trucking company[4] and learned that the goods were lost in transit, but this was never reported to us. The company should have[5] notified us immediately, of course.

We are sending you the 24 sets of leather luggage via express.[6] We guarantee you that this shipment will reach you by Monday, August 22.

We are sorry for the[7] inconvenience that we have caused you. As a token of our appreciation for your patience, we are deducting[8] 10 percent from the total amount of your bill. Yours sincerely, [171]

ℂ LETTER 320 ℂ (Related to Lesson 54, Letter 4)

[shorthand outlines]

Within, entitled, fund, ideas, legally, library.

Dear Mr. Miles: Thank you for your order for a copy of the new book, *How to Decrease Your Taxes*. It is being[1] mailed to you this week, and you should receive it within two weeks' time.

When you receive your copy, please note especially[2] Chapter 6. It is entitled "Setting Up Your Own Retirement Fund." I am sure that this chapter will give[3] you many ideas on how to reduce your taxes legally and save for the future at the same time.

When you[4] have had an opportunity to examine the book carefully, we feel sure that you will want to add it to[5] your library. If you do, just write us your check for $8.95 and send it to us in the[6] envelope that is enclosed. If you do not want to keep the book, just return it to us; you will be under no[7] obligation, of course. Very sincerely yours, [148]

ℂ LETTER 321 ℂ (Related to Lesson 54, Letter 5)

[shorthand outlines]

Coverage, decided, reducing-term, understand, will you please.

Dear Mr. Tate: Thank you for spending several hours' time with me last Tuesday evening. I appreciate your taking[1] the time to explain the various types of life insurance that are available to me and the coverage[2] that each type affords.

After careful consideration, I have decided that I would like to purchase a[3] $50,000 reducing-term life insurance policy. I understand that at my age the premium[4] will be $20 per month. Enclosed is the completed application form and a check for $20.[5]

Will you please send me the policy as soon as possible. I will feel more secure when I receive it. Very[6] sincerely yours,   [124]

❲ LETTER 322

Arrived, plant, condition, myself, shipment, transportation.

Dear Mr. Lee: Thank you for calling to our attention the fact that some of the goods that you ordered from our[1] company last month arrived at your plant in Columbia, South Carolina, in very poor condition. We were,[2] of course, very sorry to hear that the goods arrived in less-than-perfect condition, but we were very glad that[3] you took the time to tell us about the problem.

I am looking into the matter myself, Mr. Lee, and I[4] personally guarantee that your next shipment will arrive in the very best condition. In the meantime, please[5] return any items that are not acceptable from your last shipment. We will pay the transportation charges[6] and will replace all damaged goods.

We have enjoyed serving you during the past several years, and we certainly[7] wish to keep your business and your goodwill. Very cordially yours,   [151]

❲ LETTER 323

Annual, begins, inventory, showrooms, original, account.

Dear Customer: The annual Jefferson Store summer sale begins July 5. As you probably know, once a[1] year we reduce the prices on all our inventory in our showrooms and offer our high-quality goods at[2] the lowest possible prices. In fact, many of the sale items are marked well below our original cost.[3] We know that you will want to take advantage of the many bargains.

Remember, this sale will last just one week. If[4] you would like to obtain a Jefferson Store charge card, send us your application in the enclosed envelope. We[5] will be glad to open an account for you. Very cordially yours, [112]

❰ LETTER 324 ❰ (Office Style)

Weeks ago, customers, poor, southern, transport, contact.

To All Department Heads: Several weeks ago I received a memorandum from one of our representatives[1] in the South. The memorandum stated that many of the items that we shipped to customers in the South[2] were arriving in very poor condition. Unfortunately, that was not the first time that we have received this[3] type of complaint about the Southern Transport Company.

I am calling a meeting of all department heads for[4] Monday, March 14, at 2 p.m. in the conference room to discuss this problem.

> Type *Monday, March 14, at 2 p.m. in the conference room* in all capital letters.

I think we must decide whether[5] we want to continue using the Southern Transport Company to deliver our products.

If any of[6] you would like to discuss this matter with me before our meeting, please contact me before March 10.

> Underscore *March 10.*

I will be glad[7] to hear any suggestions you may have. Jason Brown [149]

LESSON 55

◖ LETTER 325 ◖ (Related to Lesson 55, Letter 3)

[shorthand symbols]

Calling, attention, weight, majority, beige, contrast.

Dear Miss Pace: Thank you for calling to our attention the problems the weight of our original choice of paper[1] would have caused in printing our spring catalog.

We have looked through the samples which you sent us and have made a selection.[2] The majority of us believe that the beige paper would be best for our catalog. The color of the[3] paper should provide a good contrast to the three colors that we selected earlier. Please print the 10,000[4] catalogs on our new selection of paper.

Do not forget that these catalogs must be in our warehouse and[5] ready for mailing no later than the tenth of February.

Thank you for your assistance. Cordially yours,   [119]

◖ LETTER 326 ◖ (Related to Lesson 55, Letter 4)

[shorthand symbols]

Display, women's, you will be glad, colors, appeal.

Dear Mr. Woods: We are planning to display our new line of women's and children's clothing at the fashion shows in[1] Tucson, Arizona. We are happy that you and your staff will be there. You will be glad to see the new colors[2] in our spring fashions that are sure to appeal to your customers. We will again feature styles in lightweight materials.[3]

We are pleased to hear that your sales for the past year were much greater than they were the previous year; we are[4] happy to be a part of your success. Yours sincerely,   [90]

❡ LETTER 327 ❡ (Related to Lesson 55, Letter 5)

Problem, several months ago, apologize, sincerely, definitely, advise.

Dear Mr. Miller: Thank you for calling to our attention the problem that you have had with the Master lawn mower[1] that you purchased several months ago. We are very sorry that you have had trouble with the machine, and[2] I apologize sincerely.

We agree with you, Mr. Miller; you definitely should have a new machine.[3] If you will return the mower to the Master Service Company in Toledo, we will be glad to exchange[4] it for a new model.

Because we are near the end of the summer season, our supply of new machines is running[5] low. Therefore, we advise you not to wait. Please take the mower to the Master Service Company at your[6] earliest convenience. Very sincerely yours, [128]

❡ LETTER 328

Developed, shampoo, minor, results, media, someone.

Ms. Johnson: As you know, our newly developed shampoo is almost ready to be sold to the general public.[1] After our lab has completed a few more minor tests and has sent the test results to our main office, two[2] of our plants will start production. If sales go as well as we expect, we may also have our third plant producing[3] this shampoo by September.

Our next step is to prepare a series of ads for all media. We feel that we[4] should proceed at once; we do not feel that it would be advisable to wait until all tests are completed to[5] begin working on our advertising campaign. At our last staff meeting someone suggested that we stress that this[6] shampoo is for the entire family and that we should build this appeal into our advertisements. All of us[7] agree that this total family approach to advertising is best. We are now working on several[8] radio, television, and newspaper ads that can be used in our sales campaign.

Will you please let me have your feelings[9] about this plan. Ray Conway   [186]

ℂ LETTER 329

Damaged, table, wood, imported, experts, especially, chosen.

Dear Mrs. Kelley: We were very sorry to learn that you damaged the fine table that you bought from the Madison[1] Company six months ago. The wood for the table that you bought was imported and selected with great care[2] by our experts. The top was especially chosen for its fine grain and was rubbed by hand with a special polish[3] to bring out the natural beauty of the wood.

We will send someone from our main factory in Chicago to[4] determine if your table can be repaired to your satisfaction. If our representative feels that the top[5] is irreparable, we will send you an estimate of the cost of repairing the entire top.

Please let us know[6] on the enclosed self-addressed card when it will be convenient for you to have our representative call. Sincerely[7] yours,   [141]

ℂ LETTER 330 ℂ (Office Style)

History, entire, substantial, household, furnishings, items.

Dear Customer: On Monday morning, January 6, our store will begin the biggest sale in its history.[1] Our doors will open at 9 a.m., and everything in our entire store will be on sale at discounts up to 60[2] percent off the regular price.

You will be able to make substantial savings on men's, women's, and children's[3] clothing. In addition, you will be able to make great savings on household furniture and home furnishings.

Don't[4] wait; mark January 6 on your calendar right now.

Type *January* in all capital letters.

This will be your best opportunity of the year to[5] save money on items for you and your family. Remember, our doors will be open promptly at 9 a.m.[6]

Underscore that last sentence.

Very sincerely yours,   [124]

ℂ **LETTER 331** ℂ (Related to Lesson 56, Letter 3)

Formal, announcement, alumni, sponsoring, always, points.

Dear Mr. Lyons: It was nice to receive the formal announcement that our alumni association is[1] sponsoring a tour again this year. I have always enjoyed the tours that you have arranged in the past, and I am[2] certainly looking forward to the cruise to the West Indies this year.

Enclosed is my completed application[3] form and a deposit of $200. As you suggested in your letter, I will pay the balance one[4] month before the date of departure.

Will you please send me any brochures you have about the ship on which we will[5] be sailing and about the various points of interest that we will be visiting. Very cordially yours,   [119]

ℂ **LETTER 332** ℂ (Related to Lesson 56, Letter 4)

Few days ago, specifically, answers, tuition, formerly, records.

Dear Sir or Madam: A few days ago I received a letter saying that Eastern State College would be offering[1] three short courses specifically designed for the international traveler. I will be vacationing[2] in Europe next year, and I would like to know more about these courses.

I would like to have answers to the following[3] questions:
1. What is the exact date the courses will begin?
2. What is the cost of tuition and books?
3.[4] Will the courses be offered for graduate credit?

I was formerly a student at Eastern State College; therefore,[5] you should be able to find a copy of my records in your files.

I will be looking forward to hearing[6] from you. Sincerely yours,

[124]

ℂ LETTER 333 ℂ (Related to Lesson 56, Letter 5)

Complimentary, informative, style, appealing, distribute.

Ladies and Gentlemen: Thank you for sending me a complimentary copy of the brochure, *The Right Vacation*[1] *for You.* I found it to be interesting and informative. The informal style of writing made it[2] particularly appealing.

I am a physical education teacher here at Lexington College in Troy, New[3] York, and I would like to have copies of this brochure for my students. Would it be possible for you to send me[4] 100 copies to distribute to the students? If you can send me this large a quantity, I will be very[5] grateful. If you cannot send this many copies, may I have permission to reproduce them myself?

Thanks very[6] much for your cooperation. Very sincerely yours,

[131]

ℂ LETTER 334

Welcome, membership, identification, moment, discounts, in a few days.

Dear Mr. Williams: It is a pleasure to welcome you formally to membership in the National Travel[1] Club; your identification card is enclosed. Please take a moment now to sign the card in ink on the back. When[2] you travel, be sure to take the card with you. You will receive discounts of up to 25 percent at major hotels,[3] motels, and restaurants throughout the world.

In a few days you will receive a copy of our monthly magazine,[4] *Travel Today*. In it you will find a listing of hundreds of participating establishments as well[5] as a number of interesting articles on travel. We hope you will enjoy the magazine.

We are delighted[6] that you are a member of our organization, Mr. Williams. Whenever we can be of service to[7] you, please call the toll-free number imprinted on your card. Sincerely yours,   [153]

(LETTER 335

To serve, reference, formerly, period, industrious.

Dear Miss Washington: It is a pleasure to serve as a business reference for Miss Mary Tate, who formerly[1] worked for me.

Miss Tate was employed by my company, Bennington Associates, for a period of three years[2] before she left to take a position with a travel agency in Miami, Florida, two years ago.[3] I was very sorry to lose her, but she wanted to live and work in a warmer climate. Therefore, she decided[4] to move to the South.

Miss Tate is a well-qualified, industrious person. She works well with other people[5] and can easily accept a great deal of responsibility.

I would be quite happy to hire her again[6] if she should decide to return to Pennsylvania. Very sincerely yours,   [134]

(LETTER 336 ((Office Style)

Formally, holidays, to make, vacation, available.

To the Staff: I am happy to announce formally that our company will add two new holidays to its[1] regular schedule for the coming year.

We will be closed Thursday, July 3, which is the day before Independence[2] Day. In addition, we will be closed on August 29, which is the Friday before Labor Day.

Underscore those dates.

We are happy[3] to make these vacation days available to all our employees.

Please keep a copy of this memorandum[4] for future reference.

Type that last sentence in all caps.

James Cunningham   [88]

LESSON 57

❰ LETTER 337 ❱ (Related to Lesson 57, Letter 3)

Referred, associate, family, transportation, accommodations, myriad.

Ladies and Gentlemen: Your organization has been referred to me by Mr. William Brown, a business[1] associate of mine. Mr. Brown tells me that your company planned an interesting, exciting vacation for him[2] and his family last year and that he recommends your travel service highly. I am planning to visit[3] Africa this summer, and I would like an experienced, capable person to help me in making all the plans.[4]

Because I have never visited Africa, I am familiar with neither the transportation nor the living[5] accommodations available in the various cities I want to visit. I will need help in[6] determining the weight and style of clothing that I should plan to take with me. In addition, I will need some help in[7] deciding just how much money I should plan to take in cash and traveler's checks.

If your company would like to[8] help me in answering the myriad of questions that have occurred to me, I hope you will ask one of your[9] representatives to call me soon; my phone number is 555-6170. Sincerely yours, [198]

❦ LETTER 338 ❦ (Related to Lesson 57, Letter 4)

Announcing, memberships, natural, habitat, typical, answering.

Dear Mr. Taylor: I was delighted to receive your letter announcing that family memberships would be[1] available for Animal Kingdom this summer. My family and I have enjoyed the park during the past[2] two summers. We have always preferred seeing animals in their natural habitat rather than in a[3] typical zoo.

My son has become quite interested in photography and would like to know if you are planning tours[4] for photographers this summer. If you are, he would like to know when they will be conducted and what the cost will[5] be. I will appreciate your answering these questions, Mr. Taylor.

Enclosed is my check for $30.[6] Will you please send us our family membership card as soon as possible; we want to be among the first to[7] visit Animal Kingdom this summer. Very cordially yours, [152]

❦ LETTER 339 ❦ (Related to Lesson 57, Letter 5)

Chartered, forward, sponsored, deposit, deferred, until.

Dear Mr. Tatum: Will you please make four reservations for the tour that you have chartered to Old West City from[1] April 25 to May 5. My family and I are certainly looking forward to the trip. We enjoyed[2] our trip to the East that your travel agency sponsored last year, and we know that this year's trip will be just as well[3] planned and organized.

As you requested, we are enclosing a deposit of $400. We understand[4] that payment of the remainder of the fee for the trip can be deferred until after our return.

As the[5] date of departure approaches, I hope you will send us any additional information that you believe[6] will be of interest to my family and me. Sincerely yours, [132]

❰ LETTER 340

Transportation, system, pollution, 75 cents, automobile, decrease.

Dear Commuter: As you know, Springfield has a fine public transportation system. I am sure you are also aware[1] that we have a great deal of pollution and traffic congestion. The city government is making a[2] determined effort to get commuters to use the public transportation system and leave their cars at home.

You can[3] ride anywhere within the city limits on one of our comfortable, air-conditioned buses for only[4] 75 cents. In addition, you can ride to most of the suburbs for only $1.25.[5] When you drive your automobile to the city, it can easily cost as much as $5 in tolls and parking[6] fees. This is in addition to the regular cost of gasoline and oil.

Doesn't it make good sense to use[7] public transportation? You can save yourself money while helping to decrease pollution and traffic congestion.[8] For a free transportation guide covering all routes in the city and suburbs, just return the enclosed self-addressed[9] card. Your Public Transportation System [188]

❰ LETTER 341

Offices, associates, relocated, average, adequate, gratitude.

Ladies and Gentlemen: We are thinking about transferring our company offices to the South, and we are[1] considering several cities in Florida. We were referred to your company by Madison and[2] Associates, an organization that relocated its main offices in Tampa about two years ago.[3]

We would like to have answers to the following questions:

1. What is the average rental fee per square foot for[4] offices in the Tampa area?

2. Is there an adequate supply of well-trained office personnel?

3.[5] Is there a good public transportation system that serves the city as well as the suburbs?

If you will answer[6] these questions for us, you will have our gratitude. We will then be able to make a decision about whether[7] we should move our offices to Tampa. Very cordially yours,   [152]

❆ LETTER 342 ❆ (Office Style)

Construction, period, ceremony, cordially, refreshments, attend.

To All Employees: As you know, we have been working on the construction of a new bus terminal for a[1] period of more than two years. We are delighted to announce that our work is now completed and we will have a[2] formal opening ceremony on Saturday, May 3.

Underscore that date.

Every person who has worked in any way on the[3] construction of the new terminal is cordially invited to attend the grand opening.

There will be a[4] formal ribbon-cutting ceremony at 10 a.m. This will be followed by a short speech by the mayor and[5] members of the city government. Refreshments will then be served, and tours of the new facilities will be[6] conducted during the remainder of the day.

We hope each of you will plan to attend. Mark the date, May 3, on your[7] calendar now.

Type that last sentence in all capital letters.

James Farmer   [145]

LESSON 58

LETTER 343 (Related to Lesson 58, Letter 3)

Invitation, certainly, proposal, fuel, already, adequate.

Dear Miss Moses: Thank you for your invitation to take part in the open meeting on July 17. I[1] will certainly be prepared to express my feelings on the proposed changes in the city's bus schedule.

I am,[2] of course, in favor of almost any proposal that would result in less pollution and reduced traffic[3] congestion. As you will remember, however, we had to increase the bus fares only last year because of increases[4] in the cost of fuel. This resulted in our having fewer riders on each of our bus lines.

We already[5] provide adequate bus service to the city and suburbs. In fact, most buses are running at less than 50[6] percent capacity. Adding more buses will add significantly to our costs, and there is no guarantee[7] that ridership would increase.

Under the circumstances, I will speak against the proposed changes. Yours truly,   [159]

LETTER 344 (Related to Lesson 58, Letter 4)

Weeks ago, courteous, guarantee, notification, capacity, expended.

Gentlemen: Several weeks ago I received a letter from your advertising department. The letter stated[1] in part: "Before you begin your next trip, just call (800) 555-8016. One of our courteous,[2] efficient reservation clerks will be glad to guarantee your reservation at any one of our[3] conveniently located motels."

I took your advice; I should not have. I called your number before I left on a[4] short business trip. When I arrived at the

Lexington Motel in Burlington, Vermont, the clerk had not received[5] notification of my reservation. The motel was already filled to capacity, and the clerk made no[6] effort to help me find another room. I would have expended less time and energy if I had made the[7] reservation myself.

I do not plan to patronize Lexington Motels in the future. Yours truly, [158]

(LETTER 345 ((Related to Lesson 58, Letter 5)

Vacation, pleasant, forward, wonderful, gracious, weekend.

Dear Max: It was nice to receive your letter in today's mail. We, too, had a fine time on our short vacation with[1] you and Janet. It's always pleasant to get away from the city for several days. We are looking forward[2] to having you join us on our boat again in August. Although we will have fewer days together, I am sure[3] that we will have a wonderful time.

Unfortunately, Betty and I will not be able to accept your gracious[4] invitation to spend the Labor Day weekend at your cabin in the mountains. We have already made plans[5] to fly to the West Coast to see our relatives there. Perhaps you will give us a rain check.

If you are in the city[6] anytime during July, please stop by to see us. Sincerely yours, [133]

(LETTER 346

Third, reviewed, actually, period, performance, gross.

Mr. Trent: I am happy to tell you that the members of our staff are all ready for the sales meeting to be[1] held in Vail, Colorado, the third week in July.

We have reviewed our expense budget for the year, and we have[2] actually spent less money this year than we did during the corresponding period last year.

Our sales performance[3] also presents a bright picture. Although we have made fewer actual sales, our gross revenue is up by[4] more than 15 percent. This means that we are making bigger sales and are getting a better return from each sales[5] call.

If you would like to have more information before the sales meeting, please call me. Helen Edwards   [118]

❧ LETTER 347

Memorandum, group, budgets, corresponding, prepared, relationship.

Miss Edwards: Thank you for your memorandum concerning the performance of the sales staff during the first six months[1] of the year. In general, I am very well pleased with the performance of your group.

In this day of tight budgets,[2] I am happy that our company has been able to increase its gross revenue. I am somewhat concerned,[3] however, that we have made fewer actual sales during the first half of the year than we did during the corresponding[4] period of last year. This could be the result of our spending less money in order to make our profit[5] goal.

I think you should be prepared to answer questions concerning the relationship between the number of[6] sales calls made and the number of actual sales at the meeting in Vail, Colorado, next week. Fred Trent   [138]

❧ LETTER 348 ❧ (Office Style)

Annual, conference, mountain, register, meetings, promptly.

To the Staff: Our annual sales conference will be held at the Mountain Lodge in Vail, Colorado, the week of[1] July 20.

Underscore that date.

Please plan to arrive sometime in the early afternoon on Monday, July 20. When you[2] register at the lodge, be sure to pick up your sales information kits. They will be all ready for you at the main[3] registration desk. It is very important that you review this material before the meeting on Tuesday[4] morning.

Type that last sentence in all capital letters.

There will be an informal reception for all members of the staff at 6 p.m. on Monday in[5] the lobby of the lodge. Dinner will follow at 7 p.m. Our regular meetings will begin promptly at[6] 8 a.m. every morning. We plan to have our work completed by 4 p.m. each day so that you can take full[7] advantage of the many fine recreational facilities in the area.

We are planning an[8] interesting, informative meeting, and we know that everyone will gain a great deal from it. Max Tate   [177]

LESSON 59

❨ LETTER 349 ❩ (Related to Lesson 59, Letter 3)

Confirm, St. Louis, you will be able, guaranteeing, let us know.

Dear Miss Jefferson: We are happy to confirm your reservation for a large room at the Hotel Washington[1] in St. Louis for June 2, 3, and 4. We will reserve one of our special conference rooms that contains a sofa,[2] a table, a large desk, and four chairs. You will be able to conduct your interviews in this room just as though[3] you were in your own office.

The rate is $50 per day, and we are guaranteeing your reservation[4] for late arrival.

We will be happy to have you with us, Miss Jefferson. If there is anything we can do[5] to help make your stay with us more enjoyable, please be sure to let us know. Very sincerely yours, [118]

ℂ LETTER 350 ℂ (Related to Lesson 59, Letter 4)

Unpaid, forgive, returned, drawer, certain, statement.

Dear Miss Miller: Enclosed is my check for $138.50 to cover my unpaid balance[1] at the Nashville Motel. Please forgive me for being more than one month overdue in paying the bill.

When I[2] returned home to Memphis last month, I wrote a check, inserted it in an envelope, and placed it in the top drawer[3] of my desk. I was certain that I had mailed the check to you before I received your first statement. When I received[4] a second statement from you, I knew that something was wrong. I looked in my desk, and there was the envelope.

I[5] promise to take care of my obligations more promptly and efficiently in the future. Very sincerely[6] yours,   [121]

ℂ LETTER 351 ℂ (Related to Lesson 59, Letter 5)

Formally, we have not yet, happened, maybe, misplaced.

Dear Ms. Martinez: Last month we mailed you a letter formally inviting you to become a member of the[1] State Travel Club. Because we have not yet heard from you, we are wondering what could have happened. Perhaps the letter[2] was lost in the mail. Maybe it was misplaced when it arrived at your home. Or possibly you have not yet decided[3] whether or not you want to become a member of our organization.

If you are still thinking about[4] joining our organization, I hope you will consider the following advantages:

1. We issue you[5] a $25,000 travel accident insurance policy.

2. We make hotel, motel, and travel[6] reservations for you free of charge.

3. We supply you with a valuable identification card that[7] en-

ables you to cash checks when you are out of town.

When you consider the many advantages of membership[8] in the State Travel Club, we are sure you will want to mail us your completed application today. Another[9] blank is enclosed for your convenience. Sincerely yours, [190]

❐ LETTER 352

Tired, frequently, economy, restaurants, cable, stereo.

Dear Traveler: Are you tired of paying high rates for motel rooms? Many people who travel frequently feel that[1] they are overcharged by many of the nationally known motels that line our nation's interstate highways.

Our[2] company, Economy Motels, is doing something about the problem. We are offering only the basic[3] items that travelers want. At Economy Motels you will not find swimming pools or fancy restaurants.[4] You will not find cable television or stereo music. What you will find, however, is a clean, quiet[5] room with a comfortable bed and a private bath.

By offering only the basic items that the frequent[6] traveler wants and needs, we can lower our own costs significantly. We then pass our savings along to you,[7] our customer. For a free listing of the 500 Economy Motels, just fill out and return the enclosed[8] self-addressed card. Sincerely yours, [167]

❐ LETTER 353

Young, reservation, recommendation, following, competent, dependable.

Mr. Case: Yesterday a young man by the name of James Long came to my office and applied for a job as a[1] reservation clerk at my hotel. He stated that he had worked for you for several years and that you would be[2] willing to give him a recommendation.

I would appreciate it, Mr. Case, if you would answer the[3] following questions for me:

1. Is Mr. Long a competent, dependable person?
2. Can he work without direct[4] supervision?
3. If you had the opportunity, would you hire him again?

If you will let me have your[5] answers to these questions, you will have my gratitude. If I can be of similar help to you in the future,[6] I will be pleased to do so. Sincerely yours,   [128]

❐ LETTER 354 ❐ (Office Style)

Lower, strange, everything, between, London.

Dear International Travelers: Overseas air rates are getting lower each day. Does that sound strange to you? It[1] probably does because the cost of almost everything we buy these days seems to be getting higher.

Transatlantic[2] Airlines, which first started flying between New York and London only three years ago, will fly you to Europe[3] for less than $200. How can we do this? The answer is simple. No airline likes to fly with empty[4] seats. Empty seats represent a great expense.

Indent the next three sentences: *We do everything we can to avoid flying with even one empty[5] seat. We actually guarantee a seat to anyone who wants to fly to London and arrives one hour before[6] departure time. If the plane is already filled, we will fly you free of charge on the next day's flight.*

The next time[7] you want to fly to London, come to International Airport before 1 p.m. Our flights leave daily at 2[8] p.m. Sincerely yours,   [164]

LESSON 60

⊄ LETTER 355 ⊄ (Related to Lesson 60, Letter 3)

Inviting, amount, experienced, answers, provide, emergency, identification.

Dear Mrs. Bennington: Thank you for your letter inviting me to become a member of the International[1] Travel Club. In the next year or so I will be doing a great amount of international traveling,[2] and I will definitely need the services of an experienced organization such as yours.

I am[3] seriously considering applying for membership in the International Travel Club, but before[4] I do, I would like to have answers to the following questions:

1. Do you have offices in cities throughout[5] South America?
2. Do your members receive travel accident life insurance?
3. Does your organization[6] provide its members with an emergency medical identification card and a list of physicians[7] in the various countries they plan to visit?

When I receive answers to these questions, I will be able[8] to make a decision on whether or not to apply for membership in your organization. Will you please[9] let me hear from you as soon as possible. Sincerely yours,   [191]

⊄ LETTER 356 ⊄ (Related to Lesson 60, Letter 4)

Glad to hear, retirement, beautiful, region, superb, do you want.

Dear Mr. Gates: We were very glad to hear that you plan to visit us on the 21st of April to discuss[1] purchasing a lot on which to build your retirement home. As you probably know, Lakeside Park is the largest,[2] most beautiful retirement development in the entire region. We have many superb lots on which you can[3] build your home.

Before you come to see us, please consider the following questions:

1. Do you want a lot directly[4] on the lake? Lots located on the lake are approximately twice the price of lots that are only a few[5] blocks away from the water.

2. Do you want a lot with shade trees? The price of each lot is related to the number[6] of trees it contains.

3. Do you want a large lot or a small one? We have sites that vary in size from three acres[7] to only 10,000 square feet.

We are looking forward to seeing you on the 21st of April at 10[8] a.m. in our offices at 1402 Main Street here in Mobile. After we discuss the various questions[9] you have, we will take a drive through our beautiful retirement community. Sincerely yours,   [197]

❆ LETTER 357 ❆ (Related to Lesson 60, Letter 5)

Flattered, director, satisfied, unqualified, recommendation.

Dear Miss King: Thank you very much for your letter of August 18. I am flattered that you would like me to apply[1] for the position of tour director with your travel company. As you know, I have been working for[2] another organization for more than ten years, and I am very well satisfied with my work and with the[3] company. At this time I have no plans to make a change.

However, one of my former associates, Mr. A.[4] R. Smith, is looking for a position as a tour director. Mr. Smith worked with me for more than five years, and[5] I can give him an unqualified recommendation. If you would like to get in touch with Mr. Smith, you may[6] call him at (260) 555-2602, or you may write to him at 92 14th Street in Danville,[7] Colorado.

Thank you very much for considering me for a position with your organization.[8] Best wishes on finding just the right person for the position you have open. Sincerely yours,   [177]

❡ LETTER 358

(shorthand outline)

Sports, quantities, equipment, especially, products, catalog.

Dear Mr. Tate: Did you know that skiing is one of America's fastest-growing sports? What does this mean to you[1] as the owner of a sporting goods company? It means that you have an opportunity to sell large quantities[2] of ski equipment to new customers each year. This means increased profits for you.

The Western Manufacturing[3] Company can supply you with all types of ski equipment. In addition, we can furnish you with high-quality[4] clothing especially designed for skiing. Our line of goods has proved to be very popular in sporting[5] goods stores throughout the country.

Don't you think you should consider carrying our products this season? If you would[6] like to have a copy of our latest catalog, just sign and mail the self-addressed card. When we receive it, we[7] will mail your catalog to you immediately.

Take advantage of the new interest in skiing; begin selling[8] our products this winter. Yours truly,   [167]

❡ LETTER 359

(shorthand outline)

Article, foreign, tourists, sponsored, percentage.

Mr. Davis: I read an interesting article in this week's _Business News_. The article states that the number[1] of foreign tourists visiting the United States will be up by more than 25 percent during the coming[2] year. I believe this represents a real opportunity for our travel company. We have not sponsored[3] guided tours for foreign tourists in the past, but I believe we should give serious consideration to doing[4] so at this time.

Most foreign tourists see New York and one or two other cities in the East; some visit cities[5] in the West. However, a smaller percentage visit cities in other parts of the nation. I believe[6] this is a market that is well worth exploring.

Will you please look into the possibility of our company's[7] sponsoring guided tours for foreign visitors from New York to Atlanta, Birmingham, and Houston. I will[8] be looking forward to having your ideas on this subject. Marsha Sloan   [173]

❡ LETTER 360 ❡ (Office Style)

Central, contest, Europe, box, productivity, valuable.

To the Staff: We are happy to announce that the Central Manufacturing Company is sponsoring a contest[1] for its employees. The first prize will be a free trip to Europe.

On January 2 we will place a[2] suggestion box in the main dining area. If you have any suggestions on how to increase productivity[3] at our company, just place them in the suggestion box. At the end of each of the next three months

No, make that *six months.*

we will select[4] what we consider to be the best suggestions. If we use any of your ideas, we will pay you[5] $1,000 immediately. At the end of this period, we will select the best suggestion of all. The[6] person who made that suggestion will receive an all-expense-paid vacation to Europe.

Indent the next two sentences: *To enter the contest,*[7] *just write your suggestions for increasing company productivity on a slip of paper. Then place the paper*[8] *in the suggestion box in the main dining area.*

We know you will all enjoy the contest and that our[9] company will receive many valuable ideas. James Green   [191]

PART **4**

The letters in Part 4 vary in length—some are short, some are average, and some are long.

It is suggested that the students use the block style for the letters in Chapter 13, the full block style for those in Chapter 14, and the simplified style for those in Chapter 15. The teacher may vary the style requested for the letters in Chapter 16.

Some of the letters in Part 4 contain errors in grammar or in fact. These letters are labeled "Alertness Exercise." Each error is indicated by an asterisk, and the correct transcription is indicated at the end of the letter.

Chapter 13
RECREATION AND LEISURE

Chapter 14
BUSINESS EQUIPMENT
Lesson 66   Ages and anniversaries
Lesson 67   The dash

Chapter 15
GOODWILL AND PUBLIC RELATIONS
Lesson 71   Adjacent numbers
Lesson 72   Parentheses

Chapter 16
GENERAL
Lesson 76   Fractions, mixed numbers, and hyphenated numbers
Lesson 77   Exclamation point

❰ LETTER 362 ❰ (Related to Lesson 61, Letter 4)

[shorthand]

Camera, photography, excellent, satisfactorily, until.

Dear Mrs. Adams: Thank you for purchasing a new Owens camera from the Eastern Photography Shop. You[1] made a very wise investment in this fine camera. We are sure that you will receive many years of excellent[2] service from it.

It is quite important, Mrs. Adams, that you read the warranty carefully. As you know,[3] the camera is guaranteed for a one-year period. The camera will probably need no service for[4] many years. However, if it should fail to operate satisfactorily, you must return it to an[5] authorized dealer for repair. We suggest that you bring it back to our store. If you should have to have your camera[6] repaired by a dealer who is not authorized by the Owens Camera Company, the warranty will be[7] canceled.

If you should have any questions about the operation of your fine camera, please feel free to call[8] us at any time during regular store hours. We are open from 9 a.m. until 8 p.m. Monday through[9] Saturday. Very sincerely yours,   [187]

❰ LETTER 363 ❰ (Related to Lesson 61, Letter 5)

[shorthand]

Subscribed, quiet, device, attached, indeed, quite.

Gentlemen: Last month I subscribed to the service of the Home Television Theater. I enjoy watching movies[1] in the peace and quiet of my living room, and I was assured that you would provide six new, uninterrupted[2] movies each month.

The device that your representative attached to my television set works satisfactorily,[3] and there were indeed six movies last month. However, the quality of the movies left a great deal to[4] be desired. There was only one new movie broadcast last month.

The other five were quite old. Several of the movies[5] have been in circulation for at least two years.

Do you plan to present newer, better pictures? If you do,[6] I will continue to subscribe to your service. If you do not, I will definitely ask that the service be[7] canceled. I will be looking forward to hearing from you. Yours truly, [153]

❿ LETTER 364

[shorthand]

Stenographer, resort, reluctance, submit, automobile, climate.

Miss Chase: For the past year I have been working as a stenographer here at the East Coast Travel Resort. It has[1] been quite nice working with the many fine people at the hotel, and it is with reluctance that I must submit[2] my resignation.

As you know, about six months ago I was injured in an automobile accident. Although[3] I have made good progress in my recovery, my doctor feels that it would be a good idea for me to[4] move to a warmer climate. Therefore, I am planning to move to Texas sometime within the next three months.

I will,[5] of course, stay until a replacement has been properly trained. Thank you for your consideration during the past[6] year. Marlene West [123]

❿ LETTER 365 ❿ (Alertness Exercise)

[shorthand]

Accept, resignation, promoted, within, period, understand.

Mr. Harrington: It is with a great deal of reluctance that I must accept your resignation as a sales[1] representative with our organization. I have been very well pleased with your work, and I am quite sure that[2] you would have been promoted to a position in top management within a period of three or four years'[3] time.

I can easily understand your desire to return to the West Coast, where your family lives. I am sure[4] that you will be able to find a suitable position with a company there in a very short period[5] of time.

If I can be of help to you in any way, Mr. Smith,* I will be happy to do so. Paul[6] Madison   [121]
*Harrington

❬ LETTER 366 ❬ (Office Style)

Leisurely, countryside, horseback, memorable, surprisingly.

Dear Friend: If you like quiet, leisurely walks in the country-side, you are sure to enjoy a vacation at Twin[1] Oaks Vacation Resort. If you like to go horseback riding or just relax in the sun, you will love Twin Oaks. If[2] you want a truly memorable vacation at a surprisingly low cost, Twin Oaks is the place for you.[3]

Located just 100 miles from Pittsburgh, Pennsylvania, Twin Oaks is quite easy to reach by car, by bus, or by[4] train.

> Indent the next two sentences: *You can stay a day, a week, or a month at a price that will be easy on your budget. For only*[5] *$75 per day you will have a beautifully decorated room, three delicious meals, and access to all*[6] *our recreational facilities.*

Plan your next vacation at Twin Oaks Vacation Resort.

Make that just *Twin Oaks.*

You will be glad[7] you did. Sincerely yours,   [144]

LESSON 62

❬ LETTER 367 ❬ (Related to Lesson 62, Letter 3)

Information, yellow, recommend, closest, circled, further.

Dear Mr. Cunningham: Thank you for writing to us for information about the route to take and places to[1] visit on your upcoming vacation. We are happy to send you the information you need.

Enclosed are maps[2] of the states of Louisiana, Alabama, and Florida. We have marked in yellow the route that we[3] recommend. This route is the closest to the Gulf of Mexico, and it is also near three major amusement parks[4] and several golf courses.

We have circled on the maps the sites of ten trailer parks that cater to vacationers.[5] The enclosed folders give the rates charged at each of these trailer parks. We recommend that you make your reservations[6] at each of the trailer parks immediately. If you wait until summer, you may find that they are already[7] booked to capacity for the entire season.

If we can be of further help to you, Mr. Cunningham,[8] please do not hesitate to let us know. Sincerely yours,   [170]

⟪ LETTER 368 ⟪ (Related to Lesson 62, Letter 4)

Galleries, museums, except, Christmas, fixed.

Dear Miss White: Thank you for writing to us about the art galleries and museums in Chicago. We are[1] delighted that you are interested in art and that you are planning to visit our city in the near future.

Enclosed[2] are several folders on the art galleries and museums in Chicago. The National Museum[3] of Modern Art is open every day of the year except Christmas. It opens at ten in the morning and closes[4] at seven in the evening. There is no fixed admission charge. However, it is recommended that visitors[5] each contribute $2. The museum does not have an exhibit of motion pictures. However, it[6] does have a collection of classic television shows in which you may be interested.

If we can be of further[7] assistance to you as you plan your trip, please feel free to contact us. Very cordially yours,   [157]

⊄ LETTER 369 ⊄ (Related to Lesson 62, Letter 5)

[shorthand symbols]

Memorandum, visitors, substantially, encourage, whether, actually.

To the Staff: Six months ago I sent a memorandum to each of you stating that we had leased ten rooms at the[1] Wellington Hotel on an annual basis. The rooms were to be used for out-of-town business visitors.

Only[2] six of these rooms were occupied on any given day during the past four months. However, our company[3] has had many out-of-town business visitors who have stayed at other hotels. The rates that each department pays[4] at other hotels in the area are substantially more than the basic rate of $65 per[5] day that we are charged at the Wellington.

I encourage each of you to make use of the accommodations at[6] the Wellington Hotel whenever you have out-of-town visitors. Our company must pay for the rooms whether[7] or not they are actually used. Max Golden   [148]

⊄ LETTER 370

[shorthand symbols]

Away, remember, until, representative, named, memorial.

To the Staff: It is my sad duty to tell you that Mr. William Carson, who worked for our company for many[1] years, passed away last evening at the home of his daughter in Baltimore, Maryland. Many of you will[2] remember that Mr. Carson served as special assistant to the president of our organization for more[3] than ten years until his retirement in 1978.

He came to work for us in 1950, when[4] the company was quite small. He worked as a sales representative for five years before being named director[5] of marketing in 1955. He held this position until 1965.

A brief memorial[6] service will be held for Mr. Carson in the main auditorium on Friday, May 26, at 3[7] p.m. Mrs. Carson and her daughter will be present. I am sure that those of you who knew the family[8] personally will wish to attend. Martin Brown [168]

❏ LETTER 371 ❏ (Alertness Exercise)

Reserve, single, accommodate, those, annual, terminal.

Dear Mr. Lee: Thank you for your letter of April 21 asking that we reserve a single room for you[1] for the evenings of June 2, 3, and 4. I wish that we could accommodate you on those dates, Mr. Lee, but,[2] unfortunately, we will not be able to do so. The National Manufacturing Association is[3] holding its annual convention here in Cleveland during that time, and they have reserved all our rooms.

Because you[4] have been a regular customer of ours for many years, we are very sorry that we cannot serve you at[5] this time. We suggest, however, that you try the Lexington Hotel, which is located near the air terminal.[6] It is possible that they will have rooms available during the time you will be here.

We hope you will give us[7] the opportunity to serve you the next time business or pleasure brings you to Chicago,* Mr. Lee. Very[8] sincerely yours,   [163]
*Cleveland

❏ LETTER 372 ❏ (Office Style)

You will not be able, fall, forward, presentation, excellent.

Miss Gates: I was very sorry to learn that you will not be able to attend our fall sales meeting in Burlington,[1] Vermont, next month. I was looking forward to hearing your presentation on how you increased the sales in your[2] region by more than 50 percent in only a year's time. Several of the people here in the main office[3] have heard your presentation, and they tell me that it is excellent.

If it is possible for you to do so,[4] I hope you will plan to make this presentation at the spring meeting in May.

No, make that *in April.*

Jeffrey Nelson [97]

Add this sentence to the letter: *We will be looking forward to seeing you on your next visit to Detroit.*

LESSON 63

◖ LETTER 373 ◖ (Related to Lesson 63, Letter 3)

Guided, Europe, lodging, deposit, scheduled, cancel.

Dear Miss Lee: Thank you very much for your letter asking for more information about our guided tours of Europe.[1] We are delighted to give you the information you need.

We have tours to London, Paris, and Rome leaving[2] on June 1 and July 21. Each tour lasts three weeks, and the low fee of $2,000 covers transportation,[3] meals, lodging, and sight-seeing.

If you want to make a reservation for one of these tours, you should send us[4] your deposit of $200 at least one month before the scheduled date of departure. The balance is[5] due at any time before the tour begins. You may cancel your reservation if you find that you will not be[6] able to make the trip; however, the deposit is not refundable.

We are enclosing a special brochure[7] that gives more information about this once-in-a-lifetime vacation. We hope you will be with us either[8] on June 1 or July 21. Very sincerely yours, [171]

❰ LETTER 374 ❰ (Related to Lesson 63, Letter 4)

[shorthand]

Inquiry, to spend, along, fuel, marinas, personally.

Dear Mr. Stein: Thank you for your inquiry about renting one of our houseboats for the months of June, July, and[1] August. We are very happy that you would like to spend your vacation this year taking a leisurely cruise along[2] the rivers of northern California.

Here are the answers to the questions you asked in your letter:

1. You[3] can rent a boat for the entire summer for $2,000. The price includes the cost of fuel and docking at[4] any of the marinas along the rivers.

2. When you rent one of our boats, you do not have to carry[5] insurance on the houseboat or its contents. However, you are personally responsible for any damage[6] to the boat due to negligence on your part. In addition, if you want personal liability insurance,[7] you must purchase it yourself.

3. You must have a license to operate a boat, of course.

If you want further[8] information, please call me at 555-6602. Very sincerely yours,   [175]

❰ LETTER 375 ❰ (Related to Lesson 63, Letter 5)

[shorthand]

Mailed, application, received, satisfied, stated, publishers.

Ladies and Gentlemen: For the past year I have been a member of the National Book Club. I mailed my application[1] to you last January, and I received five very good books for the low introductory price of[2] $1. I was very well satisfied with these books, and I certainly intended to keep my membership[3] in your organization. Your circular stated that you would offer the latest books from all major publishers[4] at discount prices.

Unfortunately, I have found your selections to be quite limited.

In addition,[5] the prices quoted in your circulars are only slightly lower than those charged in our local bookstore. I had[6] a very difficult time finding five books on your list that I wanted to add to my library during the[7] year.

As you can see, I am quite unhappy with your service. Under the circumstances, I am asking that my[8] membership be canceled immediately and that my name be deleted from your mailing list. Yours truly, [179]

◀ LETTER 376

Cabins, children, facilities, equipped, within, distance, will you please.

Gentlemen: Several days ago I received a circular stating that there were new cabins on the south side[1] of Clear Lake that could be rented for family vacations. My husband, my two children, and I are planning to[2] spend two or three weeks vacationing in this area in June or July, and we would like to know more about[3] the facilities at Clear Lake. Will you please answer the following questions for me:

1. Are the cabins completely[4] furnished and equipped with cooking utensils, dishes, and bedding?

2. Are the cabins within walking distance[5] of the lake and other recreational facilities?

3. What is the weekly charge for renting a cabin[6] during the summer?

Will you please let me hear from you by return mail. I want to complete my vacation plans in[7] the next week or so. Very cordially yours, [148]

◀ LETTER 377 ◀ (Alertness Exercise)

Proposed, recreational, corporation, as you say, aware, actively.

Dear Mr. Keith: Thank you for writing to me about the proposed recreational park that the General[1] Amusement Corporation hopes to build just east of the city near Ford Road. I can easily understand your concern.[2] As you say, the traffic in your vicinity has increased greatly in the past few years. We are, of course, well[3] aware of the problem.

Unfortunately, our city has lost several major businesses in the past few[4] years, and the City Council has been working very hard to find new industries. We always keep in mind, of course,[5] that we want only businesses that will benefit our city without creating problems for us.

We have worked[6] actively to get the General Amusement Corporation to build a recreational park in this[7] area. A park of this type would create thousands of new jobs and would bring in several million dollars annually.[8] We are sure that the benefits far outweigh the problems. You may be sure, however, that we will not allow[9] the construction of the park to begin until we have resolved any possible traffic problems.

Thanks for[10] your interest, Mr. Jones.* We will keep you informed about new developments concerning your area as they[11] occur. Sincerely yours,   [224]
*Keith

❡ LETTER 378 ❡ (Office Style)

Council, municipal, discussing, amusement, agenda.

Dear Mr. Keith: The next meeting of the City Council will be on Wednesday, April 4, at 7 p.m. in[1] Room 703 of the local municipal building. We will be discussing the recreational park[2] that the General Amusement Corporation hopes to build in your area.

Make that *in your neighborhood.*

There are many items on the[3] agenda for that evening, and it will help us if you will ask one member of your group to prepare a short[4] presentation outlining your objections to the proposed park.

We are looking forward to seeing you and the other[5] members of your group at our meeting. Very cordially yours, [112]

Insert this paragraph at the beginning of the letter: *Thank you very much for writing to us again, Mr. Keith. We were glad to hear from you.*

LESSON 64

❬ LETTER 379 ❬ (Related to Lesson 64, Letter 3)

Conducting, experiment, personnel, until, quite, discouraged.

To the Staff: As you know, for the past six months we have been conducting an experiment to determine whether[1] a four-day work-week would be good for our company. The advertising department, the accounting department,[2] and the personnel department have been open from eight in the morning until six in the evening Monday through[3] Thursday. They have been closed all day on Friday, Saturday, and Sunday.

During the first few weeks of the experiment,[4] everyone was quite happy with the new schedule. However, most people became discouraged during the second[5] month. We had a substantial increase in absences, and about 25 percent of the staff members arrived[6] late each morning.

Just two weeks ago we discussed the work schedule with every person affected. Everyone[7] wanted to return to the regular five-day week. Beginning the first week in January, therefore, all[8] departments will again work a five-day week from nine in the morning until five in the afternoon.

Thanks for your[9] cooperation and support during this trial period. James Burlington [194]

◖ LETTER 380 ◖ (Related to Lesson 64, Letter 4)

[shorthand symbols]

Announcement, seriously, decision, indoor, in addition, anticipated.

Dear Miss Woods: Thank you very much for sending me a copy of the announcement about the opening of the[1] new River Tennis Club. My family and I are seriously considering joining the club. Before we[2] make a final decision, however, there are several things we would like to know.

Will you please answer the[3] following questions for us:

1. Will the tennis club have both indoor and outdoor tennis courts?

2. Will the club be open[4] all year?

3. What are the hours that the club will be open each day?

In addition, we would like to know what the[5] anticipated membership fee will be during the second year of operation.

When we receive your answers[6] to these questions, we will be able to decide whether or not we want to become members of the River[7] Tennis Club. We will be looking forward to hearing from you by return mail, Miss Woods. Sincerely yours,   [158]

◖ LETTER 381 ◖ (Related to Lesson 64, Letter 5)

[shorthand symbols]

Years ago, admit, skeptical, durability, unconditional, sturdy.

Dear Mr. Davis: As you will recall, three years ago I purchased a Davis plastic swimming pool from your[1] company. I must admit that at first I was quite skeptical about the durability of the pool. However,[2] the price was amazingly low, and I accepted your unconditional two-year guarantee.

I am very[3] glad to report that the pool has given my family and me three years of excellent service. The pool is[4] in almost the same condition that it was in when I installed it three years ago. You certainly may consider[5] me a satisfied customer. The money I spent for this sturdy pool was very well invested.

You may[6] use my letter as a testimonial if you wish to do so. Sincerely yours,   [135]

[135]

❲ LETTER 382

Membership, limited, facilities, family, clubhouse.

Dear Mr. Lloyd: Thank you for your request for information about the Troy Country Club. We are very happy[1] to answer your questions.

1. Membership in the Troy Country Club is open to anyone who applies. Because[2] of limited facilities, however, we can have only 1,000 members at any given time.

2.[3] The membership fee is $750 per year. All members of your family may use the[4] facilities of the club.

3. The clubhouse and the golf course are open every day of the year. However, the swimming[5] pool is open only during the months of June, July, and August.

If you would like to become a member[6] of the Troy Country Club, please let us know as soon as possible. At the present time we have ten family[7] memberships available. However, we expect them to be taken within the next week or so. Very sincerely[8] yours,
[161]

❲ LETTER 383 ❲ (Alertness Exercise)

Charter, constructing, surrounded, exercise, sauna, expressed.

Dear Mrs. Madison: You are invited to become a charter member of the West Side Health Club.

As you[1] probably know, we have been constructing a beautiful swimming pool and health club at 602 West 14 Street here[2] in San Francisco, California. The pool will cover almost half a city block and will be surrounded by[3] beautiful shrubs and trees. We will have an exercise room, a sauna, and a game room. In short, the West Side Health Club[4] will be just the place for you and your family to enjoy the summer.

Many people have expressed an interest[5] in joining the East* Side Health Club; however, membership will be limited to the first 1,000 people who[6] apply. Don't wait; join today. Just complete the enclosed application form and return it to us along with your[7] first year's family membership fee of $500. You will be guaranteeing yourself and your family[8] a wonderful summer. Sincerely yours,   [168]
* West

Ⅽ LETTER 384 Ⅽ (Office Style)

Almost, practical, dozens, physically, psychologically.

Dear Miss Long: How is your tennis game? Almost everyone who plays tennis would like to play a better game. Now you[1] have the opportunity to learn the secrets of one of the world's best tennis players, Kenneth Greene.

That's spelled *G-r-e-e-n-e.*

Mr. Greene[2] has just completed his practical, easy-to-read book, *Improving Your Tennis Game.*

Be sure to underscore the book title.

Chapter 1, "Getting Yourself[3] Ready To Play Tennis," gives dozens of tips on how to prepare yourself physically and psychologically for[4] the challenging game of tennis.

Chapter 2, "Selecting the Right Racket," tells you how to select the tennis racket[5] that is best for you. It describes the advantages and disadvantages of the various types of rackets[6] on the market today.

There are eight other chapters that deal with every aspect of this fascinating sport.[7] Don't miss this opportunity to become a better tennis player. Get your copy of *Improving Your Tennis[8] Game* today. It is available at your local bookstore for only $10.95. Sincerely[9] yours, [181]

LESSON 65

❮ LETTER 385 ❮ (Related to Lesson 65, Letter 3)

Denmark, scheduled, transportation, guided, countryside, fascinating.

Dear Miss Kelly: Thank you for your inquiry about our vacation tours to Denmark. We are very glad to tell[1] you about them.

We have three tours scheduled for this summer; each lasts two weeks. The tours leave New York on June 1, July[2] 5, and August 16. The low fee of $2,000 includes air transportation to and from Denmark,[3] accommodations in first-class hotels, and two meals per day. The price also includes guided tours of the cities and[4] admission to all museums and parks.

In addition to the scheduled events, you will have seven days on your[5] own. You can rent a car or a bicycle for a ride through the countryside, or you can visit historic sites[6] or attend the theater. If you wish, you can spend the time just relaxing or getting to know the people of this[7] fascinating country.

The enclosed circular gives full details about each of the tours. When you have had an[8] opportunity to read the circular, just call one of our representatives at 555-9630[9] if you have any questions. We hope you will plan to take your vacation this year with us in Denmark. Sincerely[10] yours, [201]

◖ LETTER 386 ◖ (Related to Lesson 65, Letter 4)

Position, qualifications, college, graduated, international, bilingual.

Dear Miss Lexington: Thank you very much for writing to us about the position you have open in your travel[1] agency. We are delighted to tell you that we have a person who has all the qualifications for[2] the job. His name is A. R. Garcia.

Mr. Garcia was born in Mexico and attended college in[3] Texas. He was graduated only two years ago and has been working for an international travel[4] agency in Spain for the past year. He recently returned to the United States and is looking for a[5] position with a good travel agency here.

Mr. Garcia's references tell me that he is very good at[6] detailed work. In addition, he works well with other people and is bilingual. If you would like to discuss the[7] position with Mr. Garcia, you may reach him after 4 p.m. Monday through Friday at 555-8706.[8] If you prefer, you may write to him. His address is 863 23d Street, San Antonio,[9] Texas 78205. Sincerely yours, PS. If you should hire Mr. Garcia, our fee will[10] be equivalent to one month's salary.   [208]

◖ LETTER 387 ◖ (Related to Lesson 65, Letter 5)

Inquiring, magazine, continuing, semiannual, bimonthly, proportionately.

Dear Mr. Young: Thank you for inquiring about the advertising rates for *The National Travel Magazine*.[1] We are enclosing a brochure that shows the cost of advertising in each issue.

As you will note, you can[2] advertise your sporting goods in one edition only, or you can advertise on a continuing basis. If[3] you choose to advertise in one edition only, the prices quoted on page 3 of the brochure are applicable.[4] If you decide to advertise on a

semiannual, bimonthly, or monthly basis, the rates are[5] proportionately lower. These rates are given on pages 4, 5, and 6 of the
brochure.

For further information[6] about the advantages of advertising in
The National Travel Magazine, just call our[7] representative, Miss
Janet Smith, at 555-9906. Very sincerely yours,   [156]

❡ LETTER 388

Perfect, Christmas, bicycle, almost, exercise, discount.

Dear Mrs. Lopez: If you are looking for the perfect gift for your
son this Christmas, we suggest that you purchase[1] a new Madison
bicycle. A Madison bicycle makes the perfect gift for almost anyone. Bicycling[2] is a great deal of fun, and it is extremely good
exercise.

At the Eastern Sporting Goods Shop we have a[3] complete line
of Madison bicycles. They are priced from $100 to $500. If you
place[4] your order before November 15, however, you will receive
a 10 percent discount off the regular[5] price. By ordering early you
will assure yourself that you will get just the bicycle you want in
the color[6] you want.

Make your son's Christmas this year the happiest ever; buy him a
new Madison bicycle from the Eastern[7] Sporting Goods Shop. We
are located at 60 East 21 Street here in Lexington, Kentucky, and
we[8] are open daily from nine to six. Sincerely yours,   [170]

❡ LETTER 389 ❡ (Alertness Exercise)

Citizens', club, activities, we are sure, you will find, volunteer.

Dear Mrs. Lee: Welcome to the Senior Citizens' Club of Jacksonville. We are very happy to have you as a[1] new member.

Enclosed is a list of the many activities planned for the coming year. We are sure that you will[2] find many things that will be of special interest to you. We have scheduled a large number of social activities[3] in the senior citizens' building. In addition, we have three out-of-town trips planned for the members of the[4] club.

We hope that you will also want to consider participating in the volunteer programs at the local[5] libraries, museums, and hospitals.

If you have any friends here in Jackson* who are 65 years of[6] age who would like to participate in any of our programs, please ask them to call Miss Martha Smith at[7] 555-6860.

We will be looking forward to seeing you at our next bimonthly meeting on Saturday,[8] November 21, at 1 p.m. Sincerely yours,

*Jacksonville   [170]

❰ LETTER 390 ❰ (Office Style)

Stenography, procedures, Spanish, English, unqualified.

Dear Ms. Poland: Thank you for your inquiry about Miss Marie Gomez,

> That's spelled *G-o-m-e-z*.

one of my former students here at[1] Interboro Institute.

Miss Gomez studied typing, stenography, and office procedures with me. She is[2] bilingual and can type and take shorthand in both Spanish and English. Miss Gomez graduated last year with a degree[3] in secretarial science. I am happy to say that she was in the top 10 percent of the graduating[4] class.

I can give Miss Gomez my unqualified recommendation. If you hire her to work as an[5] administrative assistant in your travel agency

> Comma.

you will be making no mistake. Very sincerely yours,[6]   [120]

CHAPTER

BUSINESS EQUIPMENT

LESSON 66

(LETTER 391 ((Related to Lesson 66, Letter 3)

Inviting, exhibit, accept, reprographic, booth, afternoon, forward.

Dear Professor Lyons: Thank you very much for inviting our company to have an exhibit at the[1] twentieth annual fall conference of business teachers. We are delighted to accept.

We are planning to have[2] a complete exhibit of all our reprographic equipment on display from 9 a.m. until 6 p.m.[3] on October 12, 13, and 14. Enclosed is a check for $100 to cover the cost of the[4] booth for the three-day conference.

Will it be possible for us to set up our exhibit in the afternoon[5] on October 11? If we can set up the booth before the conference starts, we will be ready to[6] demonstrate our equipment for those teachers who arrive early for the first meeting on October 12.

We are looking[7] forward to exhibiting our equipment at the conference; thanks for the invitation. Sincerely yours,[8]   [160]

TRANSCRIPTION PREVIEW

Typing Style. Transcribe: twentieth annual fall conference (spell out anniversary).

◖ LETTER 392 ◗ (Related to Lesson 66, Letter 4)

[shorthand symbols]

To me, started, thinking, calculators, myself, quite.

Dear Mr. Wheeler: Your recent letter was of great interest to me. It started me thinking about the age of[1] the typewriters, calculators, and duplicators in my office. I checked into this matter myself, and I[2] found that the average age of our machines was more than 10 years. Frankly, this was quite a surprise to me.

I believe[3] it would be a good idea for you to send one of your representatives to my office to discuss the[4] features of the various machines you sell and the cost of your machines. Will you please ask someone to call me at[5] 555-8106 anytime between the hours of nine and five Monday through Friday. I will be looking[6] forward to hearing from you. Very sincerely yours,   [130]

TRANSCRIPTION PREVIEW

Typing Style. Transcribe: 10 years (significant statistic).

◖ LETTER 393 ◗ (Related to Lesson 66, Letter 5)

[shorthand symbols]

Instituting, series, self-improvement, employees, described.

Dear Mr. Brown: Thank you for your very interesting letter about the new self-teaching course in typing that your[1] organization, the Interstate Business College, is offering to companies such as ours.

We are indeed[2] interested in instituting a complete series of self-improvement courses for the employees of our[3] company. We have a number of students who work for our company who did not complete high school. Some of them are[4] only sixteen or seventeen years of age, and I am sure that they would profit greatly from courses such as the[5] one described in your letter.

Will you please ask one of your representatives to come to see me to discuss a[6] series of courses that could be offered in our office building for the benefit of our employees. Very[7] sincerely yours, [143]

Typing Style. Transcribe: sixteen or seventeen (spell out ages).

⟨ LETTER 394

To bring, congratulate, anniversary, procedures, arrange, will you please.

Dear Miss Wilson: It was very nice to receive your invitation to bring my business students to visit your[1] company's main manufacturing plant. I want to congratulate your company on its 125th[2] anniversary. This is indeed a very significant occasion.

I would like to bring my office[3] procedures class to visit your manufacturing plant on Tuesday, September 24. We can arrange to[4] be in the plant at ten in the morning. Will you please let us know if this date and time are satisfactory for[5] you. We are certainly looking forward to seeing how modern business machines are actually made. Very[6] cordially yours, [122]

TRANSCRIPTION PREVIEW

Typing Style. Transcribe: 125th anniversary (ordinals that are more than two words are transcribed in figures).

◖ LETTER 395 ◖ (Alertness Exercise)

[shorthand outlines]

Interested, formerly, college, graduate, computer, technology.

Mrs. White: Yesterday I talked with a friend of mine who is interested in working for our company. Her name[1] is Miss Marie Davis, and she formerly worked at the Eastern Office Machines Company in Newark, New Jersey.[2]

Miss Davis is twenty-three years of age and is a college graduate. Her main interest is computer[3] technology, but I believe she would be a very good marketing representative for our company.

If[4] you would like to meet Miss Smith,* you may get in touch with her by calling 555-8106. If you wish, you[5] may write to her at 1900 West Main Street. Jane Tate   [110]
*Davis

◖ LETTER 396 ◖ (Office Style)

[shorthand outlines]

Suggested, though, capable, marketing, territory.

Miss Tate: Thank you very much for referring Miss Marie Davis to us. As you suggested, I called Miss Davis[1] last week, and she came in for a personal interview.

Paragraph.

Even though Miss Davis is relatively young, I believe[2] that she is quite capable of handling one of our more difficult marketing territories in the East.[3]

Be sure to capitalize *East.*

Miss Davis will join our staff on February 25 and will be working out of the main office for two[4] or three months. After that time she will be assigned her own marketing territory.

Thanks very much, Miss Tate, for[5] providing us with this excellent lead. May White [109]

LESSON 67

❰ LETTER 397 ❰ (Related to Lesson 67, Letter 3)

Pleasure, information, systems, single, communications, within.

Dear Mr. Schultz: It was a pleasure to receive your request for information about the new Cunningham business[1] telephone systems that our company manufactures. At the present time our company makes only[2] internal telephone systems for use in a single building; we do not handle lines between the four cities in[3] the South in which you have offices—Houston, Dallas, Atlanta, and Miami.

However, there is one good way[4] that our company can help you save money—through interoffice communications in your main building here in[5] Atlanta. We can install an internal communications system that will connect every office within[6] the building. An executive in any office can call any other person in the building simply by[7] dialing a four-number extension. Each person in the building can communicate with any other person[8] easily and quickly.

If you are interested in this internal office communications system, we will[9] be glad to have one of our well-trained, experienced representatives come to your office to discuss our service[10] with you. You will be surprised at how little it costs. Very truly yours, [214]

TRANSCRIPTION PREVIEW

Typing Style. Dashes after *in which you have offices* and after *help you save money.*

❰ LETTER 398 ❰ (Related to Lesson 67, Letter 4)

Months ago, electronic, report, they wanted, deserved, formally.

Dear Depositor: Just six months ago we opened our first electronic cash machine at the Greenville National[1] Bank. We are very glad to report that the cash machine was an immediate success. In fact, it was so[2] popular that we sometimes had a line of people waiting to use the machine. We knew that we should install more[3] machines in order to give our depositors the kind of service they wanted and deserved.

On Monday, March[4] 27, we will formally open three new cash machines in convenient locations throughout the city—in[5] the Eastern Shopping Center, in the Central Shopping Mall, and in the uptown airlines terminal.

These new cash machines[6] will be open at all hours of the day and night. We are sure that they will make banking at the Greenville National[7] Bank even easier and more convenient for you than ever before. Sincerely yours,   [157]

TRANSCRIPTION PREVIEW

Typing Style.   Dash after *throughout the city.*

❰ LETTER 399 ❰ (Related to Lesson 67, Letter 5)

Requested, notification, typewriters, satisfied, lengthy, circumstances.

Mr. Porter: As you requested, I sent a letter of notification to each department head stating[1] that we would not be replacing all the typewriters in their offices this year. Each department head was satisfied[2] with the decision except one—Mr. Tate of the accounting department.

Mr. Tate wrote a lengthy report[3] stating that the average age of the typewriters in his division is 11 years. He feels that it[4] is false economy to try to keep half of these old machines operating for another year. He further[5] states that he spent nearly $500 on typewriter repairs alone during the past fiscal year.

Under[6] the circumstances, I recommend that we replace all the typewriters in Mr. Tate's department. Will you please[7] let me know your feelings about this matter. Nora Carson   [151]

TRANSCRIPTION PREVIEW

Typing Style.   Dash after *except one.*

ℂ LETTER 400

Interview, position, he wanted, resignation, advanced, degree.

Miss Adams: Several months ago you brought a young man by the name of Max Cunningham to my office to[1] interview for a position as a marketing representative for our office equipment. He was from[2] Seattle—or was it Spokane?

At the time I talked with him, we did not have a position open in the South, where[3] he wanted to work. This morning, however, I received a letter of resignation from Betty Green, our[4] representative in New Orleans, Louisiana. She is leaving our organization in order to complete[5] an advanced degree in business administration. Her position will be open after the first of June.[6]

Will you please contact Mr. Cunningham to see if he is still looking for a marketing position. Please let[7] me know as soon as you contact him. A. C. Hughes   [149]

TRANSCRIPTION PREVIEW

Typing Style.   Dash after *Seattle.*

❡ LETTER 401 ❡ (Alertness Exercise)

[shorthand symbols]

Copy, useful, worthwhile, valuable, personal.

To All Department Heads: Enclosed is a copy of a new sales manual that I think the members of your[1] department will find particularly useful. It is entitled *Selling Techniques That Work*. There are two parts that should[2] be quite worthwhile—the part on getting the customer's attention and the part on closing a sale.

When you have had[3] an opportunity to read the manual yourself, please route it to the various members of your department.[4]

If you feel that there is enough valuable information in *Marketing* Techniques That Work*, we will ask our[5] purchasing agent to get enough copies in order for each employee to have a personal copy. Ellen[6] James   [121]
*Selling

❡ LETTER 402 ❡ (Office Style)

[shorthand symbols]

Coming, products, offices, emphasis, calculators, computers.

Mr. Moore:

> That's spelled *M-o-o-r-e.*

During the coming year three cities will be used as test marketing sites for our new office machines[1] products—Philadelphia, Baltimore, and Washington.

We will open sales offices in each of these cities[2] before the first of December, and we hope to have a complete sales force hired before the middle of January.[3]

> Make that *before the first of January.*

We will place special emphasis on our new line of electronic adding machines, calculators, and desk-top[4] computers. If our sales are good in these three cities during the coming year, we will expand our operation[5] to include the entire East Coast the following year.

Will you please set up a meeting of our New York marketing[6] staff sometime before the end of October. I want everyone concerned to understand the scope of this project[7] thoroughly. Anne Washington   [146]

LESSON 68

❧ LETTER 403 ❧ (Related to Lesson 68, Letter 3)

Disturbed, between, proper, installed, contacted, capabilities.

Ms. Winters: I was quite disturbed to receive your memorandum of Monday, January 5, concerning the[1] use of the computer that we are leasing from the National Business Machines Company in Cincinnati,[2] Ohio. No one knows better than I that our office staff is not making full use of the computer at this[3] time. Between you and me, I think the problem is that we did not give our employees proper training at the time[4] the computer was installed.

Last week I contacted the National Business Machines Company and asked that they[5] send one of their people to our offices next week to help our staff learn the capabilities of the machine.[6] We are planning to have an all-day training session next Wednesday.

Under the circumstances, I suggest that you[7] delay making a final decision about the matter until the end of March. J. D. Gomez   [158]

❧ LETTER 404 ❧ (Related to Lesson 68, Letter 4)

Interesting, computer, inordinate, amount, observing, increase.

Mr. Welsh: In today's mail I received a very interesting letter from Mr. R. D. Chang of the General[1] Computer Company. In the letter Mr. Chang askcd: "Do your office employees spend hundreds of hours every[2] month posting customers' purchases to their accounts? Do your employees spend an inordinate amount of[3] time checking and reviewing account totals? Do your employees need several days to prepare end-of-month reports?"[4]

It seems as though Mr. Chang might have been observing our office operations; we certainly are having[5] those kinds of problems.

Mr. Chang suggests that a General computer can help us to increase our office[6] efficiency and save money at the same time. Under the circumstances, I think it would be wise for us to contact[7] the General Computer Company and ask for a demonstration of a new computer. What do you[8] think? Martin Trent   [163]

❮ LETTER 405 ❮ (Related to Lesson 68, Letter 5)

Frankly, amusing, expensive, required, those, competitor.

Dear Mr. Mason: I received your letter in the mail this morning. Frankly, I found it quite amusing. Yes, my bank[1] did lease an expensive computer only to find out that we were not getting our money's worth. Yes, we did purchase[2] a small computer only to find that it was not capable of performing all the required work in our[3] bank.

We leased the first computer and purchased the second computer from your company, the General Computer[4] Company. I am sure our problems were not significantly different from those of many other banks.[5] Fortunately, we were able to get just the right computer at the right price from a competitor of yours[6] about six months ago.

We are quite satisfied with the computer, and we are not planning to change models in[7] the near future. Very truly yours, [147]

❏ LETTER 406

Discharge, excellent, closely, situation, two or three, excessive.

Mr. Kelly: I was very sorry to learn that you feel that you should discharge Edward Smith. When Mr. Smith came[1] to us from the Western Manufacturing Company, I had high hopes that he would be an excellent employee.[2] However, you have been working closely with him for almost six months and know the situation much better[3] than I.

I can easily see why you do not want to keep an employee who is late two or three times each week.[4] I can also understand your concern about his excessive absence and his poor attitude. Frankly, I do[5] not know how to handle those kinds of problems.

I suggest, however, that you have a confidential conversation[6] with Mr. Smith and give him one more chance. If his attitude does not improve, then you definitely should go[7] ahead with dismissal procedures. Ellen Marks   [150]

❏ LETTER 407 ❏ (Alertness Exercise)

Exhibit, different, automatic, allows, extensions, building.

Dear Miss Temple: We are happy to invite you to this year's business machines exhibit that will be held during[1] the week of September 17 in the Scott Hotel in Chicago, Illinois. At this year's exhibit we[2] will be showing our new line of interoffice telephones.

We know that you will be interested because these[3] telephones are different *than** those that we have shown in past years. Every phone is equipped with an automatic dialing[4] feature that allows you to reach up to nine extensions in your building without actually dialing the full[5] extension number. You need only to touch the special button in the lower left corner of the keyboard plus[6] one number button that you have especially assigned to the extension that you call frequently.

We are sure[7] you will be fascinated by this new improvement in interoffice telephone systems, and we are looking[8] forward to explaining it to you in further detail at our exhibit in Chicago in September. Very[9] cordially yours,   [184]
*from

❡ LETTER 408 ❡ (Office Style)

Electronic, calculators, patronage, promptly, discontinued.

Dear Mr. Morris:

That's spelled *M-o-r-r-i-s.*

Thanks for your recent order for one of our Model 11 electronic calculators.[1] We appreciate your order and your patronage over the years. We wish we could fill your order promptly;[2] unfortunately, we cannot do so.

The model that you ordered has been discontinued, and we are completely[3] out of stock.

Delete *completely.*

We suggest, however, that you let us send you a Model 16, which is only slightly[4] different from the Model 11. It has all the same features. In addition, it has a memory key that[5] we think you will find quite handy. The Model 16 ordinarily sells for $95. Because you[6] are a valued customer of ours, we will send you one of these fine new calculators for $85,[7] which is only $10 more than the cost of the Model 11.

Please let us know what you would like us to[8] do by jotting a note at the bottom of this letter and returning it to us in the self-addressed envelope[9] that is provided. Very sincerely yours,   [189]

LESSON 69

❰ LETTER 409 ❰ (Related to Lesson 69, Letter 3)

[shorthand symbols]

Radio, tuning, carefully, tax, if you wish, we are sure, just.

Dear Mr. Edwards: Thank you for your order for a new Model 12 National radio. We are happy to[1] tell you that the radio is on its way to you now. We are also sending a complete set of instructions[2] for tuning and adjusting the radio. The set will give much better service if you read the instructions[3] carefully before operating the radio.

The complete cost of the radio is $90. This includes[4] the price of the radio itself, the sales tax, and the shipping charges. You may pay the $90 now[5] if you wish. If you prefer, you may pay for the radio in three equal payments of $30.

We are[6] sure that the radio will give satisfactory service for many years. If you should have any trouble with[7] it during the first year, just return it to us. We will either repair it or replace it free of charge. Very[8] sincerely yours, [163]

❰ LETTER 410 ❰ (Related to Lesson 69, Letter 4)

[shorthand symbols]

Music, create, atmosphere, frankly, skeptical, ahead.

Dear Mr. Madison: Several months ago I leased a new National music system from your company.[1] At the time you assured me that the music would create just the right atmosphere in our store and would actually[2] increase sales. Frankly, I was somewhat skeptical, but I went ahead with the installation anyway.

I am[3] happy to say that the system is working perfectly. Many people have commented that they enjoy the music[4] and that it makes shopping more enjoyable for them. In addition, our sales have increased nearly 5 percent[5] since we installed the system.

If you have further ideas about how to make my business more profitable, I[6] hope you will tell me about them. Very cordially yours, [130]

❐ LETTER 411 ❐ (Related to Lesson 69, Letter 5)

Thanks, posture, models, will you please, discuss, secretarial.

Dear Mr. Carter: Thanks for your letter of Tuesday, April 21, inviting me to try two or three of[1] the posture chairs that your company sells. I plan to purchase new chairs for my entire suite of offices in the[2] next few months, and I would like to try several models of chairs.

Will you please ask one of your representatives[3] to come to my office at 186 Tenth Avenue any day during the next week or so. I would like[4] to discuss the cost of purchasing 5 executive chairs, 10 secretarial chairs, and 12 chairs for our[5] reception area. I need to know the various styles and colors available as well as the cost of each.[6]

I will be looking forward to hearing from you soon. Sincerely yours, [133]

❐ LETTER 412

Identification, photograph, resent, understand, procedure, handle.

To All Department Heads: On Monday, August 12, we will begin using the newly installed identification[1] system for all customers who wish to pay for their purchases by check.

Whenever a customer pays for[2] any item by check, we will take a photograph of the customer and the check itself. It will take only[3] a few seconds' time and should help us to reduce our losses from bad checks.

Many people may resent having[4] to have their pictures taken when they want to pay for a purchase by check. However, when you explain to them that this[5] is a program designed to keep our costs down and will help to keep our prices down, I am sure they will understand.[6]

Enclosed is a procedure chart that describes how to handle all checks written in the store. Will you please post a[7] copy of the chart by every cash register and be sure that the employees in your area understand[8] the procedure thoroughly. Jane Price   [167]

❡ LETTER 413 ❡ (Alertness Exercise)

System, actually, unusual, stolen, reduce, cooperation.

Dear Customer: On Monday, August 12, we will begin using a new identification system for all[1] customers who pay for purchases by check. We will actually take a small photograph of the person and the[2] check. This photograph will be for our records only and will be used only in unusual cases.[3]

Unfortunately, we have received a significant number of bad checks during the past year. In addition, we have[4] had several cases in which payment for purchases was made with checks that had been stolen. Our new procedure[5] should help us to reduce those *kind** of problems.

We hope you will understand the necessity for our having to[6] take this action at this time; we will appreciate your cooperation. Sincerely yours,   [137]
*kinds

❡ LETTER 414 ❡ (Office Style)

Glad to say, computer, in addition, economically, successful.

To All Department Heads: Our new checkout procedure has been in operation for a year now, and I am glad[1] to say that it is working very satisfactorily.

Delete *very.*

Through the use of the computer, we have been able[2] to decrease our customers' waiting time by as much as 75 percent. In addition, we have been able[3] to operate more efficiently and economically. In the past we have had to hire as many as[4] 20 part-time cashiers to work on Fridays and Saturdays. During the past year we have had to hire part-time[5] employees on only two occasions.

Our procedure has been so successful that we are planning to institute[6] it in all our stores throughout the South.

Thanks for your cooperation during the past year; your cooperation[7] has been invaluable. Marie Davis   [147]

Send a copy of this memo to James Simms and Mary Smith.

LESSON 70

⊄ LETTER 415 ⊄ (Related to Lesson 70, Letter 3)

Memorandum, postponement, accepted, cancel, ahead, posted.

Mr. Case: Thanks for your memorandum concerning the postponement of the executive committee meeting.[1] Unfortunately, I will not be able to attend the meeting on Wednesday, July 10. Several months ago[2] I accepted a speaking engagement in Cleveland, Ohio, and I do not feel that it would be a good[3] idea for me to cancel it at this time.

If you wish to go ahead with the meeting, please keep me posted[4] concerning any action that the committee takes. If you decide to select another date for the meeting, I[5] suggest the following Monday morning at 9 o'clock. A. M. Davis   [113]

⫷ LETTER 416 ⫷ (Related to Lesson 70, Letter 4)

Attention, confusion, offices, birthday, preceding, to celebrate.

To the Staff: It has come to my attention that there is some confusion over the date of our next company[1] holiday, Presidents' Day. We have been closing our offices on February 22, which is Washington's[2] Birthday. Several years ago, however, the government began using the Monday preceding February[3] 22 as the official date to celebrate all presidents' birthdays. All post offices and banks[4] are closed on this day, and our board of directors has decided that it would be a good idea for our company[5] to celebrate Presidents' Day on a Monday each year.

There are two major advantages for doing this:[6]

1. We will always have a three-day weekend.

2. Our offices will not be open on a day that the post offices[7] and banks are closed.

Our offices will be closed all day February 18 this year. We will be open for[8] business as usual on Friday, February 22. Harry Simmons [174]

⫷ LETTER 417 ⫷ (Related to Lesson 70, Letter 5)

Acknowledge, memorandum, postdated, ourselves, cited.

Miss Drake: This is to acknowledge your memorandum of December 28 concerning our company's[1] accepting postdated checks for payment of goods.

I can easily understand why it is necessary for our[2] company to charge interest on accounts that are not paid for three or four months. When we must pay 14 percent[3] interest ourselves, we can hardly make it a policy to let our customers take months to pay for goods without[4] an interest charge.

In the two cases you cited in your memorandum, however, I believe we are faced with[5] a very special situation. Lexington and Associates made two purchases from us recently. One[6] was for $300; the other was for $800. As you know, Lexington and Associates[7] is a small business machines company that has been a good customer of ours for many years. Several months[8] ago their store was destroyed by fire. Unfortunately, the company was underinsured. I felt that it was[9] a good idea for us to let them have some extra time to pay their bills while they are recovering from this fire.[10]

I will, of course, accept no further postdated checks unless I have the prior approval of the company[11] controller. Ellen Ward

[224]

❡ LETTER 418

Postpone, finance, committee, members, actually, until.

Mr. Jennings: I am very sorry that we must postpone our next meeting of the finance committee. As you[1] know, many of the members of this committee actually postponed their vacations in order to be able[2] to attend the meeting. It is not likely that we will be able to get the complete committee together[3] again until September.

I hope you will reconsider your decision and allow the meeting to take place[4] as originally planned. Mary Stein   [87]

❡ LETTER 419 ❡ (Alertness Exercise)

Thanks, poor, speedy, recovery, early, agreement.

Dear Miss Day: Thanks for your letter of Wednesday, October 21, in which you explain your reason for having[1] to postpone your business trip to Albany. I am very sorry that you have been in poor health, and I wish you[2] a speedy recovery.

Unfortunately, I will not be able to wait until December to select[3] an advertising agency. I would like to come to an early agreement so that we can begin our[4] advertising plans immediately. I must make a decision within the next few weeks, and I hope you will let[5] me know if you will be able to send someone from your company to discuss the plans in detail with me.

I[6] will be looking forward to hearing from you, Miss Smith.*
Sincerely yours,   [133]
*Day

❡ LETTER 420 ❡ (Office Style)

You will not be able, machines, extremely, associate, arrangements.

Dear Mrs. Anderson: I am very sorry that you will not be able to wait until December in order[1] to complete your plans to advertise your office machines next year. I am extremely sorry that it was[2] necessary for me to postpone my business trip to Albany.

I will, of course, send someone to represent our[3] advertising agency. My associate, Miss Anne Tailor,

> That's *A-n-n-e T-a-i-l-o-r.*

can come to your office on a day that will be[4] convenient for you.

> Send a copy of this letter to Miss Tailor.

Please call my office collect at (212) 555-8608 to make arrangements[5] for Miss Tailor's visit. Sincerely yours,   [107]

CHAPTER

GOODWILL AND PUBLIC RELATIONS

LESSON 71

⟨ LETTER 421 ⟨ (Related to Lesson 71, Letter 3)

Clearance, annually, permitted, reductions, different, gratitude.

To All Department Heads: As you know, our department store has held two 3-day clearance sales annually for the[1] past several years. The first is held after the Christmas season in January, and the second is held after[2] Independence Day in July.

In the past we have never permitted anyone to take advantage of[3] the special reductions in our prices until the first day of the sale. However, this year we are planning something[4] different. As a way of expressing our gratitude to our preferred customers, we are having a special[5] sale for them. On Monday evening, January 10, which is the day before our regular sale begins, we[6] will close our doors at 5 p.m. and reopen them at 6 p.m.—but only to our preferred customers. These[7] customers will be able to take advantage of the special prices that will be available to the[8] general public the following day.

Will you please be sure that each member of your sales staff understands our plans for[9] this special sale. If this sale proves to be successful, we will probably have a similar sale for our pre-ferred[10] customers this summer and again next winter. Max Hugo

[211]

TRANSCRIPTION PREVIEW

Typing Style. Transcribe: two 3-day clearance sales (spell out the first number).

❡ LETTER 422 ❡ (Related to Lesson 71, Letter 4)

Circulars, finishing, technical, presses, schedule, originally, discount.

Dear Mr. Harrington: You will be happy to know that we shipped your 1,000 four-page circulars to you this[1] morning. I am very sorry that there was a one-week delay in finishing this job for you.

Until ten days[2] ago we were sure that we could finish our work and ship the circulars to you on time. However, we experienced[3] several technical problems with our printing presses, and we were not able to meet our schedule. Because[4] we were not able to fill your order by the date that we had originally promised, we are giving[5] you a 10 percent discount on the cost of the circulars.

You have been a good customer of ours for many[6] years, and we want to keep your goodwill. We will make every effort to be sure that there is no delay in filling[7] your orders in the future. Cordially yours,

[148]

TRANSCRIPTION PREVIEW

Typing Style. Transcribe: 1,000 four-page circulars (spell out the shorter number).

⊄ LETTER 423 ⊄ (Related to Lesson 71, Letter 5)

Selected, bid, quite, disappointed, accept, area, next time.

Dear Ms. Long: Thank you for your letter of Friday, August 1, telling us that you had not selected our bid for[1] the construction of the addition to your motel. We were, of course, quite disappointed. However, we can[2] easily understand that you feel you should accept the lowest bid.

Our company is presently building four[3] 9-unit apartment buildings just east of the city. They are located on Country Road. When you are in the[4] area, we hope you will stop by to see them. We are very happy with the job, and we think you will be impressed[5] with the high quality of the design and of the work.

The next time you have a large construction job, we hope you[6] will give us the opportunity of making a bid. Next time we may be able to submit a bid that you[7] feel is acceptable. Sincerely yours,   [147]

TRANSCRIPTION PREVIEW

Typing Style.   Transcribe: four 9-unit apartment buildings (spell out the first number).

⊄ LETTER 424

Certainly, experiencing, frankly, transfer, regional, headquarters.

Miss Burns: Your idea certainly sounds like a good one to me. I am aware, of course, of the housing shortage that[1] we are experiencing here in Springfield. Frankly, I do not expect the problem to be resolved for several[2] years.

I definitely believe that we should lease at least three 2-bedroom apartments on a long-term basis[3] for the use of the executives we want to transfer from our regional offices throughout the United[4] States to our company headquarters here in the city. I am confident that we would actually reduce our[5] expenses in the long run. In addition, it will be easier to get our competent, promising, and[6] capable executives to transfer to the company headquarters.

I want to place this matter on the agenda[7] for the next regularly scheduled meeting of the board of directors on October 23. Alvin[8] Moore   [161]

TRANSCRIPTION PREVIEW

Typing Style. Transcribe: three 2-bedroom apartments (spell out the first number).

❬ LETTER 425 ❬ (Alertness Exercise)

Comments, manuscript, prepared, appreciate, discussed, justified.

Mrs. Carter: Thank you for your comments about the manuscript that I prepared for the brochure that we are planning[1] to distribute to those who attend our convention in Baltimore, Maryland, in April. I certainly[2] appreciate the time you took to go over the material, and I can easily understand your concern[3] about the cost of printing 1,000 eight-page brochures.

I have discussed the matter with the company that[4] does all the printing, and they assured me that the cost of an eight-page brochure will be only about 25[5] percent higher than the cost of a four-page brochure. Frankly, I think that the additional investment of[6] 20 percent* is justified. Therefore, I am recommending that we go ahead with our original plans. May[7] Stone   [141]
*25 percent

◖ LETTER 426 ◗ (Office Style)

[shorthand symbols]

Reports, congratulate, excellent, thorough, statistical, extend.

Mr. Lopez: In today's mail I received the three 200-page reports that you prepared for our public[1] relations department. I want to congratulate you on the excellent job that you did. The reports are accurate,[2] complete, and thorough. The statistical information is presented in an interesting, informative[3] way, and the charts and tables are easy to understand.

There is no doubt in my mind that this year's reports are vastly[4]

No, delete *vastly;* on second thought, leave it in.

superior to those that we prepared last year. Please extend my congratulations to each member of your[5] staff who helped to prepare these fine reports. James Clayton [110]

Send a copy of this memorandum to Miss Smith.

LESSON 72

◖ LETTER 427 ◗ (Related to Lesson 72, Letter 3)

[shorthand symbols]

Copies, revised, delighted, editions, arranging, choosing, submit.

Dear Mr. Lang: Yesterday I received the 14 copies of the two books that I revised. Needless to say, I[1] am delighted that the new editions are now in print.

You and your staff members (all five of them) did an outstanding[2] job in arranging the material on the pages and in choosing the interior colors. The books[3] certainly are attractively printed and bound.

I have enjoyed working with you and will be sure to submit

my[4] next manuscript for publication to you and your publishing firm. Thank you for doing an outstanding job.[5] Cordially yours,

[102]

TRANSCRIPTION PREVIEW

Punctuation. Place parentheses around *all five of them* to deemphasize the expression.

❬ LETTER 428 ❬ (Related to Lesson 72, Letter 4)

Pleasure, provided, graduated, enjoyment, radio.

Dear Miss Wheeler: It was a pleasure seeing you when you came to the Webber Department Store last week to pick up[1] one of the special gifts that we provided for each of you who graduated in the top 10 percent of your[2] class at Eastern Business College. We hope that you will receive many hours of enjoyment from the radio that[3] you chose as your special gift.

We also hope that you will take the opportunity to open a charge account[4] with our department store. All you need to do is: (1) fill out the enclosed application, (2) sign it in the space[5] indicated, and (3) return the completed form to us in the envelope that is provided.

We look forward[6] to receiving your application and to seeing you in our store in the near future. Sincerely yours, [139]

TRANSCRIPTION PREVIEW

Punctuation. Place parentheses around the numbers accompanying the enumerated items: *(1), (2), (3).*

⊄ LETTER 429 ⊄ (Related to Lesson 72, Letter 5)

[shorthand symbols]

Community, theater, report, performances, empty, extend, theatrically.

Mr. Wilson: I am very glad to see that the first production of the Wichita Community Theater[1] was a financial success (see the attached report). We were sold out for every one of the performances except[2] one. That particular performance was on a cold, snowy evening in November. Even on that day there[3] were only 20 empty seats.

I want to extend my sincere congratulations to everyone who worked so[4] hard to make this show successful both theatrically and financially.

We are looking forward to our next[5] production in January. If all goes well, our second show should be even more successful than our first. James[6] Lexington   [121]

TRANSCRIPTION PREVIEW

Punctuation. Place parentheses around *see the attached report* to de-emphasize the expression.

⊄ LETTER 430

[shorthand symbols]

Begin, submitted, include, standard, format, let me.

Mr. Garcia: Will you please begin this year's financial report that is to be submitted to the board of[1] directors at its next meeting. We will need to include: (1) gross sales, (2) operating expenses, and (3) net[2] income for the fiscal period. You will need to submit the report in a standard format (see the attached[3] sheet).

If you have any questions about the report, please let me know as soon as possible; I will be glad to[4] help you obtain any statistics that you need. Paul Craft [90]

TRANSCRIPTION PREVIEW

Punctuation. Place parentheses around the numbers accompanying the enumerated items: *(1), (2), (3)*.

❡ LETTER 431 ❡ (Alertness Exercise)

Executive, committee, redecorated, formerly, blocks, proposed.

To the Members of the Executive Committee: On Friday, January 21, the executive[1] committee of International Enterprises will hold its monthly meeting. Because the boardroom is being[2] redecorated at this time, we will meet in the executive suite of the George Washington Hotel (formerly[3] the Holiday Hotel). The George Washington Hotel is located at 602 East 21 Street, which[4] is only four blocks from our office building.

At the meeting we will discuss: (1) our proposed sales budget for the[5] coming year, (2) last year's sales performance, and (3) staff additions for the next three months.

The meeting will begin at[6] 2:30 p.m. (on Thursday*). Please note the date and time on your calendar now. Henry Strong [137]
*Friday

❡ LETTER 432 ❡ (Office Style)

Today's, budget, regions, summary, fortunate.

Dear Dr. Reed: Seldom do we take the opportunity to tell our good customers just how much we appreciate[1] them. It seems as though the only time many of our customers hear from us is when they are behind in[2] their payments. That is certainly not the case with you, however.

On checking our records, I found that you have been[3] a regular customer of ours for the past five years and that you have purchased many items from us. I hope[4] you have been pleased with every one of your purchases.

I also found that you have handled your account in a very[5] fine manner. Not once have you missed a payment or even been late with a payment. This is a commendable[6] record, Dr. Reed.

If you should need a credit reference at any time, please do not hesitate to call on[7] you.* We will give you a very good recommendation. Sincerely yours,   [153]

*us

❰ LETTER 438 ❰ (Office Style)

Very glad, developments, appreciated, gracious, in the future, decided.

Gentlemen: Thank you for sending your representative, Mr. C. R. Greene,

That's G-r-e-e-n-e.

to our offices last week. We were[1] very glad to learn about all the new developments in the field of electronic computers.

Please send a copy of this letter to Mr. Greene.

We want you[2] to know how much we appreciated talking with Mr. Greene. It was a pleasure to learn about the new[3] developments without having any pressure placed on us to purchase a new computer system for our company.[4] Mr Greene was a gracious representative who shared information with us and let us make up our own[5] minds about the purchase of a new computer.

Mr. Jackson: In today's mail I received a copy of next year's sales budget for each of our five sales regions[1] (see the summary on the attached sheet). Frankly, I think the sales budget is much too high for three of the five regions.[2] I think we will be fortunate indeed to reach 90 percent of the projected budget.

Under the[3] circumstances, I suggest that you ask each of the regional managers to review their particular budgets[4] very carefully. If they accept the budgets as stated, I think they will regret having done so by the[5] end of the year.

Make that *fiscal* year.

Please let me know the findings as soon as possible. L. C. Carpenter   [116]

Send a copy of this memorandum to Mr. R. A. Smith.

LESSON 73

❰ LETTER 433 ❰ (Related to Lesson 73, Letter 3)

Formal, reception, retiring, contribution, wonderful, possible.

Miss Miller: I was happy to read that you are planning to have a formal reception and dinner for Ms. Judy[1] Gray, who will be retiring shortly. You may count on my being there. Enclosed is the top half of the form you[2] mailed to me; I will retain the bottom half to serve as my admission ticket. I am also enclosing a[3] check for $25 for my ticket and for my contribution toward a gift.

Ms. Gray is a wonderful[4] person; she has affected my life and my attitude greatly over the years. I am sure that she has also[5] had a great effect on the lives of the other people with whom she has worked.

If you need any help with the[6] arrangements for the reception or the dinner, please let me know. I will be more than willing to help in any way[7] possible. James Reed   [144]

❰ LETTER 434 ❱ (Related to Lesson 73, Letter 4)

[shorthand]

Months ago, beautiful, automobile, recommended, maintenance.

Dear Mr. Powers: Eleven months ago you purchased a beautiful new Lexington automobile from our[1] agency. We are confident that you will receive excellent service from this car and that you are very well[2] pleased with it.

However, we recommended when you bought the car that you bring it to our service department in[3] six months for a routine maintenance check. Five months ago we mailed you a reminder stating that it was time for[4] a checkup, and we even scheduled an appointment for you. Unfortunately, you did not acknowledge our letter,[5] and you did not bring in your car for service.

It is necessary for even the very best cars to be[6] checked on a regular basis. If you fail to have your car serviced properly, its performance can be severly[7] affected.

Please take a moment right now, Mr. Powers, to call our service department at 555-8672.[8] We will make an appointment for you to bring your car in for that checkup that is now five months[9] overdue. Sincerely yours, [184]

❰ LETTER 435 ❱ (Related to Lesson 73, Letter 5)

[shorthand]

Years ago, certificates, annual, mature, maturity.

Dear Ms. Pierce: Nearly two years ago you invested your ready cash in three 2-year time certificates at the[1] First National Bank. During those two years your money has been hard at work for you. You have earned 10 percent annual[2] interest on the money you invested with us.

On March 3 your three certificates will mature. You have[3] several options available. They are as follows:

1. You may redeem the principal plus the interest afte_ date of maturity.

2. You may retain your time certificates, and we will rei_ your funds for an[5] additional two-year period.

3. You may place your funds in a regular checking account special[6] savings account.

The enclosed circular gives all the details about each of th_ options. When you have read the[7] circular, just fill out the attach_ form, sign it, and mail it to us in the envelope that is provided.

We will[8] be looking forward to hearing from you. Sincere_ yours, [17_

❰ LETTER 436 ❱

[shorthand]

Sweater, color, actually, return, accepted, congratulate.

Dear Mr. Case: Several days ago I purchased a new red sweater from your store at 406 West 21[1] Street in Dover, Delaware. When I took the sweater home, I found that it was not the right color. It was[2] actually much too light to use with the suit that I was trying to match.

Because the sweater was on sale, I was sure[3] that I would not be able to return it. However, I decided that it was worth a try. I took it back[4] to the store yesterday. The clerk not only accepted the sweater for full credit but also helped me find[5] another red sweater that was exactly the right shade to match my suit.

This kind of service can have only a very[6] positive effect on your business, Mr. Case. I congratulate you on having friendly, courteous people[7] who are willing to take a little extra time to be sure that each customer is satisfied with each purchase.[8] You may be sure that I will do the majority of my shopping for new clothes in your store. Sincerely yours,[9] [180]

❰ LETTER 437 ❱ (Alertness Exercise)

[shorthand]

Seldom, how much, behind, items, account, record.

He is a likable person who will have a very good effect[6] on your business in the future.

You will be glad to know that after much discussion, we have decided that[7] we should go ahead with the purchase of a new computer shortly after the first of the year. We will be calling[8] Mr. Greene to come to our offices once again to accept our order. Very sincerely yours, [178]

LESSON 74

⊄ LETTER 439 ⊄ (Related to Lesson 74, Letter 3)

Congratulations, throughout, recruitment, college, mentioned, representatives.

Bob: I want to extend my congratulations to you, to your staff, and to the four students who traveled throughout[1] the state on your recruitment program for our college. When you mentioned to me that you wanted to take students with[2] you this year, I knew that you would have very good results.

When you told me which students you wanted to take, I knew[3] you had made wise choices. The students—James Smith, Betty Brown, Max Tate, and Janet Garcia—are excellent[4] representatives for our college.

Thank you for sending the list of potential students. I am impressed that you obtained[5] commitments from so many good students in our area; we have received many of their application forms[6] already.

Keep up the good work. Frank Long [127]

⊄ LETTER 440 ⊄ (Related to Lesson 74, Letter 4)

Congratulatory, remodeled, enlarged, hardware, family, impressed.

Gentlemen: This is just a congratulatory note to tell you how much we enjoyed visiting and shopping[1] in your newly remodeled and enlarged hardware store. My family and I attended your grand opening on[2] Saturday, April 10, and were impressed with the size and beauty of your store.

Thank you for providing the citizens[3] of Medford, Massachusetts, with such a fine hardware store in which to shop. Thank you, too, for the special invitation[4] to your sale. Very cordially yours,   [88]

ℂ LETTER 441 ℂ (Related to Lesson 74, Letter 5)

Membership, surprised, earlier, ideals, outweigh, happenings.

Gentlemen: Enclosed is my check for $50 for my membership dues for the coming year. I was not surprised[1] that the dues were raised; in fact, I was surprised that they had not been raised earlier.

I believe in the ideals[2] and goals of our organization, and I understand the reason for the increase in dues. The benefits that[3] I derive far outweigh the cost of my dues. If it were not for our professional organization, I would[4] not be able to keep up to date with the happenings and laws in real estate.

Thank you for doing such a fine[5] job. Very truly yours,   [104]

ℂ LETTER 442

Thank you very much, request, you have been, certainly, goodwill, guidelines.

Dear Mr. Green: Thank you very much for your recent request that we increase your credit line from $500[1] to $1,000. We certainly wish we were able to do this. You have been a good customer of[2] ours for many years, and we certainly want to retain your good-will and your business.

Unfortunately, our board[3] of directors recently issued new guide-lines concerning open lines of credit. We will not be able to[4] extend credit lines above their present limits during the coming year.

Please accept our apologies for not[5] being able to grant your request. We look forward to serving you in the future. Sincerely yours, [118]

❮ LETTER 443 ❮ (Alertness Exercise)

Always, glad to hear, luggage, definitely, quite.

Dear Miss Adams: Thank you for your letter of Wednesday, May 21. We are always glad to hear from our good[1] customers.

We are, of course, sorry to learn that you have not been satisfied with the leather luggage that you purchased[2] in our Framingham department store last month. We want all the items we sell to give proper, adequate service,[3] and we definitely want to keep your goodwill.

The next time you are in the area, please bring the luggage to[4] our store. One of our representatives will inspect the luggage to determine just what the problem is. If your[5] dissatisfaction is caused by some defect in the quality of the material or by poor work, we will,[6] of course, be quite happy to replace the luggage free of charge.

We are looking forward to seeing you in your* store[7] in the near future. Sincerely yours, [147]
*our

❮ LETTER 444 ❮ (Office Style)

Seldom, policy, customers, personal, arise.

Dear Miss Green:

> Check the spelling on that name; it may be *G-r-e-e-n* or *G-r-e-e-n-e*.

It was a pleasure hearing from you in today's mail. We seldom get such a nice letter as the one[1] you wrote to us concerning our sales representative, Miss Janet Adams. Needless to say, we are very happy[2] that you received such fine service from Miss Adams when you were in our store on August 24.

> Check that date.

We make it[3] a policy to give each of our customers personal, efficient service every time they are in our store.[4] We want our customers to feel that they are quite special to us—because they are.

We hope you will receive many[5] years of excellent service from the furniture that you purchased from us. If you should have any difficulty[6] with anything you buy in our store, please let us know immediately. We will take whatever steps are necessary[7] to correct any problems that may arise. Very sincerely yours,   [154]

LESSON 75

❴ LETTER 445 ❴ (Related to Lesson 75, Letter 3)

Ordinarily, circumstances, control, automobile, accident, hospital.

Gentlemen: It is with regret that I acknowledge that my bill with your company is long past due. I[1] ordinarily pay my bills on time. However, circumstances beyond my control have caused me to be quite late with[2] my payments to your company and to several others as well.

On February 25 I was involved[3] in a serious automobile accident. I have been in the hospital since that date and will not be[4] released until August.

Enclosed is a check for $20 to be applied toward my past-due balance. I will[5] send a check for $20 each month if this is satisfactory with you. Under the circumstances, I[6] have no other course of action open to me.

Thank you for your patience and understanding at this very trying[7] time. Yours sincerely, [144]

❮ LETTER 446 ❮ (Related to Lesson 75, Letter 4)

Problem, you ordered, remember, always, drapery, beige.

Dear Ms. Chase: Thank you for writing to me about the problem you had with the drapes that you ordered from my home[1] furnishings store several weeks ago. I remember you very well; I took your order myself. It was a pleasure[2] helping you. I am very sorry that you were not happy with the drapes when Miss Wilson delivered them to[3] you recently. We always try to give the very best service to our customers.

The material that you[4] chose when you were in my store was the material that was used when we made your new drapes. Sometimes materials[5] look somewhat different after the drapes have been made. The lighting in your home can have a great effect on the way[6] the colors appear. The No. 608 drapery material is beige and is fairly coarse. We do not[7] use soft, delicate fabrics for draperies because they do not wear well.

I suggest, Ms. Chase, that you let us install[8] the drapes that you ordered so that you can see how they look in your home. After a week's time, we will remove the[9] drapes if you wish. We must charge you our actual cost of making the drapes, but we will allow you a 40 percent[10] discount on any new ones that we make for you.

We are very sorry for the misunderstanding, and we[11] want to keep your business and your goodwill. Under the circumstances, however, I am sure you can understand[12] our position in this matter. Very cordially yours, [250]

❮ LETTER 447 ❮ (Related to Lesson 75, Letter 5)

Superb, presentation, comments, attended, practicality, honorarium.

Dear Dr. Weston: Thank you for doing a superb job with your presentation at our fall conference. We heard[1] many fine comments after your talk. Those who attended were impressed with the practicality of your speech and[2] the valuable suggestions you offered. I agree with their comments, of course.

Enclosed is a check for your expenses[3] and the honorarium.

Thank you again, Dr. Weston, for a job well done and for sharing your ideas[4] with us. Very truly yours, [85]

❡ LETTER 448

Entitled, prompt, efficient, explanation, inconvenienced, satisfaction.

Dear Mr. Lee: Thank you for writing to me about the problem you have had getting your automobile serviced[1] at our shop. We are, of course, very sorry that you have not received the service to which you are entitled. All[2] customers should receive prompt, efficient service whenever they bring their cars to us for repairs.

We could tell you[3] that the manager of our service department has been ill for several months and has not been on the job. This[4] is true, of course, but it is not a satisfactory reason for our not giving you proper service.

We could[5] tell you that there has been a strike in our manufacturing plant and that spare parts have been difficult to obtain.[6] This is also true, but it is not a satisfactory explanation to a customer who has been[7] inconvenienced.

We will tell you that we want to do everything in our power to make you a satisfied customer[8] once again. If you will bring your car to our shop on Monday morning, September 6, at 8 a.m., we will[9] repair your car to your satisfaction and have it ready for you by 5 p.m. the same day.

Please call us to[10] confirm the appointment. Sincerely yours, [207]

(LETTER 449 ((Alertness Exercise)

[shorthand symbols]

Different, assess, relationship, almost, regularly, rapidly.

Dear Miss Edwards: Now that December is here, most companies are beginning to look back at the year to determine[1] what progress has been made and what they have actually accomplished. Our company is no different from most[2] others. We are beginning to assess our accomplishments during the year.

We looked specifically at our business[3] relationship with your organization. We were delighted to find out that our two firms had done almost[4] twice as much business this past year as we had the *coming** year. We knew that we had been able to serve your company[5] more regularly in recent months, but we had not realized that the amount of business had grown so rapidly.[6]

We want to take this opportunity to thank you for the business you have given our company this past[7] year. In addition, we want to promise you that we will do everything in our power to give you even better[8] service during the coming year.

Whenever we can be of special help to you in any way, just let us[9] know; we will be pleased to be of service to you, of course. Sincerely yours,   [193]
*previous

(LETTER 450 ((Office Style)

[shorthand symbols]

Pleasure, satisfied, especially, routine, maintenance, dependable.

Dear Miss Peterson:

That could end in *s-e-n;* be sure to check it.

It was a pleasure receiving your letter of Thursday, May 1. We are glad to hear from[1] satisfied customers.

Make that *always glad to hear from satisfied customers.*

We are especially happy that you received such good service when you brought your car to our[2] shop for routine maintenance last week. We strive to give every customer efficient, dependable service, and[3] I am happy to see that we succeed in nearly every case.

Your car will need routine maintenance again before[4] spring. We hope you will call for an appointment two or three days before you want to bring it in. We will make an[5] appointment for you and have your car ready for you the same day you bring it in.

Very best wishes to you, Miss[6] Peterson, and thank you for your complimentary letter. Sincerely yours,   [134]

Dear Dr. Reed: Seldom do we take the opportunity to tell our good customers just how much we appreciate[1] them. It seems as though the only time many of our customers hear from us is when they are behind in[2] their payments. That is certainly not the case with you, however.

On checking our records, I found that you have been[3] a regular customer of ours for the past five years and that you have purchased many items from us. I hope[4] you have been pleased with every one of your purchases.

I also found that you have handled your account in a very[5] fine manner. Not once have you missed a payment or even been late with a payment. This is a commendable[6] record, Dr. Reed.

If you should need a credit reference at any time, please do not hesitate to call on[7] you.* We will give you a very good recommendation. Sincerely yours, [153]

*us

◖ LETTER 438 ◖ (Office Style)

Very glad, developments, appreciated, gracious, in the future, decided.

Gentlemen: Thank you for sending your representative, Mr. C. R. Greene,

That's *G-r-e-e-n-e.*

to our offices last week. We were[1] very glad to learn about all the new developments in the field of electronic computers.

Please send a copy of this letter to Mr. Greene.

We want you[2] to know how much we appreciated talking with Mr. Greene. It was a pleasure to learn about the new[3] developments without having any pressure placed on us to purchase a new computer system for our company.[4] Mr Greene was a gracious representative who shared information with us and let us make up our own[5] minds about the purchase of a new computer.

1. You may redeem the principal plus the interest after[4] the date of maturity.

2. You may retain your time certificates, and we will reinvest your funds for an[5] additional two-year period.

3. You may place your funds in a regular checking account or a special[6] savings account.

The enclosed circular gives all the details about each of these options. When you have read the[7] circular, just fill out the attached form, sign it, and mail it to us in the envelope that is provided.

We will[8] be looking forward to hearing from you. Sincerely yours,   [170]

❦ LETTER 436

Sweater, color, actually, return, accepted, congratulate.

Dear Mr. Case: Several days ago I purchased a new red sweater from your store at 406 West 21[1] Street in Dover, Delaware. When I took the sweater home, I found that it was not the right color. It was[2] actually much too light to use with the suit that I was trying to match.

Because the sweater was on sale, I was sure[3] that I would not be able to return it. However, I decided that it was worth a try. I took it back[4] to the store yesterday. The clerk not only accepted the sweater for full credit but also helped me find[5] another red sweater that was exactly the right shade to match my suit.

This kind of service can have only a very[6] positive effect on your business, Mr. Case. I congratulate you on having friendly, courteous people[7] who are willing to take a little extra time to be sure that each customer is satisfied with each purchase.[8] You may be sure that I will do the majority of my shopping for new clothes in your store. Sincerely yours,[9]   [180]

❦ LETTER 437 ❦ (Alertness Exercise)

Seldom, how much, behind, items, account, record.

Mr. Jackson: In today's mail I received a copy of next year's sales budget for each of our five sales regions[1] (see the summary on the attached sheet). Frankly, I think the sales budget is much too high for three of the five regions.[2] I think we will be fortunate indeed to reach 90 percent of the projected budget.

Under the[3] circumstances, I suggest that you ask each of the regional managers to review their particular budgets[4] very carefully. If they accept the budgets as stated, I think they will regret having done so by the[5] end of the year.

Make that *fiscal* year.

Please let me know the findings as soon as possible. L. C. Carpenter   [116]

Send a copy of this memorandum to Mr. R. A. Smith.

LESSON 73

⊄ LETTER 433 ⊄ (Related to Lesson 73, Letter 3)

Formal, reception, retiring, contribution, wonderful, possible.

Miss Miller: I was happy to read that you are planning to have a formal reception and dinner for Ms. Judy[1] Gray, who will be retiring shortly. You may count on my being there. Enclosed is the top half of the form you[2] mailed to me; I will retain the bottom half to serve as my admission ticket. I am also enclosing a[3] check for $25 for my ticket and for my contribution toward a gift.

Ms. Gray is a wonderful[4] person; she has affected my life and my attitude greatly over the years. I am sure that she has also[5] had a great effect on the lives of the other people with whom she has worked.

If you need any help with the[6] arrangements for the reception or the dinner, please let me know. I will be more than willing to help in any way[7] possible. James Reed   [144]

❰ LETTER 434 ❰ (Related to Lesson 73, Letter 4)

[shorthand outlines]

Months ago, beautiful, automobile, recommended, maintenance.

Dear Mr. Powers: Eleven months ago you purchased a beautiful new Lexington automobile from our[1] agency. We are confident that you will receive excellent service from this car and that you are very well[2] pleased with it.

However, we recommended when you bought the car that you bring it to our service department in[3] six months for a routine maintenance check. Five months ago we mailed you a reminder stating that it was time for[4] a checkup, and we even scheduled an appointment for you. Unfortunately, you did not acknowledge our letter,[5] and you did not bring in your car for service.

It is necessary for even the very best cars to be[6] checked on a regular basis. If you fail to have your car serviced properly, its performance can be severly[7] affected.

Please take a moment right now, Mr. Powers, to call our service department at 555-8672.[8] We will make an appointment for you to bring your car in for that checkup that is now five months[9] overdue. Sincerely yours, [184]

❰ LETTER 435 ❰ (Related to Lesson 73, Letter 5)

[shorthand outlines]

Years ago, certificates, annual, mature, maturity.

Dear Ms. Pierce: Nearly two years ago you invested your ready cash in three 2-year time certificates at the[1] First National Bank. During those two years your money has been hard at work for you. You have earned 10 percent annual[2] interest on the money you invested with us.

On March 3 your three certificates will mature. You have[3] several options available. They are as follows:

He is a likable person who will have a very good effect[6] on your business in the future.

You will be glad to know that after much discussion, we have decided that[7] we should go ahead with the purchase of a new computer shortly after the first of the year. We will be calling[8] Mr. Greene to come to our offices once again to accept our order. Very sincerely yours,   [178]

LESSON 74

❰ LETTER 439 ❰ (Related to Lesson 74, Letter 3)

Congratulations, throughout, recruitment, college, mentioned, representatives.

Bob: I want to extend my congratulations to you, to your staff, and to the four students who traveled throughout[1] the state on your recruitment program for our college. When you mentioned to me that you wanted to take students with[2] you this year, I knew that you would have very good results.

When you told me which students you wanted to take, I knew[3] you had made wise choices. The students—James Smith, Betty Brown, Max Tate, and Janet Garcia—are excellent[4] representatives for our college.

Thank you for sending the list of potential students. I am impressed that you obtained[5] commitments from so many good students in our area; we have received many of their application forms[6] already.

Keep up the good work. Frank Long   [127]

❰ LETTER 440 ❰ (Related to Lesson 74, Letter 4)

Congratulatory, remodeled, enlarged, hardware, family, impressed.

Gentlemen: This is just a congratulatory note to tell you how much we enjoyed visiting and shopping[1] in your newly remodeled and enlarged hardware store. My family and I attended your grand opening on[2] Saturday, April 10, and were impressed with the size and beauty of your store.

Thank you for providing the citizens[3] of Medford, Massachusetts, with such a fine hardware store in which to shop. Thank you, too, for the special invitation[4] to your sale. Very cordially yours,   [88]

❡ LETTER 441 ❡ (Related to Lesson 74, Letter 5)

Membership, surprised, earlier, ideals, outweigh, happenings.

Gentlemen: Enclosed is my check for $50 for my membership dues for the coming year. I was not surprised[1] that the dues were raised; in fact, I was surprised that they had not been raised earlier.

I believe in the ideals[2] and goals of our organization, and I understand the reason for the increase in dues. The benefits that[3] I derive far outweigh the cost of my dues. If it were not for our professional organization, I would[4] not be able to keep up to date with the happenings and laws in real estate.

Thank you for doing such a fine[5] job. Very truly yours,   [104]

❡ LETTER 442

Thank you very much, request, you have been, certainly, goodwill, guidelines.

Dear Mr. Green: Thank you very much for your recent request that we increase your credit line from $500[1] to $1,000. We certainly wish we were able to do this. You have been a good customer of[2] ours for many years, and we certainly want to retain your goodwill and your business.

Unfortunately, our board[3] of directors recently issued new guidelines concerning open lines of credit. We will not be able to[4] extend credit lines above their present limits during the coming year.

Please accept our apologies for not[5] being able to grant your request. We look forward to serving you in the future. Sincerely yours, [118]

❆ LETTER 443 ❆ (Alertness Exercise)

Always, glad to hear, luggage, definitely, quite.

Dear Miss Adams: Thank you for your letter of Wednesday, May 21. We are always glad to hear from our good[1] customers.

We are, of course, sorry to learn that you have not been satisfied with the leather luggage that you purchased[2] in our Framingham department store last month. We want all the items we sell to give proper, adequate service,[3] and we definitely want to keep your goodwill.

The next time you are in the area, please bring the luggage to[4] our store. One of our representatives will inspect the luggage to determine just what the problem is. If your[5] dissatisfaction is caused by some defect in the quality of the material or by poor work, we will,[6] of course, be quite happy to replace the luggage free of charge.

We are looking forward to seeing you in your* store[7] in the near future. Sincerely yours, [147]
*our

❆ LETTER 444 ❆ (Office Style)

Seldom, policy, customers, personal, arise.

Dear Miss Green:

> Check the spelling on that name; it may be *G-r-e-e-n* or *G-r-e-e-n-e*.

It was a pleasure hearing from you in today's mail. We seldom get such a nice letter as the one[1] you wrote to us concerning our sales representative, Miss Janet Adams. Needless to say, we are very happy[2] that you received such fine service from Miss Adams when you were in our store on August 24.

> Check that date.

We make it[3] a policy to give each of our customers personal, efficient service every time they are in our store.[4] We want our customers to feel that they are quite special to us—because they are.

We hope you will receive many[5] years of excellent service from the furniture that you purchased from us. If you should have any difficulty[6] with anything you buy in our store, please let us know immediately. We will take whatever steps are necessary[7] to correct any problems that may arise. Very sincerely yours, [154]

LESSON 75

ℂ LETTER 445 ℂ (Related to Lesson 75, Letter 3)

Ordinarily, circumstances, control, automobile, accident, hospital.

Gentlemen: It is with regret that I acknowledge that my bill with your company is long past due. I[1] ordinarily pay my bills on time. However, circumstances beyond my control have caused me to be quite late with[2] my payments to your company and to several others as well.

On February 25 I was involved[3] in a serious automobile accident. I have been in the hospital since that date and will not be[4] released until August.

Enclosed is a check for $20 to be applied toward my past-due balance. I will[5] send a check for $20 each month if this is satisfactory with you. Under the circumstances, I[6] have no other course of action open to me.

Thank you for your patience and understanding at this very trying[7] time. Yours sincerely, [144]

⊄ LETTER 446 ⊄ (Related to Lesson 75, Letter 4)

Problem, you ordered, remember, always, drapery, beige.

Dear Ms. Chase: Thank you for writing to me about the problem you had with the drapes that you ordered from my home[1] furnishings store several weeks ago. I remember you very well; I took your order myself. It was a pleasure[2] helping you. I am very sorry that you were not happy with the drapes when Miss Wilson delivered them to[3] you recently. We always try to give the very best service to our customers.

The material that you[4] chose when you were in my store was the material that was used when we made your new drapes. Sometimes materials[5] look somewhat different after the drapes have been made. The lighting in your home can have a great effect on the way[6] the colors appear. The No. 608 drapery material is beige and is fairly coarse. We do not[7] use soft, delicate fabrics for draperies because they do not wear well.

I suggest, Ms. Chase, that you let us install[8] the drapes that you ordered so that you can see how they look in your home. After a week's time, we will remove the[9] drapes if you wish. We must charge you our actual cost of making the drapes, but we will allow you a 40 percent[10] discount on any new ones that we make for you.

We are very sorry for the misunderstanding, and we[11] want to keep your business and your goodwill. Under the circumstances, however, I am sure you can understand[12] our position in this matter. Very cordially yours, [250]

⊄ LETTER 447 ⊄ (Related to Lesson 75, Letter 5)

Superb, presentation, comments, attended, practicality, honorarium.

Dear Dr. Weston: Thank you for doing a superb job with your presentation at our fall conference. We heard[1] many fine comments after your talk. Those who attended were impressed with the practicality of your speech and[2] the valuable suggestions you offered. I agree with their comments, of course.

Enclosed is a check for your expenses[3] and the honorarium.

Thank you again, Dr. Weston, for a job well done and for sharing your ideas[4] with us. Very truly yours,   [85]

❰ LETTER 448

Entitled, prompt, efficient, explanation, inconvenienced, satisfaction.

Dear Mr. Lee: Thank you for writing to me about the problem you have had getting your automobile serviced[1] at our shop. We are, of course, very sorry that you have not received the service to which you are entitled. All[2] customers should receive prompt, efficient service whenever they bring their cars to us for repairs.

We could tell you[3] that the manager of our service department has been ill for several months and has not been on the job. This[4] is true, of course, but it is not a satisfactory reason for our not giving you proper service.

We could[5] tell you that there has been a strike in our manufacturing plant and that spare parts have been difficult to obtain.[6] This is also true, but it is not a satisfactory explanation to a customer who has been[7] inconvenienced.

We will tell you that we want to do everything in our power to make you a satisfied customer[8] once again. If you will bring your car to our shop on Monday morning, September 6, at 8 a.m., we will[9] repair your car to your satisfaction and have it ready for you by 5 p.m. the same day.

Please call us to[10] confirm the appointment. Sincerely yours,
[207]

⊄ LETTER 449 ⊄ (Alertness Exercise)

[shorthand symbols]

Different, assess, relationship, almost, regularly, rapidly.

Dear Miss Edwards: Now that December is here, most companies are beginning to look back at the year to determine[1] what progress has been made and what they have actually accomplished. Our company is no different from most[2] others. We are beginning to assess our accomplishments during the year.

We looked specifically at our business[3] relationship with your organization. We were delighted to find out that our two firms had done almost[4] twice as much business this past year as we had the *coming** year. We knew that we had been able to serve your company[5] more regularly in recent months, but we had not realized that the amount of business had grown so rapidly.[6]

We want to take this opportunity to thank you for the business you have given our company this past[7] year. In addition, we want to promise you that we will do everything in our power to give you even better[8] service during the coming year.

Whenever we can be of special help to you in any way, just let us[9] know; we will be pleased to be of service to you, of course. Sincerely yours,   [193]
*previous

⊄ LETTER 450 ⊄ (Office Style)

[shorthand symbols]

Pleasure, satisfied, especially, routine, maintenance, dependable.

Dear Miss Peterson:

         That could end in *s-e-n;* be sure to check it.

It was a pleasure receiving your letter of Thursday, May 1. We are glad to hear from[1] satisfied customers.

Make that *always glad to hear from satisfied customers.*

We are especially happy that you received such good service when you brought your car to our[2] shop for routine maintenance last week. We strive to give every customer efficient, dependable service, and[3] I am happy to see that we succeed in nearly every case.

Your car will need routine maintenance again before[4] spring. We hope you will call for an appointment two or three days before you want to bring it in. We will make an[5] appointment for you and have your car ready for you the same day you bring it in.

Very best wishes to you, Miss[6] Peterson, and thank you for your complimentary letter. Sincerely yours, [134]

LESSON 76

ℂ LETTER 451 ℂ (Related to Lesson 76, Letter 3)

Concerning, program, businesses, interested, forward.

Dear Miss Lexington: Thank you for your letter of Thursday, August 21, concerning the new group life insurance[1] program that your company is now offering to businesses in the state of Illinois. I am, of course,[2] interested in life insurance coverage for myself and my employees.

I sent a questionnaire to each[3] employee last week, and about two-thirds of them stated that they would be interested in participating in a[4] company-sponsored group life insurance program. However, we will need a great deal more information before[5] we make a final decision.

Will you please ask one of your representatives to call on our company sometime[6] after the first of December to discuss the various plans that you have available. We will be looking[7] forward to hearing from you. Cordially yours,   [149]

Typing Style. Transcribe: two-thirds.

❧ LETTER 452 ❧ (Related to Lesson 76, Letter 4)

Flood, carefully, statement, amount, premium, losses.

Dear Ms. Anderson: Enclosed is your new flood insurance policy. Please read it carefully and put it in a[1] safe place.

Also enclosed is our statement for the policy. You may pay the entire amount at one time, or you[2] may pay monthly. If you choose to pay the premium in 12 installments, there will be a 9½ percent[3] interest charge.

We are sure that you will be pleased with your flood insurance policy, Ms. Anderson. We hope, of course,[4] that you will never suffer losses due to flooding. However, you can rest assured that should a flood occur, you[5] are fully protected. If you have any questions about our insurance policy, just call us at[6] 555-6161. Sincerely yours, [127]

Typing Style. Transcribe: 9½ percent.

❧ LETTER 453 ❧ (Related to Lesson 76, Letter 5)

Recent, hardware, shipment, contained, returning, original.

Dear Mr. Stern: Thank you for your letter acknowledging my recent order for hardware supplies from your company.[1] The first shipment arrived today, and everything was in good condition. However, I had ordered a box[2] of 3/16-inch drill bits, and the box I received contained 5/16-inch drill bits.

I am returning the box[3] to you; I hope you will send the proper size to me by return mail. I am looking forward to receiving the[4] other items that were on my original order. Cordially yours,   [93]

TRANSCRIPTION PREVIEW

Typing Style. Transcribe: 3/16-inch; 5/16-inch.

⟪ LETTER 454

Exercise, attempting, polls, concerned, ballot, responsibility.

Dear Mr. Mason: You can exercise one of the most valuable rights you have next Tuesday—the right to vote. The[1] League of Voters is attempting to get at least two-thirds of the eligible voters of Brown County to the[2] polls on Election Day. We are not concerned about which people you vote for; we are only concerned that you cast[3] your ballot.

We are making free transportation available to anyone in the county who needs it. If[4] you would like to have someone drive you to and from the polls next Tuesday, just call 555-8619.

Don't fail[5] to exercise your valuable right to vote. It is your right and your responsibility. Sincerely yours,   [119]

TRANSCRIPTION PREVIEW

Typing Style. Transcribe: two-thirds.

◖ LETTER 455 ◖ (Alertness Exercise)

[shorthand symbols]

Accounts, average, evidently, depositors, computation, approval.

Miss Stern: As you know, our bank began paying 5½ percent interest on funds in checking accounts on July[1] 21. However, we have paid interest only on those accounts that had an average daily balance of[2] $400.

Evidently, there has been some misunderstanding about the way we compute the interest. We[3] have had 20 or 30 telephone calls concerning this matter during the past few days.

Will you please compose[4] a letter to each of our depositors explaining the computation of the interest on checking accounts.[5] We will enclose a copy of your letter with every bank statement next month. Please submit a copy of the letter[6] you write to me for approval, Miss James.* I will appreciate your help in this matter. Leslie Yale   [138]
*Stern

◖ LETTER 456 ◖ (Office Style)

[shorthand symbols]

Acknowledge, mortgages, raising, minimum, devastating.

Miss Adams: This is to acknowledge your memorandum of Monday, December 15,

Check the date of that memorandum.

concerning the increase[1] in the interest rate for home mortgages.

I will, of course, see that all members of my department are aware of[2] the changes in the rate. However, I believe that we will definitely hurt our business by raising the rate[3] 1½ percent at this time. In addition, I think that the increase in the minimum down payment is[4] much too high.

I suggest that you consider reducing the mortgage rate

> Make that *consider reducing either the mortgage rate.*

or the required down payment.

If we increase[5] both rates at one time, I am sure that it will have a devastating effect on our business. James Davis   [118]

LESSON 77

❬ LETTER 457 ❬ (Related to Lesson 77, Letter 3)

Thoughtful, remember, graduation, thrilled, occupy, unfortunately.

Dear Marvin: How very thoughtful it was of you to remember me at graduation time! I was thrilled to receive[1] the wonderful set of reference books that you sent to me. The books will occupy a prized place on my bookshelf.[2]

I have decided to take a three-month vacation in Europe before beginning full-time work here in Oregon.[3] I plan to leave Portland on June 28. My travels will take me to England, France, and Germany. If all[4] goes well, I will probably spend some time in Spain and Italy too.

Unfortunately, I will not be in the[5] Denver, Colorado, area this summer. However, I will definitely make plans to visit you and[6] your family when I return from Europe. Thanks so much for your nice letter and the wonderful graduation[7] present. Sincerely yours,
     [144]

TRANSCRIPTION PREVIEW

Punctuation. Exclamation point after the first sentence.

❡ LETTER 458 ❡ (Related to Lesson 77, Letter 4)

[shorthand]

Petition, variance, ordinance, supermarket, residential, neighborhood.

Gentlemen: I certainly will not sign a petition for a variance in the city zoning ordinance![1] I am quite opposed to having a supermarket located within 200 feet of my home.

This is a[2] quiet residential neighborhood, and I definitely want to keep it that way. A supermarket located[3] on the corner of Fifth Avenue and Elm Street would create a great deal of traffic congestion. In addition,[4] I am sure that my property would actually decrease in value in the long run.

I am taking this[5] opportunity to tell you that I will do everything in my power to keep the city from issuing a[6] variance to your company. Cordially yours, [129]

TRANSCRIPTION PREVIEW

Punctuation. Exclamation point after the first sentence.

❡ LETTER 459 ❡ (Related to Lesson 77, Letter 5)

[shorthand]

Determine, addition, understand, firm, let me, we hope you will.

Dear Mr. Simmons: It was a pleasure visiting you last week to determine exactly what will be involved[1] in building an addition to your home. We understand that you want the following things:

1. A new living room[2]
2. A new bedroom
3. A two-car garage

After discussing your plans with our people, we believe that we could[3] make all the additions for approximately $20,000. Although this is not a firm bid, I believe[4] that it is within 5 percent of the actual cost.

If you would like my company to proceed with the[5] plans and make a firm bid on the work, please let me know.

We hope you will choose our company to do the work for you.[6] You will be making no mistake! Sincerely yours,   [129]

TRANSCRIPTION PREVIEW

Punctuation. Exclamation point after the last sentence.

(LETTER 460

Disappointed, representatives, quality, discourteous, assure, personally.

Dear Miss Edwards: How disappointed we were to receive your recent letter! No, we were not disappointed that[1] you wrote to us; we were disappointed that our sales representatives had not given you the high-quality[2] service to which you are entitled.

I have discussed the problems you outlined in your letter with Miss Mary Wilson,[3] who is the head of the women's shoe department. I am sure that she will discuss with her staff the poor, discourteous[4] treatment you received in that department on your last visit to our store.

We assure you, Miss Edwards, that[5] you will receive the very best service on your next visit to our store. Please stop by my office the next time[6] you are in the store; I would like to have the opportunity to speak with you personally. Very sincerely[7] yours,
                [141]

TRANSCRIPTION PREVIEW

Punctuation. Exclamation point after the first sentence.

⟨ LETTER 461 ⟨ (Alertness Exercise)

Pleasure, agreement, additional, actually, campaign.

Dear Mr. Kelly: It was a pleasure meeting you on your recent visit to Massachusetts! I am sure that[1] my advertising agency will be able to work out an agreement that will be profitable for both[2] our companies when we meet in St. Paul on the last day of June.

Before I can complete my plans for our meeting,[3] I will need additional information. Will you please answer the following questions for me:

1. How much money[4] do you actually plan to spend on advertising next year?

2. When would you like to begin your first advertising[5] campaign?

3. What advertising media do you want to use?

When I receive your answers to these questions,[6] I will be able to complete my plans for the meeting on June 31.* I will be looking forward to[7] hearing from you. Sincerely yours,   [146]
*30

⟨ LETTER 462 ⟨ (Office Style)

Manuscript, commended, condition, prepare, publication, posted.

Dear Mr. Woodward:

Check the spelling on that name.

Congratulations on finishing the manuscript for your new book! You are to be commended[1] for the work that you have done.

We received the last chapter in the mail yesterday, and we are having our copy[2] editor, Miss Mary Smith, begin her work today. The manuscript is in such good condition that we believe[3] it will take only light editing to prepare it for publication.

> Make that *only a little editing;* no, leave it as it
> was.

We will keep you posted on the progress[4] we are making. Thanks for doing such a good job; it makes our work easier! Sincerely yours, [97]

LESSON 78

❆ LETTER 463 ❆ (Related to Lesson 78, Letter 3)

Hospital, personally, pledge, loyal, maintain, contribution.

Dear Mr. Reid: As head of this year's fund-raising drive for the Nashville General Hospital, I want to thank you[1] personally for signing and returning your pledge card. It is loyal friends like you who help us maintain our[2] high-quality services. Your contribution will help us defray the exceedingly high costs of operating[3] our hospital during the coming year.

You may send your contribution to us in the enclosed self-addressed[4] envelope. If you wish, however, you may send your contribution in four equal quarterly payments. We will be[5] happy to send a reminder when each installment is due.

Incidentally, we are extremely proud of our[6] hospital and would be happy to take you on a guided tour of our facilities at any time. Very[7] cordially yours, [143]

❆ LETTER 464 ❆ (Related to Lesson 78, Letter 4)

Antique, always, answer, questions, total.

Dear Ms. Martin: The tour that the International Travel Agency is planning for antique dealers certainly[1] sounds interesting to my husband and me. We own an antique shop in Dallas, and we are always trying to[2] find unusual items for our store. In addition, we both enjoy traveling in foreign countries.

Before[3] we make up our minds about joining the tour this summer, we need to have some additional information. Will[4] you please answer the following questions for us:

1. What is the total cost per person (double occupancy)?[5]
2. What is the last date on which we may make reservations?
3. Do you provide travel insurance for the members[6] of your group?

Just as soon as we receive the answers to these questions, we will make a decision about joining[7] your tour. Very cordially yours,   [147]

◖ LETTER 465 ◖ (Related to Lesson 78, Letter 5)

Explanation, behind, consumer, understand, attorney.

Dear Mr. Carson: Thank you for your check for $500 and your explanation of the reason you have[1] been late with your payments to the Mason Department Store. We were, of course, very glad to receive your check. However,[2] you are still behind $500 in your payments.

As a consumer, I can easily understand[3] how a person could assume more debt than he or she could pay. As an attorney, however, I must be sure that[4] the legal rights of my client are protected. Because your account is still five months past due and there is little[5] likelihood that you will be able to meet the suggested payment[6] schedule, we are proposing a new payment[6] schedule.Your new monthly payment will be $50 rather than $100. Two copies of the schedule[7] are enclosed. Please sign one copy and return it to us with your first payment of $50 in the enclosed[8] envelope.

If for any reason you cannot make a payment on time, it is

essential that you notify[9] us immediately. We look forward to receiving each of your checks on a regular basis. Yours truly,[10] [200]

ℂ LETTER 466

Delighted, identification, to make, clerks, automatically.

Dear Ms. Lexington: I am delighted to tell you that your application for credit with our store has been approved.[1]

Enclosed is an identification card for you to use whenever you wish to make a purchase in our[2] store. Please sign the card on the back and carry it with you whenever you shop at our store. When you make a purchase,[3] just present the card to one of the clerks. Your purchase will be approved automatically, and you will be billed at[4] the end of the month.

You may use your credit up to a limit of $300. Should you wish to extend[5] your line of credit or make a single large purchase that exceeds your credit limit, just let us know. Sincerely[6] yours,   [121]

ℂ LETTER 467 ℂ (Alertness Exercise)

Concerned, resources, discuss, levels, legislation.

Dear Mr. Ryan: Are you concerned about the quality of the air you breathe? Are you concerned about the fuel[1] shortage? Are you concerned about protecting all our natural resources?

If you are concerned about these things,[2] you should be a member of the National Ecology Association. Our association has more[3] than 25,000 members from every state in the nation. We conduct meetings to discuss just what can be[4] done on the local, state, and national levels to help conserve our resources and protect our environment.[5] We try to encourage the passage of legislation that we think is beneficial to the interests of all[6] Americans.

If you are interested in becoming a member of a local chapter of our organization,[7] just write to the National Ecology Group* at 406 Third Avenue, New York, New York[8] 10020. We will be glad to send you more information. Sincerely yours,   [174]
*Association

❰ LETTER 468 ❰ (Office Style)

Application, routine, accounts, positive, basis.

Dear Miss Lain:

Check the spelling on that name.

We have received your application for credit at the General Department Store.

As you know, it[1] is always necessary for any retail store to run a routine credit check on those who wish to open[2] charge accounts. It should take only a matter of a week or so to complete the check for you. Just as soon as we[3] receive a positive rating, we will open your account and send you one of our special identification[4] cards.

> Put this sentence immediately after the first sentence in the letter: *We are delighted that you wish to open an account with us.*

In the meantime, Miss Lain, we hope you will visit our store and shop on a cash basis. We will be very[5] glad to see you. Cordially yours,   [106]

LESSON 79

❰ LETTER 469 ❰ (Related to Lesson 79, Letter 3)

Contractor, elevators, previously, minimized, alleviate, overcrowding.

To All Employees: Last month the contractor began installing the eight new elevators in our office building[1] here in Cincinnati, Ohio. We are happy to say that work is progressing exceedingly well and[2] that the installation may be completed sooner than we had previously expected.

We are, however,[3] experiencing several problems that could be minimized with a little effort on everyone's part. If[4] you will use the stairs when you need to go up or down only one flight, it will help to alleviate overcrowding.[5] Arriving at work a few minutes early in the morning and leaving a few minutes before 5 p.m.[6] will also help to reduce the crowding in the elevators. The manager of each department will establish[7] temporary working hours for those people who wish to alter their schedules until the elevator[8] installation is completed.

We sincerely appreciate your continued cooperation in this matter.[9] Bill Adams   [183]

◁ LETTER 470 ◁ (Related to Lesson 79, Letter 4)

Support, extremely, disappointed, constructed, taxes, recreational.

Dear Mr. Miller: In today's mail I received your letter asking me to support the construction of a new[1] shopping center in suburban Springfield.

I am extremely disappointed that the Chamber of Commerce is[2] actively supporting this project; it is not in the best interests of the older businesses in the area.[3] There are several hundred owners of small stores in the area that would be driven out of business if the[4] center is constructed. We have paid taxes for many years, and we want to protect our business interests.

We are[5] forming a group to try to get the land in question sold for recreational use rather than for commercial[6] use. If you would like to send a representative to speak with us about our position in this matter, we[7] would be happy to hear from you. Yours truly,

[148]

❮ LETTER 471 ❯ (Related to Lesson 79, Letter 5)

[shorthand outlines]

Forwarded, manuscript, congratulate, occurred, postpone.

Dear Miss White: Mr. James Stern forwarded to me the manu-script you wrote for the March 14 issue of _Business[1] Day._ I would like to congratulate you on the thorough job that you did on the subject of women in business[2] today.

After I read the article, it occurred to me that it would be more appropriate for an issue[3] that we plan to publish early in the fall. That issue will contain a number of articles on women in[4] various types of businesses. Your article would make an extremely good lead article.

Would you consider[5] allowing us to postpone publication of the article until fall? I am sure that the article will[6] receive greater readership if we publish it then.

I will be looking forward to receiving your response.[7] Sincerely yours,   [142]

❮ LETTER 472

[shorthand outlines]

Sending us, purchased, unfortunately, prefer, let us know, appreciate.

Dear Mr. Yale: Thank you very much for sending us your check for $189.50 for[1] the office supplies that you purchased from our company last month. We were glad to receive your check.

Unfortunately,[2] I am afraid that there has been a slight error. When we checked the invoice, we found that the bill actually totaled[3] $199.50. Therefore, you have an outstanding balance with us for $10.[4]

You may send us your check for $10 now if you wish. If you prefer, however, we will add $10 to[5] your bill the next time you purchase goods from us. Please let us know what you would like to do.

We want you to know we[6] appreciate your business, Mr. Yale. Sincerely yours, [130]

◖ LETTER 473 ◖ (Alertness Exercise)

Thank you very much, furniture, delivered, several days ago, tax, to serve you.

Dear Miss Fleming: Thank you very much for coming to our store last week and purchasing several new pieces of[1] furniture for your home. The furniture was delivered to you several days ago, and we hope that you are[2] enjoying using it.

We are enclosing our bill for $1,500.* This includes the purchase price of[3] $1,000 and 5 percent sales tax. You may send us your check for the entire amount now, or you may make[4] three equal monthly payments.

We are happy to be able to serve you, Miss Fleming, and we hope to see you in[5] our store again in the near future. Sincerely yours, [110]
*$1,050

◖ LETTER 474 ◖ (Office Style)

Pleasure, very much, presentation, satisfactory, similar.

Dear Dr. Tate: It was a pleasure meeting you on your recent trip to Columbia, South Carolina.[1] Everyone who attended the meeting at which you spoke was very much impressed with your presentation.

Make that *speech;* no, leave it *presentation.*

I am[2] including a money order

No, make that *I am enclosing a check.*

for your expenses and an honorarium. I trust you will find it satisfactory.[3]

Our meeting will be in April next year,

Make that *late April.*

and we would like you to make a similar presentation[4] then. Do you think it would be possible for you to do so?

Please let us know if you will be able to speak to[5] our organization again; we will be awaiting your answer. Cordially yours, [115]

LESSON 80

(LETTER 475 ((Related to Lesson 80, Letter 3)

Weeks ago, area, computers, personally, definite, decision.

Dear Professor Sloan: Several weeks ago, Mr. Max Dempsey, our representative in your area, came[1] to your college to demonstrate our line of small computers for use in teaching various subjects in colleges.[2]

When Mr. Dempsey returned to the office, he stated that you were pleased with the computers and with the software[3] that we offer. However, we have not yet had the privilege of hearing from you personally. We are[4] wondering if you have made a definite decision about whether to purchase computers for your students[5] this year.

If you decide to install one of our small computers in your college before the end of the school year,[6] we will give you a 10 percent discount off the regular price.

Today is truly the day of the computer[7] in education. Don't be left behind; act today. You will be doing your students a service, and you will be[8] saving money at the same time. Sincerely yours, [169]

ℂ LETTER 476 ℂ (Related to Lesson 80, Letter 4)

[shorthand]

Thank you for, applying, account, routine, within, meantime.

Dear Mr. Cunningham: Thank you for coming to the Hamilton Men's Store last week. We were particularly glad[1] to see you because it was the first time that you have shopped in our store.

Thank you also for applying for a charge[2] account with us. We are now making a routine credit check, and we are sure we will be able to issue you[3] one of our credit cards within the next week or so.

In the meantime, Mr. Cunningham, if you need any type[4] of men's wear, just stop by our store. We will be more than happy to serve you. Very cordially yours,   [97]

ℂ LETTER 477 ℂ (Related to Lesson 80, Letter 5)

[shorthand]

Hardware, fixtures, apparel, accountant.

Miss Wilmington: As you know, our hardware store will be closing its doors for the last time on March 15. We have sold[1] the building and the fixtures to Edwards and Company. That company plans to use the building as a retail[2] shop for women's wearing apparel.

They will be needing an accountant, and I suggested that you might wish to[3] apply for the position. If you would like to have more information about the company, just call Mr.[4] Nate Edwards at 555-6107. He will be expecting your call. Sam Jenkins   [97]

ℂ LETTER 478

[shorthand]

Complimentary, campaign, products, admit, project.

Mr. Mason: Thank you for your complimentary note about the work that my division did during our recent[1] sales campaign. We are all pleased that you think we did an especially good job in getting the information[2] about our new line of products over to the general public.

I must admit that each member of the[3] department also feels that the campaign was handled very well. Every person is quite proud of the work that was done.[4]

You will be glad to know, Mr. Mason, that we will continue to do the same type of high-quality work on[5] each project in the future. Mary Tate   [107]

❬ LETTER 479 ❬ (Alertness Exercise)

Directors, decided, idea, members, conclude, will you please.

Miss Warden: Several weeks ago the board of directors of our company met and decided that it would[1] be a good idea for us to hold a general meeting of all our sales representatives this spring. Therefore,[2] we have decided to have a meeting of the members of our sales force in Chicago on the last day of April.[3]

We will meet in the Madison Hotel, which is located at 1600 Washington Avenue. Our[4] first meeting will start at 9 a.m., and we should conclude the meetings by 6 p.m.

Will you please see that everyone[5] in your division knows of this meeting in Chicago on April 31.* Charles O'Keefe   [117]
*30

❬ LETTER 480 ❬ (Office Style)

Application, qualifications, ideal, active, extremely.

Dear Miss Lopez: Thank you for your letter of application for a position as a salesclerk in the Baker[1] Women's Shop. Your qualifications and experience make you an ideal choice for our company.

Unfortunately,[2] we do not have an opening at the present time. However, we are expecting to add at least two[3] new sales representatives after the first of January. Would you like us to keep your application on[4] file until that time?

> Make that *until then.*

We hope you will decide to wait.

> No, make that *We hope you will decide to let us keep your application in our active files.*

I am sure you would make an extremely good employee for[5] our company.

> No, make that *organization;* oh, leave it *company.*

Very cordially yours,   [107]